EDUCATION FOR MINISTRY

Reading and Reflection Guide, Volume A

Living Faithfully
in Your World

EDUCATION FOR MINISTRY

Reading and Reflection Guide, Volume A

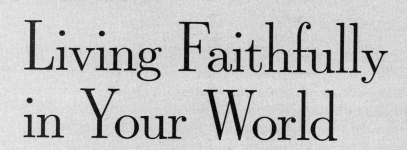

Living Faithfully in Your World

Morehouse Publishing, 4785 Linglestown Road, Suite 101, Harrisburg, PA 17112
Morehouse Publishing, 19 East 34th Street, New York, NY 10016
Morehouse Publishing is an imprint of Church Publishing Incorporated.
www.churchpublishing.org

Cover design by Laurie Klein Westhafer
Interior design and typesetting by Beth Oberholtzer

Library of Congress Cataloging-in-Publication Data

A catalog record of this book is available from the Library of Congress

ISBN-13: 978-0-8192-2918-2 (pbk.)

Printed in the United States of America

Contents

PART I: THE GUIDE

Unit One: Spiritual Autobiography and Listening

Unit Two: Theological Reflection as a Life Skill

First Interlude Unit: The Authority of the Bible

Unit Three: Developing a Sustaining Spirituality

Unit Four: Building a Theology: Integrating Belief, Behavior, and Doctrine in Everyday Life

Second Interlude Unit: Ministry and Priesthood

Unit Five: Vocation: Hearing and Responding to God's Call

PART II: RESOURCES

Supplemental Readings in the Christian Tradition

Acknowledgments

A revision by definition is not *sui generis*. Although this series of *Reading and Reflection Guides* may look different from previous editions of EfM materials, although it may be organized differently, it is nonetheless built on a framework that has evolved over the nearly forty years of Education for Ministry. Those who have some years of acquaintance with the program will recognize what the new format owes to components developed for its predecessors, among them parallel guides, common lessons, and the many variations of EfM's central discipline of theological reflection.

The developers of those foundational components are by now nearly legion and include not only founder Charles Winters and succeeding leaders like John de Beer and Edward de Bary but also the many EfM coordinators and trainers whose work with mentors all over the globe and over time has shaped the program.

The principal author of *Reading and Reflection Guide, Volume A: Living Faithfully in Your World*, the first in the cycle of four guides, is Rick Brewer, who has a long history of writing and curriculum design in EfM. Other contributors to this volume include Elsa S. Bakkum, Angela Hock Brewer, and Karen M. Meridith. In addition, several of the essays and resources included in this *Guide*, some adapted, others left as originally published in the previous edition, have long been a part of the EfM program, designed and written by a number of contributors over the years. We are grateful for their work and know that we can look to the future of EfM only because we stand on the shoulders of giants.

Karen M. Meridith, series editor
Executive Director of Education for Ministry
Sewanee, Tennessee
April, 2013

About the Author

Richard E. Brewer (Rick) is a retired Episcopal priest who served in parochial ministry and in adult Christian formation for forty years. A graduate of The University of the South and General Theological Seminary, he has lived in Oklahoma most of his life and served as priest and educator in Tulsa and Stillwater Episcopal churches. Additionally, he developed and directed the Deacon Formation Program for the Episcopal Diocese of Oklahoma.

Rick first learned about EfM in 1975 from Dr. Charles Winters, the originator and first director of the program. He has been a trainer since 1978, a coordinator, a mentor, and interim assistant director for the EfM program. He conceived and edited the Common Lesson series for the first revision of the materials. He coauthored the Parallel Guides and numerous common lessons with the Reverend John de Beer. He, along with Angela Hock, cowrote *Practically Christian: A Guide to Practical Christian Prayer, Action, and Reflection*. They codirected Opportunities for Adult Christian Education and Spirituality (OACES), Inc., which developed a variety of adult Christian formation learning guides and a comprehensive ministry formation program for the Episcopal Diocese of Nebraska. For over a decade he participated in the Progoff Intensive Journal program. Rick brings this extensive experience in adult Christian formation to the revision of the new materials for EfM.

Program Overview

The Education for Ministry (EfM) program is a four-year study and group reflection process for the formation of Christian ministry through the development of knowledge, attitude, skill, and identity as Christians. Published texts and essays provide the primary knowledge content in the study of the Christian tradition.

The first year studies the Hebrew Scriptures (Old Testament). The second year offers a study of the New Testament. Year Three provides study of Christian (church) history. Theology, ethics, and interfaith encounter constitute study in the fourth year.

Texts for Each Year

- **Year One:** *A Short Introduction to the Hebrew Bible* by John J. Collins. *The Holy Bible*, Old Testament and Apocrypha.

- **Year Two:** *Introducing the New Testament* by Mark Allan Powell. *The Holy Bible*, New Testament.

- **Year Three:** *Christianity: The First Three Thousand Years* by Diarmaid MacCulloch.

- **Year Four:** *Theology for a Troubled Believer* by Diogenes Allen. *The Christian Moral Life: Practices of Piety* by Timothy F. Sedgwick. *My Neighbor's Faith* edited by Jennifer Howe Peace, Or N. Rose, and Gregory Mobley.

Note: The most recent Oxford Annotated edition of New Revised Standard Version of the Bible is recommended, but any translation may be used as long as it includes the Apocrypha. Paraphrased Bibles are not recommended for study.

Reading and Reflection Guide

- A *Reading and Reflection Guide* provides weekly reading assignments, reflection questions, and additional supportive resources for the group.

- The entire group uses the same *Guide* each year—Volume A, B, C, or D. Each volume has a particular focus: Volume A, "Living Faithfully in Our World," works with the contexts of a person's life; Volume B builds on "Living Faithfully in an Intercultural World"; Volumes C and D explore "Christian Maturity" and "Our Journey into God," respectively.

- Each volume contains **Part I**, the reading and reflection assignments, and **Part II**, supporting materials, such as methods of spiritual autobiography and theological reflection.

- Five primary units in each volume have six sessions each.
- Two interlude units in each volume have two sessions each.
- An organization session at the beginning and a closing session at the end bring the total to thirty-six sessions in a year.

Focus of the *Reading and Reflection Guide* Units

- The first session of each primary unit is either an essay or other material for all in the group to read to help set the stage for the focus of the unit:
- **Unit One**–identity and meaning (individual, corporate, and historical);
- **Unit Two**–theological reflection as a life skill; orientation to attitudes to prayer, worship, and spirituality;
- **First Interlude**–the authority of the Bible, praying with the Bible;
- **Unit Three**–spirituality, prayer, and worship;
- **Unit Four**–integrating behavior and belief into a congruency that supports faithful living;
- **Second Interlude**–ministry and the priesthood of all believers;
- **Unit Five**–vocation: hearing the call and passion of our lives in relation to God.

A Four-fold Discipline for the Practice of Ministry

In each six-week unit, the five weeks following the introductory essay incorporate a pattern for the year's work that encourages the development of a four-fold discipline for the practice of ministry in the world:

- Read
- Focus
- Respond
- Practice

In each case **Read** and **Focus** are specific to an individual's year of study in the EfM program while the **Respond** and **Practice** are intended for all levels. Addressing the **Respond** and/or **Practice** work in the seminar meeting may encourage a conversation of great depth since each individual, having previously considered the question from the context of his or her assigned reading in the Christian tradition, will bring a different perspective to the group's work together.

Introduction

Reading and Reflection Guide, Volume A, Living Faithfully in Your World, attends to the different worlds (contexts) in which each person lives. These worlds have distinctive qualities and features that distinguish one from another.

Family life, especially the family of origin, provides a primary contextual reality. Work presents another context, while the world of play, recreation, and entertainment make up yet another sphere. The physical world including our body constitutes another powerful world. Over time these worlds change and morph into significantly different contexts, yet past events, people, and values endure even when they have faded into the past.

Once a person recognizes the various worlds she or he inhabits, faithful living can be explored. It is important to begin an examination of faith issues in our worlds by clarifying the difference between faith and belief. Urban T. Holmes and John Westerhoff, in a remarkable book called *Christian Believing,* made the distinction between faith and belief in the following way:

> It is important to distinguish between *faith* and *belief.* Religious faith is an attribute of personhood. As long as we have records of humanity we have records of religious faith. Faith, deeply personal, dynamic, and ultimate, has always been present among all peoples at all times in history.
>
> Faith—the word appears two hundred and thirty-three times in the Authorized Version of the Bible (belief appears only once)—is best understood as fidelity, as trusting obedience. Faith implies a deliberate and positive existential involvement; it precedes belief. The word for "belief" in Latin is *opinio.* "To believe" is *opinor, opinari*—that is, to have an opinion or to make an intellectual assertion.
>
> *Credo* should never have been translated as "belief." The only reason it was so translated is that in classical theology, faith and belief were once considered synonymous. In any case, *credo* literally means "I set my heart." To have religious faith—*credo*—is to pledge allegiance, to hold dear, to prize, to love intimately, to give our loyalty, to commit our lives.
>
> Faith can be and indeed must be expressed in words and ideas. *Beliefs are intellectual expressions of a people's faith.* But beliefs are *not* faith. Traditionally, theology has said that seekers ask two basic questions: First, "Is there a God?"—a question which demands a simple "yes" or "no" answer; *faith* is the affirmative response. Second, "What is God?"—a question of *belief* whose answer is complex, diverse, and inadequate.
>
> Faith is like falling in love. But suppose you are the father of an adolescent daughter, with a typical, built-in suspicion of all her suitors. Your daughter tells

you that she is "in love" with a man, but you want more than that. You ask: "Tell us what he is like." What you are asking for is a statement of belief.[1]

In the coming weeks, our work will move through five integrated units. Each has a purpose and builds on the work done in the prior unit(s). Unit One, "Spiritual Autobiography and Listening," focuses on reflecting on experience from the standpoint of a variety of worlds (contexts). Its purpose is to provide the resources needed to create a spiritual autobiography using contextual lenses. In addition, as individual spiritual autobiographies are shared, this unit explores listening as a fundamental skill for ministry. Unit Two, "Theological Reflection as a Life Skill," lays the foundation for developing another fundamental skill for ministry, reflecting from a theological standpoint on all of one's life. This unit provides the models and methods that EfM uses to integrate experience with the Christian heritage. Unit Three, "Developing a Sustaining Spirituality," encourages prayer and worship as spiritual disciplines and explores how spirituality sustains and supports a life of faith. Unit Four, "Building a Theology," provides resources for the intentional examination and construction of a personal theology through the integration of belief, behavior, and doctrine. Unit Five, "Vocation," reflects on vocation as lived in daily life. This unit offers a vocational development model for use in discerning and responding to God's call.

In Volume A, the first interlude unit, between Units Two and Three, assigns reading for the group in Christopher Bryan's *And God Spoke*, which offers a perspective on how Anglican Christians approach the Bible. The second interlude unit , between Units Four and Five, assigns reading for the group in L. William Countryman's *Living on the Border of the Holy*, which considers ministry in the context of the priesthood of all believers.

The year promises to be challenging, exciting, frustrating, encouraging, and sometimes perhaps even disturbing. The work is done together in a reflecting community of colleagues committed to helping one another know better what it means to live as an adult Christian in our worlds.

---

1. Urban T. Holmes and John Westerhoff, *Christian Believing* (New York: Seabury Press, 1979), 16.

PART I

The Guide

Week One: Orientation and Planning for the Year

This session is provided as a resource for mentors who may want to begin with a session to help organize the group and distribute materials. The components are suggestions of pieces that could be included in a Preparation Session. This is not a design that must or needs to be done, or done in this order, unless a mentor would find some or all of it helpful. After the Preparation Session, group members read according to the *Guide*.

Unit One begins with Week Two.

Worship   **TRADITION**

Prayer for a Pilgrim Who Struggles with the Journey[2]
Joyce Rupp

Pilgrim God, there is an exodus going on in my life—desert stretches, a vast land of questions. Inside my heart, your promises tumble and turn. No pillar of cloud by day or fire by night that I can see.

My heart hurts at leaving loved ones and so much of the security I have known. I try to give in to the stretching and the pain. It is hard, God, and I want to be settled, secure, safe and sure. And here I am feeling so full of pilgrim's fear and anxiety.

O God of the journey, lift me up, press me against your cheek. Let your great love hold me and create a deep trust in me. Then set me down, God of the journey; take my hand in yours, and guide me ever so gently across the new territory of my life.

God of my life, create in me the heart of a pilgrim. There is a part of me that fights letting go. Do not allow me to become so rooted or so accustomed to my daily tasks and inner securities, that I miss your voice calling me to greater growth and deeper maturity in faith. I want to hoard my blessings, to hang onto my gifts, to hide my talents and the blessings of my life.

I want to take them out, one by one, only when I know that it is safe and I won't get hurt or emptied. Stir afire in me such a great love for you and your people that I will constantly celebrate life and appreciate its beauty, even when it is painful.

---

2. Joyce Rupp, *Praying Our Goodbyes: A Spiritual Companion through Life's Losses and Sorrows* (Notre Dame, IN: Ave Maria Press, 2009), 125.

Allow me to "see visions and dream dreams" so that I can live with your vision and not be overwhelmed by the struggles of the journey. God of the Exodus, I know you are near.

Grant me the courage to change, whether that change is an inner or outer one. Deepen my awareness of your faithful presence and bless my pilgrim heart. Amen.

Check-in

Take a few minutes to consider the following:

- What events during the break have especially affected you?   **ACTION**

- What for you is the essence of EfM?   **POSITION**

Journal briefly or make notes, as you wish.

Distribute textbooks.   **TRADITION**

- **Year One:** *A Short Introduction to the Hebrew Bible* by John J. Collins. *The Holy Bible*, Old Testament and Apocrypha.

- **Year Two:** *Introducing the New Testament* by Mark Allan Powell. *The Holy Bible*, New Testament.

- **Year Three:** *Christianity: The First Three Thousand Years* by Diarmaid MacCulloch.

- **Year Four:** *Theology for a Troubled Believer* by Diogenes Allen. *The Christian Moral Life: Practices of Piety* by Timothy F. Sedgwick. *My Neighbor's Faith* edited by Jennifer Howe Peace, Or N. Rose, and Gregory Mobley.

Distribute the *Reading and Reflection Guide, Volume A* to everyone. Go over:

- Using the weekly *Reading and Reflection Guide*

- Overview of the Year, found on pages 169–92 in Part II of the Guide

Note that the readings for some sessions, in particular those at the beginning of each unit, will be found in the *Reflection and Reading Guide* rather than in the textbooks. Most participants will find looking ahead on a regular basis at the next several assignments, especially in the case of the Interlude books, will help them plan adequate time for reading before the sessions.

Review Attitudes toward Change and Transition   **CULTURE**

William Bridges notes that change is situational and external—new job, different goals, and new rules. Transition is internal—what happens and is happening emotionally and individually as a result of the change. Without a transition, a change is just a rearrangement of the furniture. Unless transition happens, the change isn't "owned" and it "won't work," because it doesn't "take." Transition is a natural process of disorientation and reorientation.

Bridges's Rule No. 1: When you're in transition, you find yourself coming back in new ways to old activities.

Returning participants come back to EfM with new texts while others come as newcomers to the program, which represents change and transition in itself.

Review Bridges's Outline on Change

CHANGE

**All changes, even the most longed for, have their melancholy;
for what we leave behind is part of ourselves;
we must die to one life before we can enter into another.**
—*Anatole France*

1. Identify who is losing what.
2. Accept the reality and importance of the subjective losses.
3. Don't be surprised at "overreaction."
4. Acknowledge the losses openly and sympathetically.
5. Expect and accept the signs of grieving.
6. Compensate for the losses.
7. Give people information, and do it again and again.
8. Define what's over and what isn't.
9. Mark the endings.
10. Treat the past with respect.
11. Let people take a piece of the old way with them.
12. Show how endings ensure continuity of what really matters.[3]

Personal Reflection

CULTURE/ACTION

Bridges's Rule No. 2: Every transition begins with an ending. Our whole way of being—the personal style that makes you recognizably "you" and me "me"—is developed within and adjusted to fit a given life pattern.

Rule No. 3: Although it is advantageous to understand your own style of endings, some part of you will resist that understanding as though your life depended on it.

Think about how you tend to act at the end of an evening at a friend's house or leaving a job or a neighborhood. Do you try to drag things out by starting new conversations and activities as others seem to be ready to leave, or do you say suddenly that it was a nice evening and dash out? (Share what you choose.)

---

3. William Bridges, *Transitions: Making Sense of Life's Changes*, 3rd ed. (Cambridge, MA: Da Capo Press, 2009), 23–36

Learning Goals and Needs   POSITION

Think of the implications of stories told.

- What goals do you have for your participation in EfM this year?

- What will help you to make this transition in your own life?

Possible theological reflection suggestions:

1. Explore "transition" from theological perspectives, using the traditional terms of creation, sin, judgment, repentance, and resurrection; or

2. Explore "transition" as a provocative word using the theological reflection method found on page 250 in Part II of this guide.

Covenant   POSITION

Questions to consider toward forming norms:

- What environment will best facilitate your goals for this year?

- What commitments will you make to your fellow travelers on this journey?

Note: The Respectful Communications Guidelines from the Kaleidoscope Institute, found on page 254 in Part II, may be a helpful resource in setting the group's own norms for community life.

Schedule   ACTION/POSITION

- Thirty-four seminar sessions in five six-week units and four Interlude sessions

- Holiday breaks

- Worship

- Spiritual autobiographies

- Theological reflection

- Anything else that needs to be scheduled

Optional Further Work on Change and Transition   CULTURE

Bridges's Rule No. 4: First there is an ending, then a beginning, and an important empty or fallow time in between.

The Neutral Zone: Attentive inactivity and ritualized routine, emptiness, old reality looks transparent, nothing feels solid anymore. The process of disintegration and reintegration is the source of renewal.

Tools: consisting of ways "in" not of ways "out"—surrender, acceptance, wilderness, retreat or liminal space, reminiscence, recollection and awareness, notice hunches, coincidences and synchronicities toward autobiography, making meaning, discovering what you really want and long for. Traps: fast forward, reverse, depression.

Beginnings: Much as we long for external signs, we must settle for inner signals that alert us to the proximity of new beginnings—a new theme, a strange fragrance, an inner idea about an external opportunity—that bring us home to ourselves. When we are ready to make a new beginning, we shortly find an opportunity.

Ways to support the process—stop getting ready and act, begin to identify yourself with the final result of the new beginning, take things step by step, shift your purpose from the goal to the process of reaching the goal.

Personal Reflection

ACTION

Think back to the neutral zones and the best and important beginnings in your own past. What tools have been most helpful to you? What has brought you home to yourself?

Worship

Psalm 139, *Prayer of One Experiencing Adult Transition by Joyce Rupp*[4]

O Lord of revelation, once again I find myself opening up to another life process, full of pain, full of mystery and a certain aching wonder. I hear you calling me to face new beginnings, to leave the old behind, to discover new and deeper parts of my total being. O Lord God, help me to realize that I can be free, that I am being freed at this present moment. Let me look beyond my own small world and smile on the mysterious way that you allow each one of us to grow into the best of our own uniqueness. I want to live and to love the mystery. I remember the wonder and newness of discovering myself as person. I recall how I began to respect and to love the secret of who I am, of how I began to sense the greater and fuller dimensions of becoming "me." I thank you for all the tastes you have given to me of myself through the crises of my life.

O God of revelation, I offer you the struggle and the beauty of being human. I ask your blessing as my human growth continues to be revealed in the midst of my daily activities. I realize that my birth was just a beginning, just a first step in the continuous series of births that have called me to constant dying and rising, to a deeper and more meaningful life. I hear now another call to die and to live more deeply, to live more wholly, more fully, a call to be opened and freed. O God, it takes so much time to bring all of myself to birth—a lifetime—and I become so impatient. This anxiousness and this anxiety

---

4. Rupp, *Praying Our Goodbyes*, 142.

I feel . . . its healthy, you say? It's all right? It's a part of my existence? It's shaping my heart into yours? Fully human? Ah yes, my God, let me not fear the mistakes or the failures of the anxieties that come with growth; rather, let me see in all of this process the signs and the strength of your cross and your resurrection. Let me know the blessing of your presence in this ever-birthing life of mine. Amen.

For Transformation the internal and external have to match.
—Laurie Rokutani

All begin the reading and reflection according to the Guide *directions for Week Two.*

UNIT ONE

Spiritual Autobiography and Listening

Week Two

Overview

An EfM seminar differs from an academic seminar. In a college context, a primary concern is understanding and mastery of content. The EfM program invites people into small, mentored communities that help us understand our lives and shape our actions as we deepen our Christian faith. The seminar is the primary place where members through conversation, prayer, and theological reflection discover and exercise gifts for ministry among those with whom they live and work.

Adults learn what they need to know as they enter into the struggle to understand the challenges of living faithfully. Mentors are trained to facilitate conversation and provide support as participants take responsibility for their learning; a mentor is neither the teacher nor the authority on the text readings. The seminar is a place where we practice the art of framing open-ended questions and listening to one another.

Some optimal techniques help avoid book reporting or retelling of study material and assist in drawing learning from study and bringing that learning into a meaningful seminar conversation: reflecting on your reading notes and highlights; noticing key concerns that are raised for you in your study; thinking about how your study can support you in living in today's world with faith.

Introduction to Context

A truism has grown out of thinking contextually: "Context is everything." The specific particularities of each experience shape how one views the urgent questions of being human. Who are we and who am I? What is truth and how can I know it? What is real and endures? What is the end (*telos*) and purpose of my life? Answers to these basic human questions arise out of particular contexts. To live faithfully in today's world requires attention to how different contexts impact our understanding of God, self, others, and the world. A person of faith does not live in a vacuum but among the specifics of cultural and religious contexts. Peter C. Hodgson, professor of theology at Vanderbilt University, wrote of the challenge of living in today's world:

> What is the new cultural situation that we face as North American Christians? It seems that it is not that of the "underside" of history, as is in the case with Latin American, African, and Asian theologies, but rather that of the "passage" of history—the passing of Western bourgeois culture, with its ideals of individuality, patriarchy, private rights, technical rationality, historical progress, capitalist economy, the absoluteness of Christianity, and so on. It *feels* as though we

are reaching the end of a historical era since we find ourselves in the midst of cognitive, historical, political, socioeconomic, environmental, sexual/gender, and religious changes of vast importance, comparable perhaps to the great enlightenment that inaugurated the modern age.[5]

Unit One of Volume A lays the foundation for thinking contextually. A person needs to be sensitive and compassionate to the contexts in his or her own life and that of others so that there is an increased probability of staying in conversation or community with others. Grappling with the reality of contextual sensitivity increases the growing awareness of God's activity within and among all people. Each week's work provides a portion of what a person or a group might need to create the foundation for living faithfully in the world.

The first Unit, "Spiritual Autobiography and Listening," works with a person's life-context and listening skills. Contextual work has two dimensions: the context of our individual lives, and the contexts of the People of God that we encounter within our study. Listening (the essence of communication) is a foundational ministry skill. Resources and reflection questions have been chosen with the intent of developing the ability to listen to all contexts—within the reading, the lives of others, in the seminar conversations, the individual worlds which we inhabit, and to our individual selves. Listening opens the door to the other so that all may better participate in the service of others and of God.

Living faithfully in a diverse, multicontextual world presents challenges. Conflicts and violence too often arise. Empathic listening and sensitivity to another's world increase the possibility of being open to God's presence. Each week's work provides a portion of what a person or a group might need to create the foundation for living faithfully in the world.

Spiritual Autobiographies

A spiritual autobiography is your life story—the telling of your journey with the purpose of discerning and proclaiming how your experience has shaped your relationship with God. Each year in the program you are asked to recall your life story. Later, you are given an opportunity to share what you think is appropriate with your seminar group. A different structure is provided for your use for each of the four years of the program. These structured methods allow you to look at the whole sweep of your life. Constructing your autobiography provides a firm foundation for the continuing work of integrating the content of your year's study with the events of your life. Your experience is a primary resource for your theological education; the yearly review of your life story enables you to hear how the timbre and direction of that story have changed in the last twelve months. Your call, discernment,

---

5. Peter Hodgson, *Winds of the Spirit: A Constructive Christian Theology* (Louisville, KY: Westminster John Knox Press, 1994), 53.

vocation, and ministry are imbedded in your spiritual journey. This process of telling and retelling your story helps those themes come more clearly into your consciousness.

A spiritual autobiography may contain both religious material—significant people or times within the religious community—and everyday material—people and times in your life that have influenced who you are now and how you understand God's presence or absence in your life.

The work you do on your spiritual autobiography is private, "for your eyes only." This allows you to be free, without concern about how others will interpret either the context or expression.

Preparing a spiritual autobiography each year provides a way to deepen your understanding of Christian life and ministry. By virtue of your baptism you were called to ministry, guided and pushed by personal gifts, passions, skills, experiences, and interests.

Once you prepare your spiritual autobiography, you need to decide what you want to share with your seminar group. Martin Buber, a twentieth-century philosopher and Jewish theologian, is reputed to have said that he could never hold a significant conversation with another person until he had heard the other's life story. The purpose of sharing autobiographies is to build trust and understanding within the group and to begin to make connections within your own story. We need the experience of hearing other life stories to know that we are not alone in God's world. By sharing appropriate stories of our lives we form learning communities that can challenge and support us throughout our lives.

Your mentor will relate her or his own story and help the group structure the time for sharing of autobiographies. Most groups give each member around ten minutes to tell his or her story, followed by time for the rest of the group to respond. Spiritual autobiographies are the focus of most of the seminar time for the first few meetings of the year. This is a special time for your group. This component of your group's life will carry you to the next phase of your year together. This may be the first time to tell your story in this way. It may seem a bit daunting at first. Remember that you should offer what you feel comfortable sharing in the group. This is not an opportunity for "group therapy" or psychologizing, so the group should not engage in raising questions about motives or probe for information beyond what you share. Feel free to say "no" or to say that you do not wish to explore questions that others may raise out of curiosity or concern.

Sharing your spiritual autobiography is a way to say, "Here I am," and to join your EFM group as a full participant. Over the years in EFM you will probably find that your spiritual autobiography changes. You may find yourself free to talk about things that were previously guarded. You also may find that your freedom to be yourself will grow as your personal story, the life of the group, and the story of God's people relate to each other.

Preparation for Seminar Week Three and Following Weeks

Spiritual Autobiography

Background: Experience begins from the moment of birth and continues to the present moment. "Raw" experience is neutral and insignificant until a person interprets the experience and gives it meaning. Each grows up living within multiple worlds. There is the world of the family, the intellect (mind), the physical world of the body through which we know that physical universe. Lives involve living within an economic world; that is, the way in which someone gets required resources. The world of play is part of experience. Each of these worlds constitutes a context in which a person creates or discovers identity and meaning.

In EfM, participants are invited to construct a spiritual autobiography according to methods that change each year. This year, the method grows out of the formation theme of Volume A: Living Faithfully in Our World.

Recollection and Reflection: Living and growing as a person means living among several worlds or contexts. Recall "worlds" or contexts in which you have lived: intellect, family, religion, play, body. You may be able to think of some others.

- Who are the people of importance in that world?

- What concerns or questions were central to the different worlds in which you live?

- What events do you remember?

- What stands out for you as you remember moving through different stages of your life?

After bringing together memories of those times and contexts, notice any sense of who you have been and who you are. These worlds or contexts and your recollection of the experiences shape your autobiography. In EfM our interest is in fashioning a *spiritual* autobiography that reflects the answers to theological concerns about the presence or absence of God, or the experience of grace, forgiveness, repentance, or questions about evil or life after death, among other concerns.

Preparation: After working with the context/worlds to recall people and circumstances of your entire life, focus on any five to ten years: How was/is your faith impacted by your various worlds during that period; how has your faith sustained you through the selected period? When or how did you experience the presence of God? What would you consider grace in various periods of your life?

At the Seminar: Each person will have time in the next three or four weeks to offer his or her autobiography.

Education for Ministry and the Importance of Listening

Education occurs as a person reflects on experience and content. Listening initiates learning. Christian ministry begins and continues with deep listening—listening for God, listening to others, and listening to oneself. A learned ministry builds as a person "listens" to the Christian tradition and applies learning to daily living. Listening is central to both education and ministry.

Before proceeding much further, it is important to define what is meant by listening. Robert Bolton in *People Skills* takes great care in defining listening. The extended quotation below began to define listening by drawing a careful distinction between "hearing" and "listening":

> It is helpful to note the distinction between hearing and listening. "Hearing," says Professor John Drakeford, "is a word used to describe the physiological sensory processes by which auditory sensations are received by the ears and transmitted to the brain. Listening, on the other hand, refers to a more complex psychological procedure involving interpreting and understanding the significance of the sensory experience."[6] In other words, I can hear what another person is saying without really listening to him. A teenager put it this way: "My friends listen to what I say, but my parents only hear me talk."
>
> I recall a time when I was talking with someone who seemed to ignore everything I said. "You are not listening to me!" I accused. "Oh, yes I am!" he said. He then repeated word for word what I had told him. He heard exactly. But he wasn't listening. He didn't understand the meanings I was trying to convey. Perhaps you have had a similar experience and know how frustrating it can be to be heard accurately by someone who isn't listening with understanding.
>
> The distinction between merely hearing and really listening is deeply embedded in our language. The word listen is derived from two Anglo-Saxon words. One word is *hlystan*, which means "hearing." The other is *hlosnian*, which means "to wait in suspense." Listening, then, is the combination of hearing what the other person says and a suspenseful waiting, an intense psychological involvement with the other.[7]

"Listening is one of the greatest gifts we can give one another and a key component of a functioning group. Often we primarily focus on what we plan to say next rather than really listening to what others say."[8] Skillful listening involves gestures, attitudes, and attention. Effective listening builds

---

6. John Drakeford, *The Awesome Power of the Listening Ear* (Waco, TX: Word, 1967), 17.

7. Robert Bolton, *People Skills: How to Assert Yourself, Listen to Others, and Resolve Conflicts* (New York: Simon & Schuster, 1989), 31–32.

8. "Listening Skills" from *Common Lessons and Supporting Materials* (Sewanee, TN: University of the South, 1998, 2002), 6-8-1.

from a few basic, common-sense approaches which emerge from the desire to respect the dignity of others.

Make eye contact without staring.

To really hear another person, listen for several things:

- What the person describes (what facts, events, situations, or information the person is trying to convey);

- How the person feels (what emotions accompany the information);

- Where the person places emphasis and shows energy;

- What the person's body is saying (sometimes one is unaware of the mixture of reactions and important information the body gives).[9]

Any skill builds from the desire to acquire it and then practice, practice, and practice some more. Use the time from week to week to continually practice until listening becomes habitual.

Respond

Prepare your spiritual autobiography. Remember to divide the work into two phases. First, use the contextual format to remember your spiritual autobiography. This work is for your eyes only. Second, plan (and rehearse) what you will present to the other members of the group. Most groups ask each participant to speak for ten to fifteen minutes.

Practice

Determine two or three ways you can put the listening skills listed above into practice. You may go to a coffee shop or some public place where you can practice listening among strangers. Also, plan how you will apply listening among those with whom you work and live.

---

9. Ibid.

Week Three

YEAR ONE

Read

Collins, Preface, Introduction, Chapter 1, "The Near Eastern Context" and Chapter 2, "The Nature of the Pentateuchal Narrative," pages 1–35

Focus

"Critical" does not mean debunking scripture, and it does not mean proving its truth. Religious people should and will find truth in their scriptures, but they may also be interested to learn something about where their scripture came from, who wrote it, and how editors collected it for them to read. For that only a historical-critical inquiry will do the job.[10]

Become familiar with terms and names such as anthropomorphic, Torah, Pentateuch, Julius Wellhausen, Hermann Gunkel, Rolf Rendtorff, Gerhard von Rad, Erhard Blum; sources in the Hebrew scripture, e.g., documentary hypothesis, J, E, P, and D sources.

YEAR TWO

Read

Powell, Preface, Chapter 1, "The New Testament World" and Chapter 2, "The New Testament Writings," pages 9–62

Focus

Terms to note: testament; apostolic; catholic; seven categories of New Testament writings; Justin Martyr's account of Christian worship; canon; stages in the transmission of the Gospel Tradition; Marcion; exegesis; hermeneutics

In the chapter section "Exegesis and Hermeneutics" Powell states, "All the exegetical methods and academic disciplines described above are used by people who operate with different hermeneutical assumptions and interests. The methods themselves are simply tools that are employed for very different purposes by people with different attitudes and goals."[11] When reading the New Testament or reading how someone else interprets a passage, it is best (if not essential) to know the purpose in reading the text or the commentary.

---

10. http://www.wfu.edu/~horton/r102/hc-method.html.
11. Mark Powell, *Introducing the New Testament* (Grand Rapids: Baker Academic, 2009), 60.

YEAR THREE

Read

MacCulloch, Acknowledgements, Introduction, Chapter 1, "Greece and Rome," pages xxiii–46

Focus

Perspectives and concepts to notice: Christians of the Middle East; Latin-speaking church; Orthodoxy; repentance and conversion; Bible as central text of Christianity; "Books are the storehouses for human ideas"; historical truth; conventions used throughout book

Until recently, our church historians have primarily traced Christian history as the movement from Jerusalem, through the Roman Empire, and on to Europe steadily moving westward to the New World. Such a focus of history is no longer practical.

MacCulloch's book has been chosen for Year Three study precisely because of his taking a more global approach. He presents Christian history by following three paths: the movement west of Jerusalem that became the Western-Latin expression of Christianity; the path into the Middle East and Far East; and the Eastern Orthodoxies of Byzantium empires.

Points to note: *Logos*; *Hellas*; *polis*; *ekklesia*; Plato's influence on Christianity; Hellenistic Greece; *res publica* (republic); Roman Republic; imperial monarchy

The Greek understanding of *polis* provides a way to flesh out a fuller understanding of living within a social and intellectual context [cf. pages 25, 26]. It involves knowing the collective consciousness that greatly influences a person's identity. The *polis* greatly shapes how one behaves, thinks, and lives. MacCulloch writes extensively about the Greek and Roman worlds as the cultural contexts definitively impacting Christianity.

YEAR FOUR

Read

Allen, Preface, Introduction, "What Is Theology?" pages ix–xxiv

Focus

Identify the six motives Allen lists that draw people to Christianity. Reflect on which of the motives have been present in your being drawn to Christianity.

Allen notes that theological topics are sometimes organized under "rubrics." He includes such topics as creation, incarnation, Holy Spirit, etc. Compare the "rubrics" to the theological perspective questions used in the exploration phase of the theological reflection process. Identify two or three different topics that Allen names. Use the topic (rubric) to frame questions to explore a focus for theological reflection.

ALL YEARS

Respond

What purposes, attitudes, and assumptions do you bring to your reading and study of the Christian tradition?

How have your attitudes and assumptions been fashioned by the various life contexts (worlds) identified in your spiritual autobiography work? How have those attitudes and assumptions affected your reading of the Christian tradition?

Use the notes or highlights you made during your assigned reading this week to reflect on the key contexts (concerns, interests, and issues) faced by the men and women of that time. What were some concerns for those who would live in faith?

Practice

Describe what feeling "at home" means to you.

Knowing oneself includes an increasing awareness of the worlds in which each has lived or currently lives. In EfM a primary strategy for self-awareness is through the use of spiritual autobiographies. Review the information in Week Two regarding spiritual autobiographies as you are constructing your spiritual autobiography. Over the next few weeks, you will have opportunities to talk about your reflections on portions of your spiritual autobiography.

For the next few weeks the seminar will center on reflecting on your reading and reflecting on spiritual autobiographies.

When you share your autobiographical reflections, what do you need to do to communicate your thoughts? When you listen to others, what do you need to do to listen well?

Week Four

YEAR ONE

Read

Genesis chapters 1–11
Collins, Chapter 3, "The Primeval History," pages 36–43

Focus

Terms to know: primeval; two creation stories; 'adam, Atrahsis myth; Epic of Gilgamesh; Sons of God (Genesis 6); Enuma Elish

Stories delight and entertain. They come in various forms and styles. Myths, epics, legends, novellas, and fables each tell some tale that entertains as they instill values, guidance, and meaning. Often the values live implicitly within the hearers of the stories only to surface in moments of crisis that call for decisive action. Some myths come into being to explain why things are as they are; others prescribe "right" behavior; while others venture into offering explanations along with establishing meaning.

All people, to some degree or another, seek answers to fundamental questions. What is truth and can I know it? What endures? What is real? Is there purpose to my life? Where did we come from and where are we going? Stories in all their forms, one way or another, offer answers to basic concerns.

YEAR TWO

Read

Powell, Chapter 3, "Jesus" and Chapter 4, "The Gospels," pages 63–101

Focus

Points to define: The two doctrines of Jesus; kingdom of God; themes in Jesus' teaching; the historical Jesus

Terms to become familiar with: gospel as a literary genre; parables; miracle stories; pronouncement stories; passion and resurrection narratives; sayings of Jesus; the synoptic puzzle (*aka* problem); the Q source; Griesbach hypothesis; *Diatessaron*

YEAR THREE

Read

MacCulloch, Chapter 2, "Israel," pages 47–73

Focus

Terms to recognize: Maccabees; Tanakh; Apocrypha; the first and second exiles; Samaritans; the first and second temple; Septuagint; Hellenized Jews; creation out of nothingness; development of the notion of afterlife and individual soul; Hasmonean dynasty; Sadduccees; Pharisees; Essenes; Zealots

Chapter 2 concludes Part I "A Millennium of Beginnings" in which MacCulloch traces the social and intellectual "seeds" of Christianity. The two histories (Greco-Roman and Israel) continually influence Christian life and thought.

The following quote appears near the bottom of page 50 of MacCulloch's *Christianity: The First Three Thousand Years*: "Even through their hardest and most wretched experiences of fighting with those they love most deeply, [Israel is] being given some glimpse of how they relate to God."

MacCulloch connects this struggle with Jacob's formational struggle with the angel of the Lord, with God, at the River Jabok. This way of drawing meaning from experience allowed Israel to view history through the eyes of faith. History became the arena in which they could see God at work, bringing them into being as a people bound to God. Some consider this a rewriting of history only, merely a means of self-justification. There is plenty of room for that view. However, this is also a way of interpreting history, of seeing God at work in the life and experience of an individual and a group; this is salvation history—history that tells the story of God's work of redemption.

YEAR FOUR

Read

Allen, Chapter 1, "The Holy One of Israel," pages 3–18

Focus

Identify the following terms and concepts: henotheist; monotheist; transcendence; immanence; *mysterium tremendum et fascinans*; Otto; Anselm; intellectual repentance; holiness

Allen wrote that we know about God "because God makes Godself known or reveals Godself *in what God does.*"[12] Identify what God has done that reveals something about God.

---

12. Diogenes Allen, *Theology for a Troubled Believer* (Louisville: Westminster John Knox, 2010), 17.

ALL YEARS

Respond

Trust, confidence, and faith often mean the same thing.

How have issues of trust been present in your life?

In your assigned reading this week, what issues of trust do you find?

What implication does trust have in your daily life?

Practice

LISTENING SKILLS

Review of Effective Listening

Listening is one of the greatest gifts we can give one another and a key component of ministry and of a functioning group. Often we focus on what we plan to say next rather than really listening to what others say.

TWO IMPORTANT POINTS

Make eye contact without staring at the other person.

When you listen to another person, listen to four things:

- What the person describes (what facts, events, situations, or information the person is trying to convey)

- How the person feels (what emotions accompany the information)

- Where the person places emphasis and shows energy

- What the person's body is saying (sometimes one is unaware of the mixture of reactions and important information the body gives).

Ways Not to Listen

Following are some exercises for developing effective listening skills and some dos and don'ts for framing questions when you listen to another person. Included are different types of listening and the purpose each type serves. Nonlistening practices in a group reduce the sense of individual participation, detract from group cohesiveness, and contribute to conflict. The same styles detract from person-to-person engagement and limit ministry effectiveness.

1. Passive listening: not concentrating on what the person is saying.

2. Happy hooking: constantly changing the subject to center the conversation on you and not on the speaker. Many times people become very competitive and try to devise a topic that is similar but more exciting than the speaker's.

3. Mind reading: completing the other person's sentences, acting as if you understand what they are saying, giving advice before you have heard them through.

4. Inappropriate body language: jiggling your foot, clicking a pen, staring at the person, touching them without being sensitive to whether they want to be touched, saying you are interested while showing the opposite with your body, showing aggression and impatience with your body while saying you are concerned.

Ways to Sidetrack the Conversation

1. Answering emotions with logic. When someone is excited about something, he or she does not want the first response to be a critical analysis. The speaker wants the other person to share some of his or her excitement.

2. Bringing in old issues. When people want to discuss a problem, they do not want to be told that they always have similar problems or that they failed to do something about the problem three months ago.

3. Using sarcasm or cynicism, or not taking the other person's issues seriously.

An Exercise to Improve Listening Skills

PURPOSE: To provide an opportunity to practice listening skills.

1. During the week, give yourself a chance to carefully listen to something that someone tells you; a coworker, family member, neighbor, store employee, and so forth. As soon as possible after the listening opportunity has ended, write about the experience, including the following:

   a. A synopsis of the sharing

   b. What he or she heard as the speaker's feelings about the event and about sharing the event

   c. Words, images, and metaphors that stood out

   d. What you thought the speaker was saying with his or her body.

2. During the week, when someone has listened to you in a way that caused you to feel really "heard," tell the listener the following:

   a. How the listener asked questions;

   b. How the listener's body posture encouraged sharing;

   c. What other responses helped the you feel understood and helped you clarify what you were saying.[13]

---

13. Adapted from Education for Ministry *Common Lessons and Supporting Materials (2005)*, 6-8-1 to 6-8-3.

Reflecting on Listening

What image conveys your sense of how it feels to really listen?

What image conveys your sense of how it feels for someone to really listen to you?

An additional resource on Storytelling and Holy Listening from the VocationCARE program can be found on pages 228–29 in Part II of this guide.

How might listening be a holy act?

Week Five

YEAR ONE

Read

"The Priestly Creation Story" essay provided in Part II, pages 180–85.

Focus

Identify and become familiar with pronunciation: covenant; Baals, cult; Sabbath, *ex nihilo*; Zoroastrianism; Manichaeism; dualism; Plato; Neo-Platonic; *via negativa*

"The Priestly Creation Story," consisting of only ten verses in Genesis, poetically presents a full doctrine of creation. It also offers a doctrine of God. A guided study of the story draws out the meaning contained in this ancient poem. The story shows God as wholly Other yet present to creation. God transcends all that is, thereby providing a corrective to all forms of dualism. Many theological difficulties get untangled by the implications in the story.

YEAR TWO

Read

The Gospel according to Matthew *(try to set aside enough time to read this gospel in one or two sittings).*

Focus

Identify terms or references that you had to look up.

The Gospel writers tell the story of the Good News of God in Christ. The Gospel in its entirety communicates the story. However, seldom do people hear the entire story, rather they experience the Scripture verse by verse or in short pieces they hear within worship. Such reading is like watching a trailer of a film and believing you have seen the movie. Individual scenes make little or no sense without the context of the story. So too it is important to know the entire Gospel, allowing you to experience its drama. Once you have a sense of Matthew's story, you are positioned better to interpret individual scenes, teachings, and events.

YEAR THREE

Read

MacCulloch, Chapter 3, "A Crucified Messiah," pages 77–111

Focus

Points to note: cluster of words (*evaggelion, evangelium,* Gospel); Julius Africanus; *epiousios*; parables; *abba*; *Kyrios*—"Jesus is Lord, the word for God"; Paul of Tarsus; *epistole*; Paul's use of the word "church"; Johannine Christ; Jewish revolt and fall of Jerusalem

Change in the eastern region of the Roman Empire eventually upset the Roman Empire's social order. The history of Christianity began with seemingly insignificant events. The importance of those events became clear through the lenses of experience and hindsight.

YEAR FOUR

Read

Allen, Chapter 2, "Holiness for Today," pages 19–27

Focus

Compare Isaiah's vision of God with Moses's encounter with God. Identify Simone Weil; Jean Vanier; absolute value.

State in your own words the justification of the claim that "human beings are significant, have dignity, and have absolute value."[14]

ALL YEARS

Respond

Identify how or where you have evidence in recent years of debates between authority and revelation. Think more broadly than within faith communities.

How has your life experience helped you in matters of authority, whether related to the church or to politics or to culture (e.g., family, community, or nation)?

Practice

Change disrupts continuity. New ways of speaking and even newer ways of behaving create unrest. Yet without continuity change evaporates into nothingness. Society's reordering of itself after chaotic change provides the stuff of history.

Find evidence in news stories or other circumstances of changes that are challenging continuity. Practice listening for the voices on both sides of such a challenge—those embracing change and those advocating "holding true" to what has been. What do you discover when you listen for those voices?

What opportunities for ministry are there in the midst of such challenges?

---

14. Allen, *Theology for a Troubled Believer,* 27.

Week Six

YEAR ONE

Read

Genesis 12–50
Collins, Chapter 4, "The Patriarchs," pages 44–55

Focus

Identify terms or references that you had to look up.

    Reading the primary text is essential to understanding scripture. Your reading forms the basis for understanding what scholars and others say about the text. Dr. Robert Denton, professor of the Old Testament at General Theological Seminary, often reminded his students that they would be amazed by how much the text illuminates the commentary. Each person has unique experiences that shape how scripture is interpreted. While the work of biblical scholars is enormously valuable, only you can bring your distinctive experience to the learning process. Then your experience with the text can be brought into dialogue with what scholars have written. It is within that dialogue that deeper learning occurs.

Identify, note, and define: types of legends (etiological, ethnological, etymological, ceremonial); Hermon Gunkel; *Sitz im Lebem; bris*; Abraham Cycle; Jacob Cycle; Joseph Story

What sources do the "authors" of the stories of the patriarchs use to express the meaning of the story?

Notice what sources Collins uses in this chapter. (Possible candidates for the sources might be academic disciplines, biblical references, personal experience, or beliefs or conclusions he asserts.)

YEAR TWO

Read

Powell, Chapter 5, "Matthew," pages 103–23

Focus

Identify: five speeches of Jesus; Beatitudes; binding and loosing of the law; *oligopistoi;* Eusebius; *Ecclesiastical History*

YEAR THREE

Read

MacCulloch, Chapter 4, "Boundaries Defined," pages 112–154

Sprinkled throughout the chapter are references to primary sources. Find two or three of them to read. They can be found in Bettenson's *Documents of the Christian Church* and online. Christian Classics Ethereal Library, www .ccel.org, provides numerous documents of the church, for example, *The Teaching of the Twelve Apostles, Commonly Called the Didache* at http://www.ccel. org/ccel/richardson/fathers.viii.i.iii.html.

Focus

Find and become familiar with pronunciation: *Hermas* (*The Shepherd*) and the *Didache* online or in Bettenson (if you have purchased that book) or elsewhere and read what you can or want.

Terms to learn: Letter to Philemon; *Didache*; gnosis, Gnosticism, Nag Hammadi; Docetism; key points of difference between gnostic and Jewish attitudes; Marcion; Diatessaron; *presbyteroi*; *diakonos*; *episkopoi*; the importance of Antioch and Jerusalem in the early church; Clement; Ignatius; Victor; Stephen of Rome

YEAR FOUR

Read

Allen, Chapter 3, "The Maker of Heaven and Earth" and Chapter 4, "Limits of Science," pages 28–43

Focus

Identify: Von Rad; Israel's cosmology; Augustine's examination of time; contemporary cosmology; relationship of creation and salvation

State the difference between the biblical view of creation and the scientific view of the universe.

Draw a distinction between the origin of the universe and the purpose of creation.

ALL YEARS

Respond

Faith is a complex matter; like any form of life, it consists of beliefs, actions, attitudes, and patterns of behavior that are often hard to identify, much less distinguish from one another and then define. Thus, at times we may not know what it is we believe theologically or why we undertake the specific faith-practices that we do, but we nonetheless do them over and over again just as we are constantly re-enacting particular theological habits of thought in the course of our daily lives. Furthermore, our religious beliefs can almost never be separated from other beliefs, actions, and attitudes that we hold and that also shape us, such as our culturally constructed beliefs about what it means to be a woman or a citizen or a student of theology.[15]

What does living faithfully mean to you?

How have reading, reflecting, and listening expanded your understanding of what is involved in living faithfully?

Autobiography: Who are the people in your life of whom you could say, "That person is an example of living faithfully"?

Practice

Write the qualities or characteristics of living faithfully.

Listening requires attentiveness, which also requires silence. Practice attentive listening this week. Notice what it takes for you to be silent and really listen to someone else. Make some notes about that.

What do you have to do in order to achieve that? What is difficult about listening attentively?

---

15. Serene Jones and Paul Lakeland, eds., *Constructive Theology: A Contemporary Approach to Classic Themes*. A project of The Workgroup on Constructive Christian Theology (Minneapolis: Fortress, 2005), 11.

Week Seven

YEAR ONE

Read

Exodus 1–24

Collins, Chapter 5, "The Exodus from Egypt," pages 55–63.

Focus

Describe the meaning of the term "salvation history." Define any names, terms, or references that were unfamiliar to you in Exodus.

Name the images/metaphors for God that the writer of Exodus uses to tell the story of God's action of liberation for the children of Israel. Select two or three of the images for God and explore what qualities of God the image reveals.

Terms that address the historicity of the Exodus event: Manetho; Hyksos; Hecataeus; Rameses II; Habiru; *Yam Sup*; Passover

Terms that deal with the meaning of the past: charter myth; history; legend; folklore; founding myth

Words and phrases related to God: YHWH; Adonai (Lord); *HaShem*; *éhyeh áser* (I AM WHO I AM); *éhyeh; eimi ho on* (I am the one who is); absolute Being; YHWH is on the side of the weak

Themes to keep in mind: revelation of God; liberation of people

Review the first twelve chapters of Exodus looking for moments of God's self-disclosure and moments of liberation.

YEAR TWO

Read

The Gospel according to Mark

Powell, Chapter 6, "Mark," pages 125–45

Focus

Identify terms or references in Mark's Gospel that you had to look up.

In Powell's text, note: John Mark; intercalation; major themes in Mark; messianic secret; *inclusio*

Every discussion, written or spoken, draws on material to form the presentation. The content (images, story, ideas) comes from different sources, which may be other writings, personal experiences, or beliefs held. Make note of the different sources that Powell uses throughout his chapter on Mark.

YEAR THREE

Read

MacCulloch, Chapter 5, "The Prince: Ally or Enemy," pages 155–88

Focus

Terms and names to note and become familiar with pronunciation: *parousia*; *Apostolic Tradition*; Celus; *in catacumbas;* Origen; Plotinus; Mani; Manichee/Manichaean; Diocletian; Syriac Church; Osrhoene; Dura Europos; Armenia; Ephren; *Odes of Solomon*; Trdat (Tiridates)

Christianity not only survived but grew under the wave of persecutions from 100 to 300 CE. People willing to suffer and die for what they believe wield powerful inspirations. When religious conviction is stronger than the fear of pain and death, people notice. It's as if the persecutors' sword sharpens one's beliefs into passionate convictions. Clarity comes whenever a person discovers relationships that matter more than death. The witness born from martyrdom has transformative power for both believers and non-believers.

YEAR FOUR

Read

Allen, Chapter 5, "What Is Meant by 'God,'" pages 44–53

Focus

Ideas and images to know: universe as everything but God; hiddenness of God; cosmological argument for existence of God; faith as above reason

Having read the chapter, answer the question "What is meant by God?"

ALL YEARS

Respond

From time to time, a person needs to stop and take stock of what has been done and what is being learned. Conversations about important matters can bring fresh awareness and allow seeing newness within the ordinary. Insight brings a renewed energy and vitality to the creation of meaning. Understanding anew the dynamics present in daily life opens the door for a person to see how her or his life is being lived. Then, a decision can be made to continue living in that manner or to make different and possibly better decisions.

Review the thoughts and feelings that you have had over the previous several weeks. As you sift these recent experiences, consider what you have learned from listening to yourself and to others within the seminar. A corollary question: What difference does what you have learned make to how you live your life?

Practice

In whatever place works well for you to focus and be still, set a timer for fifteen minutes and allow yourself to be present to your self, your environment, and to the presence of God. Just be still. Allow images and thoughts and sounds and sensations to just be, not trying to ignore them. Just be.

After fifteen minutes, write briefly about all that you were aware of during that time of listening and presence.

UNIT TWO

Theological Reflection as a Life Skill

Week Eight

Theological Reflection as a Life Skill

Two people sitting at a table over coffee engage energetically in conversation. Clearly, even from a distance, what they are saying to one another matters. Moving closer we can begin to hear something of what concerns them. Some relationship of one kind or another seemingly occupies their minds. While we cannot make out exactly what they are talking about, the two people say enough to have us realize that one of them has recently undergone some experience that left them with the desire to make sense of the experience. Together they struggle to find meaning in what happened. Only partial phrases can be overheard: "I read about this recently on the Internet," one says. "That reminds me of something I read in the Bible recently," the other adds. Near the end of the conversation they both can be heard saying, "I can't believe that, but I can believe this!"

That scene, or one like it, occurs throughout the world and all languages. The desire to create meaning out of experience is universal. From one generation to another people need to find answers to important questions or at least simply to understand better their experience. As a person matures, the issues change but the desire to know and understand remains. We are meaning-seeking beings who hope to find wisdom that guides us.

Theological reflection is a life skill used to create meaning, in fact, to discover ultimate meaning. What makes reflection theological is not a specialized vocabulary, but the relentless, restless urge to experience wholeness which brings a person to the Holy. The word "holy" in English stems from the Old English word *haleg*, which means whole.

Education for Ministry makes a bold claim: **Each of us is a theologian**. It is not an option. The question is not whether or not we reflect theologically. The question is how proficient we are.

Throughout the four years in EfM, participants practice the discipline of theological reflection. Models and methods developed within the program guide and support theological reflection. Assignments in the coming weeks will present fundamentals of theological reflection. The intent is to provide resources and practice for the refinement of the life skill of theological reflection.

In general, the term "theological reflection," used in various ways throughout the theological world, means knowing God and knowing about God through experience. EfM over the years has developed a vocabulary in support of implementing the discipline of theological reflection. Two broad areas of development were model and method.

The EFM Four-Source Model for Theological Reflection

Sources from which one draws meaning have long been important for theological learning. Richard Hooker, a sixteenth-century Anglican theologian, used three sources: scripture, tradition, and reason. Paul Tillich, a twentieth-century theologian, indicated that the theologian's sources are the Bible, church history, history of religion, and culture. Contemporary theologian John Macquarrie, while disliking the term "sources," lists six "formative factors": experience, revelation, scripture, tradition, culture, and reason.

The EFM program suggests that theological reflection occurs at the juncture of our personal experience and the world we encounter. Both are enveloped by the divine milieu which we encounter in liturgy and spiritual points of our lives. Reflection occurs when we stand in the juncture as depicted in the following diagram:

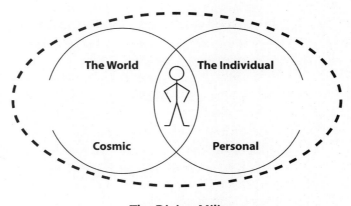

The Divine Milieu

Our experience indicates that theological reflection is more likely to occur if we differentiate personal experience and experience of the world and are careful to distinguish among four sources: Personal Experience/Action, Personal Position (Beliefs, Values), Culture/Society, and the Christian Tradition. The Action and Position sources reflect personal experiences and beliefs, while Culture and Tradition identify what we receive from the world.

Please note: Although in EfM these have often been shortened to **Action, Position, Culture, and Tradition,** in this *Guide* we will frequently use the alternate descriptors to emphasize the fullness of what is contained in each source.

ACTION

The **Personal Experience/Action** source of meaning involves what we do and experience. The specific actions we take, as well as the thoughts, feelings, and perspectives associated with the actions, come from this source.

In constructing spiritual autobiographies, each person works principally with the Action source. We remember past events and weave them into a pattern that tells our life stories. We say, "I remember . . ." or "My thoughts were . . ." or "I felt. . . ." And we say, "Then I walked to . . ." or "I did. . . ."

POSITION

The **Personal Belief/Position** source of meaning refers to that for which one consciously argues—personal attitudes, opinions, beliefs, and convictions. Phrases beginning, "I believe . . . ," "I know that . . . ," "That's the way it is . . . ," and "It's true that . . ." indicate drawing from the Position source. Included here are tentative opinions as well as passionately held convictions.

CULTURE

The **Culture or Contemporary Culture/Society** source of meaning encompasses almost all the objective content available to a person. The libraries of the world contain material that is in the Culture source. The attitudes and opinions generally held in a society also fall within this source. The Culture source draws from movies, television, magazines, advertisements, law, architecture, customs, and attire—in short, all the aspects of life that are around us. Culture is so vast that one can only deal with certain specific aspects of it; therefore, there is need to identify specific items from Culture on which to focus in a theological reflection. Culture frequently sends mixed messages and may be intertwined with aspects of our faith, such as a picture that mixes the Christmas crèche with Santa Claus and a Christmas tree.

TRADITION

The **Tradition** source refers to faith tradition, and in EfM generally refers to **Christian Tradition**, the content of the Christian heritage. It begins with the Bible and extends to the liturgies, stories, documents, music, artifacts, and history of Christianity. The Tradition source contains the literature that the Christian community has designated as authoritative. In addition to conveying truth and meaning, the contents of the Tradition source evoke awareness of the Holy, experiences of awe, or a sense of God's presence. Phrases like, "The Bible says . . ." and "According to the Prayer Book . . ." mark this source. The EFM program provides a four-year presentation of the Christian faith tradition through the participant's reading material. The Tradition source of meaning relates to the underpinnings of a faith tradition. Therefore, the term "Tradition" could be modified by Native American, if someone has that experience in their personal history; or Buddhist, or Hindu, and so forth. The important point is that Tradition as a source of meaning refers to that area of life that has nurtured or formed someone's view of God and the holy.

It is useful both to distinguish among these sources and to notice where they overlap. Each person draws on the sources as they try to make sense of the world around them. Each source functions as a kind of framework within which an individual, or even a group, interprets their experience. Often there is an inclination to keep these frameworks separate from one another. For example, what happens at work may lead to quite cynical conclusions about human nature. An individual may keep these conclusions altogether apart from how he or she views life as a family member or as a member of the church or faith group. In theological reflection we bring together these different ways of looking at the world. We look at each of the four sources of meaning so that our entire understanding may be informed by the Christian faith tradition.

Merely accessing a variety of sources—the Christian faith tradition, contemporary culture, personal experience, and personal beliefs—is not the whole of theological reflection. Doing theology requires a holistic response that involves the intellect, imagination, and emotions. The work of theology requires developing the ability to employ imagination to create metaphors, symbols, and analogies. Analogical thinking, especially practiced within a community of faith, is an essential element that constitutes theological reflection. Whenever a person gives studied attention to knowing God, the person begins to reflect theologically. How one understands God will influence an individual's view of the church (ecclesiology), worship and prayer (liturgics and spirituality), mission (missiology), human nature, and ministry. The *Guide* presents ways to practice analogical thinking by using images and metaphors and practice in connecting to the four sources of meaning in our lives—Christian Faith Tradition, Personal Experience/Action, Society/Culture, and Personal Beliefs/Positions.

A Method for Theological Reflection

For literally decades, a beginning artist tried to draw human faces using pencils and paper. While the drawings were recognizable, they resembled what one might see in a fun house mirror that distorts facial features. He decided to attend art classes to learn the basics of drawing. The first class introduced four principles: 1) all drawings are made up of basic shapes such as circles, triangles, squares, and rectangles and their oval, trapezoid, and parallelogram cousins; 2) arranging the shapes on the paper (the picture's composition) is primary; 3) shading adds depth; 4) details are drawn last. The instructor then said, "It is important to follow the composition, shading, and detail steps in order. Almost all problems arise in the composition or shading steps and not in the details. The problems you encounter in drawing can be solved by returning to the basics." The novice artist came away from the introductory lecture understanding how to solve difficulties in drawing. He also knew that to become proficient in sketching he must practice, practice, and practice again the basics of drawing.

This section begins with a story about drawing because theological reflection is an art analogous to drawing. Basic principles, developed over several decades within the EfM network, introduce the art of theological reflection. Learning the basic principles helps "correct" problems experienced as an individual or group works with theological reflection.

Disciplined thinking works with models and methods. A model shows *what* is to be done while a method guides *how* it is done. The discipline of theological reflection as practiced within EfM works from the Four-Source Model (Christian Faith Tradition, Contemporary Culture/Society, Personal Belief/Position, and Personal Experience/Action), producing a "picture" of what we are trying to do. Methods allow us to apply the model.

Each theological reflection method within EfM follows a four-phase process: *identify*, *explore*, *connect*, and *apply*.

Identify: To provide a starting point, each method begins by identifying a focus, e.g., something from **Personal Experience/Action** such a personal incident; from **Contemporary Culture/Society** such as a news story, movie, poem, work of art; from **Christian Faith Tradition** such as the Sunday scriptures, sermons, prayers of the church, hymns; or from **Personal Belief/Position** such as found on a bumper sticker or an essay or opinion page of the newspaper (a Position that occurs in a Culture piece). A note about the Position source: whether someone writes an essay, a news article, a poem, work of fiction or nonfiction, a news program or many other examples, there will be a Personal Position contained within the writing or presentation.

This week's work introduces a method that begins with a text from scripture (Christian Tradition). The focus centers on something that produces interest in exploring further. For example: A person reading the Priestly creation story might focus on verse 31 ("God saw everything that he had made, and indeed, it was very good"). The *identifying* phase would continue by recalling a specific time of experiencing life as being "very good." Next would be to develop an image that expresses what that experience of "life is very good" was like; e.g., "it was like finding an ordinary-looking box and discovering a wonderful, joyful gift." The image becomes the identified focus. At that point the reflection moves from *Identifying* (e.g., an ordinary box that contains a wonderful gift) to *Exploring* what it is like to live in a world of discovering unexpected gifts among the ordinary.

Explore: The next phase of theological reflection uses some theological questions to examine the focusing image or metaphor. The purpose, like any concentrated investigation, is to notice the features and characteristics of the identified focus. Thematic questions used in EfM are based on theological topics, often developed from basic doctrines. For example, theological themes or perspectives developed from the Hebrew Scriptures include, but are not limited to,

creation (What is the world or life like for those in the image or passage or text being considered?);

sin (What alienates, breaks, or separates in the image-world?);

judgment (What surprises, jolts, or causes one to be aware of alienation or wholeness?);

repentance (What turns someone in that image from destruction and turns them toward life?);

redemption (What brings life, renewal, restoration to someone in that image?).

Look at the image from different theological viewpoints, e.g., asking what characterizes the "world of the image" (creation perspective) or what causes alienation in the world (sin perspective) guides the conversation into an exploration of the theology contained within the image.

Use two or three of the theological themes/perspectives to explore the focus.

Connect: The point is that during the *connecting* phase associations with each of the sources of meaning in someone's life begin to occur. If someone is not yet able to discern distinctly the four sources, the reflection may produce confusion and feelings of being lost. Therefore, it is important to become proficient in distinguishing the four sources that offer wisdom or meaning in our lives: **Personal Experience, Faith Tradition, Contemporary Culture,** and **Personal Position**.

To recap to this point: The reflection began in the Christian Faith Tradition source of meaning with the passage from Genesis. Recalling an experience of "Life is very good" drew from Personal Experience to help *identify* a focus. The image of discovering a box with a joyful surprise inside further identified a focus of that passage. The *Explore* phase asked theological questions of the image to help get a sense of the dimensions of that kind of world. The *Connect* phase deliberately turns to the other two sources, Contemporary Culture and Personal Position (though connections to other sources can occur at any point and in any order).

Examination that draws from the Contemporary Culture could use movies that may have shown something about life being very good, or perhaps for another perspective, movies that have shown life as not good. Or the Culture source of meaning could draw from how advertising in America looks at life or "the good life." Once something from Contemporary Culture comes to mind relating to the identified focus of the reflection, comparing and contrasting the view presented in the Culture source of meaning and that presented in the Christian Faith Tradition source produces further food for reflection.

Finally, the *connecting phase* of this particular reflection example draws on Personal Beliefs/Positions: What do I hold as true about life? What positions do the views of Culture and Tradition cause me to take? Where do I get those beliefs?

Theological reflection can result in entertaining ideas that quickly evaporate if not put into practice. As you enter more fully into theological reflection, it is essential that the applying phase be given significant attention. It is hard work to apply what one learns to concrete and specific life situations.

Apply: The *applying phase* of theological reflection involves clarifying what the exploring and connecting phases bring into view. New learning often touches on values and behavior. Often the learning involves a change of behavior and occasionally a shift in how a person understands self, human nature, and God. Deep, significant insights need support and encouragement to enter into the change. That is one of the reasons theological reflection is done best in a supportive community.

It is good to remember that the terms "learner," "disciple," and "discipline" are closely related. Knowing God and learning how to think about God, especially for Christians, necessitate a congruency between belief and behavior. Insights require drawing out implications for living more faithfully in "thought, word, and deed."

When the *applying phase* is brought center stage, the skills, knowledge, and attitude needed to "incarnate" insights into daily life have energy. As you do your reading and focus your study, do so with the continual question of what relevance your study, reflection, and learning have to your life and ministry.

Weekly you participate in discussion with other members of your group. Theological reflection is done individually and as a group. The variety of experiences and thoughts of group members and the group dynamics enrich and add complexity to the process.

"Reflection" involves thinking carefully about what one reads, experiences, believes, or knows. Such thinking requires willingness to be open and vulnerable as one reconsiders what each believes, understands, or interprets.

Julian Marias, a Spanish philosopher of the twentieth century, said that Christianity does not give solutions, but does give light by which to seek them. Careful theological reflection illuminates experience. Theological reflection is not a problem-solving process, but a means to new or renewed awareness and understanding. As a person learns more about the Christian tradition, the increased knowledge provides fuel that generates light by which to "see" situations more clearly.

A Word about Metaphors

The use of metaphor is the method of teaching that Jesus used in the parables. In theological reflection, we employ the power of a metaphor to take us from the specific to the universal—the collective experience of human beings in God's world.

Metaphors are verbal pictures. We are not concerned here with the distinctions among images, metaphors, and similes. All of these translate meaning from one thing to another. The literal meaning of the Greek *meta + phero* is "carry over."

The metaphor functions as a bridge that connects what happens to us in our contemporary world with the other sources of meaning in theological reflection.

Metaphors provide a means to move from the known to the unknown, to understand the unfamiliar by means of the familiar. The metaphor also can offer a fresh look at what we think we already know. Religious metaphors depend on the intersection of the known, daily, human world and the unknown, mysterious, divine realm of God. Metaphors can be generated from experiences, thoughts, and feelings. The metaphor emerges from the identified reflection focus. In a group, the similarity of feelings and thoughts among members of the group makes the metaphor unifying. It paints a clear picture of contemporary life as experienced, at least on occasion, by the members of the seminar.

Theological Reflection in a Group[16]

During the first phase of reflection the subject is identified. This may be something that has happened to the group member, a particular belief the member holds, something from our Christian tradition, or an aspect of contemporary culture. Before we can begin, we need to name the subject. What exactly are we going to talk about? Where does it begin? Where does it end? How are we involved?

Identify: The more sharply defined the focus of the reflection, the more likely it is that the reflection will shape the understanding and the actions of the participants. Using the "theology of the Psalms" as a starting point for reflection is likely to lead to a very general discussion. However, using the first two verses of Psalm 37, for example, provides much finer focus:

> Fret not yourself because of the wicked, be not envious of wrongdoers!
> For they will soon fade like the grass, and wither like the green herb.

Dealing with a particular passage makes it more likely that our partner in conversation will be the tradition itself and not merely our opinions about the tradition. Similarly, when the starting point for reflection is an experience from our life, it is important to describe that experience with specificity and clarity in order to avoid merely rehashing previously held positions. The focus that is chosen for reflection should not only be clearly identified, but it should also matter to the participants. Whether the reflection begins with **Action**, **Tradition**, **Culture**, or **Position**, the focus should engage the interest and attention of the group members. Unless this happens, the reflection is likely to lack energy.

Explore: The second phase explores the subject that has been identified. What is it like? What language best describes it? What do we discover as we examine it from different vantage points? If the subject has been raised by some life event, what does this event say to us about our world? If we are

---

16. This section is adapted from *Common Lessons and Supporting Materials*, 2-11-1 ff.

reflecting on some belief that we hold, to what does this belief apply? What assumptions and values are implicit in the belief? If our starting point is a text from the Christian tradition or from another text? What does the text say to us on its own terms?

As we explore the subject of our reflection, we will often find it useful to use the language of metaphor. Using an image or metaphor deliberately encourages the evocative, intuitive quality of exploration.

Connect: The third phase makes connections between what has been discovered so far and the wider sources of meaning and truth. A reflection becomes theological by making deliberate connections between the Christian tradition and our own experience. Christian theological reflection links the Christian heritage with the personal and cultural dimensions of our lives. In this phase we are interested in the following general categories of questions:

- How does our exploration of this particular subject fit with our beliefs, with the scriptures, and with the creeds of the church?

- Does our exploration test out in everyday life? What would others in our family or at our work say about this?

The questions above are too broad to be of much practical help. More sharply defined questions help us connect and compare one source with another. A particularly helpful question is one that moves us right inside the subject of our exploration so that we can see what things look like from this perspective. We refer to questions like these as **perspective questions.** An example follows:

What kind of world is depicted in the first two verses of Psalm 37? It is a world in which there are wrongdoers, and the wrongdoers sometimes flourish, but not for long. The question "*What kind of world?*" gives us a structure for developing a conversation with other sources of meaning. For example, we can think back to our own experiences with wrongdoers. Have they in fact "faded away like the grass"? What kind of world do we seem to inhabit when we look at what happens to us and at how we actually behave?

Then we can move from questioning the **Action** source in this way to questioning the **Culture** source. What is the wisdom about wrongdoers in the magazines we read? What kind of world do our newspapers' editorial pages assume, and what of our own **Position**? What do we really believe about the place of wrongdoers in the world we inhabit?

This example illustrates *"What kind of world?"* as a question that allows us to explore the perspective of a particular source and then structure a conversation with elements from other sources by asking the same question of those sources. A question focuses our attention on a particular aspect of a given source.

In the EfM program we frequently use perspective questions designed to investigate the doctrinal themes of **Creation, Sin, Judgment,** and **Redemption**. *"What kind of world?"* is a question that opens up our perspective on the doctrine of **Creation.**

Apply: The final phase of theological reflection deals with the insights gleaned from conversation among the sources and with the implications for action decided by each individual on the basis of these insights. A desired outcome of theological reflection is a renewed understanding of what it means to be one of God's ministers in the world. To this end group members take their insights and learning from the reflection and apply them to their lives and ministries. Sometimes this involves a clear direction for action. More often the resulting application clarifies their questions, thereby preparing them to explore further their study of the Christian tradition. During this phase of reflection, questions fall into the following general categories:

- How can I apply my learning and questions?

- What am I being called to do differently?

- What do I want to take into our time of prayer?

The more specific each participant can be about the next small step necessary to apply the insights, the more likely it is that the reflection will be of lasting value.

One final note: There is no one "correct" way to do theological reflection. There will be several theological reflection methods for use during the weekly sessions. As you and your group become familiar with the dynamics and purpose of theological reflection, you can refine or develop your own methods.

Respond

Note the questions you have. What stood out for you? What did you learn about theological refection?

Practice

Analogical thinking undergirds theology, for we can only speak about God using metaphor, images, story, or pictures. Listed below are some exercises designed to help you become more comfortable in the practice of generating and discovering metaphors:

1. List biblical images—as many as possible (the vineyard, lost sheep, etc.).

2. List metaphors from everyday life. Come up with as many as you can: a caged tiger, walking a tightrope blindfolded, ice cream melting in the hot sun, traveling an unfamiliar highway without a map, and so on.

3. Describe characteristics of each metaphor. What are the feelings and thoughts in the world of the metaphor?

4. Tell a family story and ask the group to listen for metaphors within or evoked by the narrative.

5. Tell or read a news item or other print media piece and listen for metaphors.

6. Listen for sources in a sermon. In most liturgical churches, the sermon is a brief reflection on a scripture passage of the day. Which passage does the sermon draw from (Christian tradition). Where does the homilist begin: a joke (Culture), a personal experience, a personal belief, another scripture passage? What insights does the preacher offer? What call to ministry (application) does the sermon suggest?

Week Nine

YEAR ONE

Read

Exodus 16–40
Collins, Chapter 6, "Revelation at Sinai," pages 64–73

Focus

Identifications to note: Mosaic/Sinai covenant; Hittite treaties; Assyrian treaties; vassal treaty; theophany; Baal; Asherah; Festival of Unleavened Bread; Sukkoth; Book of the Covenant

Terms related to law: apodictic law; casuistic law; Yahwist Decalogue; ritual Decalogue; unwritten (oral) law

YEAR TWO

Read

The Gospel according to Luke

Focus

Define unfamiliar terms or references.

Make notes about what particularly interests you in Luke's Gospel.

Imagine the writer of Luke making a list of images for Jesus. What would be on that list?

Describe how Luke's images shade and color the gospel he proclaims.

YEAR THREE

Read

MacCulloch, Chapter 6, "The Imperial Church," pages 189–228

Focus

Important names, places, terms to note: Constantine; *Chi Rho,* Milvian Bridge; Codex Vaticannus; Codex Sinaiticus; *Hagia Eirene; Hagia S ophia;* Helena, Athanasius, Basil, Arius, Miaphysites, Nestorius; *sedes, cathedra, bascilica catechesis eremos, monachos, abila, homoousion, homoios, hypostasis, ousia, Theotokos*; monasticism; *The Acts of Thomas*; Councils; Chalcedonian Definition; dates: 312, 325, 481

History presents a narrative that the author creates from primary or other secondary sources. What sources can you identify that MacCulloch uses in this chapter?

YEAR FOUR

Read

Allen, Chapter 6, "Nature as Witness and Innocent Suffering," pages 57–67

Focus

Concepts, terms, and names to note: three elements of witness; nature's witness; inner witness; Testament: Job; *Vindicator;* William Temple

Allen presents theology, as do all theologians, by using content from other people as well as from his own thinking and experience. Identify sources he used as he presented his position in this chapter.

ALL YEARS

Respond

As you studied you likely made connections with other things that you have read, thought, or experienced. Identify the thoughts, feelings, memories, and connections to other authors that you have read. These constitute the sources you use as you form your understanding of the chapter. What do you notice about the sources you draw upon?

Defining relationships loom large in the readings of all four years. Year One read about the unfolding of the covenant through the lives of the patriarchs; Year Two confronted Mark's abrupt proclamation of the news of Jesus Christ and its power over people; Year Three watched the nascent church-state issue unfold; while Year Four read about natural theology and the injustices of innocent suffering.

The issues raised in the reading are real, ongoing, and difficult. What has your experience taught you about one or more of those issues?

What light does learning more about the Christian heritage shed on those issues?

Christians today live within a heritage of people who have placed their lives on the line because of how they experienced God and God's call on their lives. Having a theology that undergirds a living faith brings us face to face with serious life issues. A hope is that critical study of the Christian tradition will help men and women face issues such as innocent suffering.

How have your reading, study, and reflection on the Christian tradition this week contributed to deepening your understanding of faith issues, especially those raised by human suffering?

Practice

Use your assigned reading this week to:

Identify the focus of what you read;

Explore by identifying the views of the world, sin, judgment, repentance and/or redemption that may have been presented in your reading;

Connect by

identifying how the author(s) drew on his or her contemporary culture in writing the chapter;

identifying the beliefs that the author seemed to hold and how those interact with your beliefs;

recalling personal experiences related to the chapter's focus;

Apply by making notes of what you want to reflect on with the seminar group.

Week Ten

YEAR ONE

Read

Leviticus and Numbers
Collins, Chapter 7, "Priestly Theology: Exodus 25–40, Leviticus & Numbers," pages 74–83

Focus

Identify: the Tabernacle; sacrificial system; Day of Atonement; stories of Nadab and Abihu and of Korah; impurity laws; Holiness Code; relationship of ethics and holiness; Cultic Calendar; Book of Numbers

YEAR TWO

Read

Powell, Chapter 7, "Luke," pages 147–67

Focus

Note the following names, terms, ideas: Theophilus; "the beloved physician"; Luke's Gospel in relationship to the Acts of the Apostles; the major themes in the Gospel of Luke; passages from Luke widely used in Christian liturgies

What interests or concerns you in Powell's presentation of Luke's Gospel?

Which of the major themes Powell identified do you find interesting or even compelling?

What makes the Gospel according to Luke sacred literature?

YEAR THREE

Read

MacCulloch, Chapter 7, "Defying Chalcedon: Asia and Africa," pages 231–54

Focus

Learn the meaning of the following: *The Life of Balaam and Joasaph*[17]; Miaph-ysites; Dyophysite "Nestorianism"; Tome of Leo; *Henotikon*; Jacob Baradeus; Syriac Orthodox Church; Sergius; Peter the Iberian; Armenian Church; *Trisagion*; Theopaschism; Ethiopia; *abun;* Ezana; *tawahedo*; *Kebra Nagast*; King Kalleb; Dyophsite Christians; failure of the Marib Dam; School of the Persians in Edessa; Sebokht; "Mar Thoma" Church; Cosmas Indicopleustes; Thomas Christians; Evagrius Ponticus; Alopen; library pagoda of Ta Qin

Identify the central opposition for one individual or a group that defied Chalcedon.

YEAR FOUR

Read

Allen, Chapter 7, "Innocent Suffering and Life Beyond Death," pages 68–73

Focus

Concepts that provoke thoughtful reflection: transformation of suffering; sufferings as punishment for sin; prosperity as mark of righteousness; wrong doing results in suffering; injustices of innocent suffering prompt affirmation of life beyond death; omnipotence–as can do anything; almighty–as having authority over all things; problem of natural evil

Which of the concepts listed above interested you the most?

ALL YEARS

Respond

Select a theme or concept from your reading, for example, liberation, prayer, Christ, or suffering. Consider these questions:

What do you believe about the selected theme or concept?

How has your personal experience shaped that belief?

What personal values can you identify as you talk about that belief?

What personal values does the selected theme or concept challenge?

Practice

Carefully read the passage below and identify two or three places that interest you. Connect your personal experience with that focus.

Moses was keeping the flock of his father-in-law Jethro, the priest of Midian; he led his flock beyond the wilderness, and came to Horeb, the mountain of

---

17. Note: An eBook English translation of *The Life of Balaam and Joasaph* can be found at http://omacl.org/Barlaam/.

God. There the angel of the Lord appeared to him in a flame of fire out of a bush; he looked, and the bush was blazing, yet it was not consumed. Then Moses said, "I must turn aside and look at this great sight, and see why the bush is not burned up." When the Lord saw that he had turned aside to see, God called to him out of the bush, "Moses, Moses!" And he said, "Here I am." Then he said, "Come no closer! Remove the sandals from your feet, for the place on which you are standing is holy ground." He said further, "I am the God of your father, the God of Abraham, the God of Isaac, and the God of Jacob." And Moses hid his face, for he was afraid to look at God. Then the Lord said, "I have observed the misery of my people who are in Egypt; I have heard their cry on account of their taskmasters. Indeed, I know their sufferings, and I have come down to deliver them from the Egyptians, and to bring them up out of that land to a good and broad land, a land flowing with milk and honey, to the country of the Canaanites, the Hittites, the Amorites, the Perizzites, the Hivites, and the Jebusites. The cry of the Israelites has now come to me; I have also seen how the Egyptians oppress them." —Exodus 3:1–9

Theological reflection is about ministry: what we do and say that provide opportunities to hear and know God more and to act in the world in ways that reflect God. See where the following reflection outline takes you. Review the opening description of reflection movement as a reminder of the terms below.

Identify: The passage above from Christian tradition is the identified starting point. Focus by considering where the key energy/heart of the scripture passage is: what the passage seems to be about. Develop an image in words or a drawing that makes the point of the passage evident.

Explore the image using a question from the theological themes of Creation, Sin, Judgment, Repentance, or Redemption; that is,

What kind of community does the image-world suggest? (Creation)

What might get in the way of relationships in that image-world? (Sin)

What could make those in that world realize there's something wrong? (Judgment)

What would represent a change of direction? (Repentance)

What might a new, life-giving creation look like? (Redemption)

Connect

Experience—When has something happened in your life that is like the world of the image/metaphor? Compare your experience with the exploration above.

Contemporary Culture/Society—Who or what has taught you something that is helpful when life is like the image? In our world, how is there opposition to that image? How is there support for it?

What key issues do the metaphor and personal experience and contemporary culture raise?

State your beliefs and positions relative to those issues.

Apply meaning and purpose to the reflection by identifying learning and clarifying questions.

How do the beliefs and insights of the exploration support you in ministry?

Notice where you might want to make some changes in action or viewpoint about the matter covered in the reflection.

What prayer would you offer in this matter?

Week Eleven

YEAR ONE

Read

Deuteronomy
Collins, Chapter 8, "Deuteronomy," pages 84–93

Focus

As you read Deuteronomy, define the Mosaic covenant and notice how the covenant underwent renewal and reinterpretation.

YEAR TWO

Read

The Gospel according to John

Focus

Make note of anything you had to look up and any surprising ideas or images that you found in reading John's Gospel. Especially note how John's Gospel presents the message of Jesus. Compare John's proclamation (*kerygma*) with the other Gospels' proclamations.

YEAR THREE

Read

MacCulloch, Chapter 8, "Islam: The Great Realignment," pages 255–85

Focus

Rise of Islam:
  Qur'an; three possible "borrowings" of Islam from Christianity; *al-ilah* (Alllah); identify how Christian *divisions* contributed to Muslim conquests; Mosques of Umar (Dome of the Rock)

Islam's impact on Christians in East:
  Pact or Covenant (*dhimma*) of Umar; *hadith* that protected monastery of St. Catherine of Alexandria; John of Damascus; ascendency of Bagdad under Abbasid caliphs; Hunayn ibn 'Ishaq; Timothy I

Church in China:
  Ta Qin monastery; Bishop Alopen; Jesus Messiah Sutra; Discourse on the Oneness of the Ruler of the Universe; Emperor Wuzong

Christianity among Mongols:
>Khan of the Keratis's vision of St. Sergius; Kerait khan; Temujin (Genghis Khan); Kublai Khan and Dyophysite Christianity; Il-Khan Hulagu and Christians of Bagdad; Rabban Sauma; Timur's destructions

Islam and African Churches:
>North African Church; Coptic patriarchs; Ethiopian monasticism; *Qerellos*; Zagwe kings; churches of Lalibela; Takla Haymanot; Zar'a Ya'qob; *The Miracles of Mary*; Prester John myth

YEAR FOUR

Read

Allen, Chapter 8, "Suffering from Nature and Extreme Human Cruelty," pages 74–84

Focus

Key concepts to consider: David Hume's view of natural world in relation to humanity's well-being; the Stoic Epictetus's view of humankind in relation to nature; Iulia de Beausobre and her experience with suffering at the hand of human cruelty; experiencing God's love in the midst of suffering; two possible responses to the Holocaust

ALL YEARS

Respond

"Right" behavior operates within the ordering of values and expectations. Consider how different "laws" have operated in your life, especially over time, in different settings and circumstances.

Reflect on how the "laws" you learned in your first ten years shaped your beliefs about God.

Identify issues raised in your reading that you find present in contemporary society and among the people you encounter in your daily life.

Practice

Use your text reading this week to

Identify the focus of what you read;

Explore by identifying the views of the world, sin, judgment, repentance, and/or redemption that may have been presented in your reading;

Connect by

identifying how the author(s) drew on his or her contemporary culture in writing the chapter;

identifying the beliefs that the author seemed to hold and how those interact with your beliefs;

recalling personal experiences related to the chapter's focus;

Apply by making notes of what you want to reflect on with the seminar group.

Week Twelve

YEAR ONE

Read

Joshua and Judges

Focus

As you read the Book of Joshua, note what concerns the people in the book had. Especially think about the nature of God that the narrative presented and how that God shaped their understanding of their world and themselves.

YEAR TWO

Read

Powell, Chapter 8, "John," pages 169–89

Focus

Terms, ideas, and images: Book of Signs; Book of Glory; Logos; beloved disciple; abundant life; Paraclete; Sacred Heart piety; Raising of Lazarus; Washing the Feet; *Christ of Saint John of the Cross*

Major themes in John's Gospel: true revelation of God; Jesus as God; Glorification of Jesus in his death; world and Jews; loving one another

YEAR THREE

Read

MacCulloch, Chapter 9, "The Making of Latin Christianity," pages 289–318

Focus

The Rome of the Popes:
  Papa; catholic; Latin Rite; St. Lawrence; Castel Sant'Angelo; Bascilica of St. Peter; Damasus; Jerome; Gerasimos; Vulgate

A Religion Fit for Gentlemen:
  Faltonia Betitia Proba; Prudentius; *Peristephanon*; Ambrose

Augustine: Shaper of the Western Church:
  Confessions; Monica; Manichaeism; *tolle lege*; Donatists; *City of God*; Pelaguis; 410 CE; Augustine's analogy of Trinity; double processions of Holy Spirit

Early Monasticism in the West:

Martin; Sulpicius Severus; *capellae*; Cassian; Benedict; Rule of St. Benedict

YEAR FOUR

Read

Allen, Chapter 9, "The Sacrifice in Creation," pages 87–95 and William Porcher Dubose's essay "The Trinity" provided in Part II, pages 186–93.

By the time that Dubose had written his essay on the Trinity, he was nearing retirement from a long, productive, and challenging career as a professor and dean of The School of Theology of The University of the South. Before he arrived at the university, he had served as a soldier and then as a chaplain in the Confederate Army. Wounded several times and confined as a prisoner of war, Dubose knew the dark side of humanity. Upon his release as a POW, he read his own obituary—he had been reported as killed in action.

Apparent throughout DuBose's writings, his brilliance resulted in an international reputation of being one of, if not the most, original and creative American theologians. Dogma and experience, which he understood as part of what incarnation means, were in constant dialogue in all his writings.

Focus

Concepts: Power of God; creator's self-renunciation; connection between God's creative self-sacrificing and human moral action; *de facto* person and moral person; doctrine of Trinity in relation to doctrine of creation

Identifications to make with reference to the sacrifice in creation: Dorothy Sayers; Iris Murdoch; W. H. Auden; Dante; Bonaventure

Terms and phrase to note in DuBose's essay: *logos; telos;* grace of the Son; *gratia gratiata; gratia gratians;* love is grace *potential;* grace is love *actu;* three constituents of the gospel; *ex pare Dei; salvation salvans; ex parte hominis*

ALL YEARS

Respond

Compare how God is involved in the variety of worlds present in the readings with how you find God's involvement in your worlds of work, family, play, mind, and body.

Practice

As you increase your knowledge of the Christian tradition and clarify your beliefs, you will likely find yourself thinking new thoughts such as "I never knew that." New learning can be insightful and hold implications for your life as a Christian. Putting that learning into practice requires a willingness to do the hard work of honest self-examination.

Select one thing that you have learned from your study and reflection. For example, reading about the theme of justice throughout the Christian tradition can lead to the insight that God cares about those who suffer from injustice. Once you know that about God, ask how that knowledge impacts your different worlds—your relationship with play, family, work, and how you view your body.

Week Thirteen

YEAR ONE

Read

Collins, Chapter 9, "Joshua"; Chapter 10, "Judges," pages 94–115

Focus

Judges in the Hebrew Bible are more aptly described as warlords than magistrates. Collins wrote that the selection criterion for a judge was might. As you step back into the time of Judges, why would these stories be recorded and valued? State how you think the people would have seen God to be present.

YEAR TWO

Read

The Acts of the Apostles
Powell, Chapter 9, "Acts," pages 191–213

Focus

Make note of what surprises you in reading Acts; what you had to look up; and the events, images, or ideas that interest you.

YEAR THREE

Read

MacCulloch, Chapter 10, "Latin Christendom: New Frontiers," pages 319–62

Focus

MacCulloch organizes five hundred years of Latin Christianity history around several areas:

• Changing Allegiances: Rome, Byzantium, and Others

• Mission in Northern Europe (500–600)

• Obedient Anglo-Saxons and Other Converts (600–800)

• Charlemagne, Carolingians, and a New Roman Empire (800–1000)

Identify the key persons and events related to each section, especially noticing how MacCulloch's presentation sheds light on the "human capacity for relationship."

YEAR FOUR

Read

Allen, Chapter 10, "The Incarnation as Sacrifice," pages 96–106

Focus

Key concepts to identify and define: God's self-limitation; incarnation as sacrifice; "dwelling place of God"; Kierkegaard's allegory in *Philosophical Fragments*; concept from geometry to point to Jesus' divinity and humanity; miracles ("signs of wonder"; "deeds of power"; "mighty works") and natural science

ALL YEARS

Respond

How people view God impacts how they behave. Furthermore, how they understand human nature influences how they view God.

How did those in your reading this week see God—what images or metaphors did they use for God and for human nature?

List images of God that you have or have had—recognizing that there are people who do not like to think of God that way. Scripture uses a variety of images. Perhaps there is one or more that might work to convey your sense of God at this time.

What do those images suggest about how you understand the meaning of being human?

Practice

Start from a biblical text for reflection such as Romans 13; or any passage that someone in Year One or Two has encountered during the study this week; or a passage that someone particularly wants to engage; or a passage from the recent Sunday scripture reading.

Identify a scripture passage to practice the movements of theological reflection, then identify a focus in the passage—create an image or metaphor if possible;

Explore the focus with theological questions;

Connect other sources (personal experience, contemporary culture, and personal beliefs) to the focus; and

Apply the reflection by noting insights you have and how those insights might make a difference in ministry in your life.

FIRST INTERLUDE UNIT

The Authority of the Bible

Week Fourteen

The Bible and Ministry

Intentionally living out Christian identity likely will mean encountering issues that affect what one does and says. As questions and conflicts challenge what it means to live faithfully in the world, having a time and place to reflect with others moves from being something desirable to a necessity. Interlude sessions make available time and content to address specific ministry concerns and issues.

Almost without exception the concerns surface from experiences that have ministry formation implications. Ministry formation operates within four primary dimensions: identity, knowledge, skill, and attitude. For example, whenever conversations turn to religion, comments about the Bible usually follow. Within a short period of time unspoken thoughts and feelings surface: "I never can quote the Bible" (knowledge and skills issue); or "I don't feel like I am a good Christian" (identity and attitude issue).

The Bible is foundational in shaping how Christians relate to others and to God. Holy Scripture can unite Christians by providing a common source that feeds the human spirit. However, Christians differ significantly on how they approach and interpret the Bible, resulting in deep distance and division. Before open and honest conversation about the meaning of a Bible passage can occur, people have to know how each other understands what the Bible is and is not.

Marcus Borg clearly describes the situation Christians face today:

> At a basic level, the referent of the word Bible is obvious—it names Christianity's holy book, its sacred scripture. Yet what it means to affirm this is not agreed upon. Indeed, conflict about the meaning of the Bible—its origin, authority, and interpretation—is the single most divisive issue in American Christianity today.[18]

This Interlude Unit focuses on the origin, authority, and interpretation of the Bible. You have been supplied with a copy of Christopher Bryan's *And God Spoke: The Authority of the Bible for the Church Today*. He wrote it because he knew that in debates about theological and ethical questions both sides use scripture to support their positions. Listening to the debates over the years led him to address the divisions by looking at the nature of biblical

---

18. Marcus J. Borg, *Speaking Christian: Why Christian Words Have Lost Their Meaning and Power—And How They Can Be Restored* (New York: HarperOne, 2011), 55.

authority; what it means to say the Bible is the inspired Word of God; and what place the Bible has in Christian decision-making. To live faithfully in the world, an informed position about personal understanding of the Bible's origin, authority, and interpretation is valuable.

All members of the EfM group read the same book for the Interlude Sessions so that the group can give studied attention to basic questions concerning how to understand and use the scripture in Christian ministry. Two sessions are devoted to this topic. This session takes up Part One of Bryan's book: "What Do We Believe?" The next session will discuss Part Two: "What Should We Do?"

Read

Bryan, Part I, "What Do We Believe?" pages 3–90

Focus

Note how Bryan addresses these issues:

- the difficulty in interpreting the Bible;

- the relationship of the church to the Bible;

- God's self-disclosure in the Bible;

- the use of language in scripture;

- encountering God within the Bible;

- who and what is the Word of God;

- how is the Bible inspired;

- how specific books made it into the Bible;

- understanding the authority of the Bible

Respond

Identify your beliefs about the origin of the Bible; how you interpret a passage of scripture; and what the authority of the Bible is for you.

Practice

Reflection Beginning with a Personal Position

Some find it necessary, perhaps vital, to defend and protect their beliefs. They are "precious" to us, and so it is essential that there be a high degree of trust in the group where offering beliefs may occur. Deep beliefs call for reflection; some may change, some may become more certain. In an EfM group, there is generally a consensus to uphold each person with respect, and a clear understanding that reflection is not a debate nor an attempt to change anyone's mind. Reflection allows each to stand before God, searching God's presence and listening for God's voice.

Identify

1. **Personal Position:** State your belief about the Bible.

   Allow some time for silence.

   What image or metaphor depicts that belief?

Explore

2. What are the norms for human community in your metaphor world? How would people treat each other in that image? How would they worship? What would they worship?

Connect

3. The reflection then moves to the **Action** source of meaning.

   When have you felt tension in acting on the belief you have stated?

   In what situations have you been unsure how to apply your stated belief?

   What led you to the belief you hold?

   To bring in the **Culture** source, brainstorm the positive and negative cultural messages that address the topic. How does your contemporary society view the matter? How can you tell? Where are the messages?

   What does our **Christian Faith Tradition** tell us about the matter? How is the matter addressed in your particular Faith Tradition?

   Compare and contrast the positions/beliefs of your Contemporary Culture and your Faith Tradition.

Apply

4. How does this reflection help you practice Christian ministry in your daily world? What did you learn or see in a different way about your belief? What do you want to look into further?

   What difference does reflecting on these positions and images make in personal action in daily life?

Week Fifteen

Read

Bryan, Part Two, "What Should We Do?" pages 93–146
Lectio Divina essay provided on pages 67–68

Focus

Take time to find the references and descriptions of the following:

- "Listening to the Bible":

    place of community in listening to Bible;

    "four senses" of scripture;

    adapting four senses for use today

- "Studying the Bible":

    What is meant by "understanding scripture?"; studying to be transformed; social conventions and assumptions that lie behind the texts

- "Making Decisions in the Light of the Bible":

    sophrosune —"thinking soberly"; *prautes*—gentle, disciplined calmness; staying in conversation and communion even in disagreements

- "Four Notes":

    rule of faith; all things necessary to salvation; literary judgments and literal sense; preferring the more difficult reading

The Bible and Personal Transformation

Why is it always easier to see how others need to be transformed rather than to see one's own need? Why is it easier to see health and maturity in another person than it is to see those qualities in oneself? Clichés seem to form from such experiences: "It's easy for the pot to see that the kettle is black"; "The grass is greener on the other side of the fence."

Bryan advocates listening and studying scripture with an attitude of expectation. Reaching a fuller understanding of a passage from the Bible is a process of bringing head and heart together. He encourages careful study of the literal meaning of the text using every ounce of information available. Annotated Bibles, commentaries, textbooks on scripture, and Christian history all work together to ground understanding of the text. Once the literal dimension of the passage is uncovered, it is time to open the heart to more profound meaning. We learn about God so that we can know God. The same is true in our relationship with scripture.

Respond

- Find a passage from the Bible that troubles you and that you want to understand better.

- Become familiar with the passage using the biblical scholarship that you have at your disposal.

    What does the text imply for living faithfully in today's world?

    What does the text have to say about how to act in today's world?

    "Where then do we believe our lives to be leading?"[19]

Practice

Sometimes we read the Bible as we would read a textbook—scan for the important points, skim or skip over parts that seem inconsistent or incomprehensible, then move along. Rather than reading for facts or information, another way to approach the biblical text is from the standpoint of prayer. *Lectio divina* ("divine reading") offers a slower pace, a way of reading that invites us, in the words of a twelfth-century monk named Guigo II, to savor the text, to chew on it and extract all its flavor and nourishment.

In preparation for the seminar session, review the following essay on "*Lectio Divina*." Select two or three scripture texts for practicing *lectio divina*.

---

19. Christopher Bryan, *And God Spoke: The Authority of the Bible for the Church Today* (Lanham, MD: Cowley, 2002), 99.

Lectio Divina

Prayer and meditation require planning and meditation. *Lectio divina* is a method used by many people throughout the world for focusing prayer. The steps described allow one to enter into a text, allowing the text and one's heart and mind to form a conversation.

Step 1: **Select a passage of scripture** that touches you or the group of which you are a part. Some examples might be:

  a. God's love has been poured into our hearts through the Holy Spirit that has been given to us. (Romans 5:5)

  b. I have been crucified with Christ; and it is no longer I who live, but it is Christ who lives in me. And the life I live in the flesh I live by faith in the Son of God, who loved me and gave himself for me. (Galatians 2:19b–20)

  c. Come to me, all you that are carrying heavy burdens, and I will give you rest. Take my yoke upon you, and learn from me; for I am gentle and lowly in heart, and you will find rest for your souls. For my yoke is easy, and my burden is light. (Matthew 11:28–30)

Step 2: **Prayer.** Begin with prayer for the presence of the Holy Spirit to guide this period of prayer and scripture reading.

Step 3: *Lectio.* **Read.**

  a. Read over the passage you have selected very slowly, savoring each of the words.

  b. Read the same passage a second time in the same way.

  c. Read the same passage a third time, this time forming the words with your lips.

If a group is engaging *lectio divina*, two people consecutively might read the same passage aloud, using a variety of translations. The third reading could be done silently by each member of the group, according to the direction in c.

Step 4: *Meditatio.* **Contemplate.**

  a. Return to the passage and listen for the word or words that have attracted you during your reading. Group members may want to offer the words or phrases aloud, or simply hold them silently within.

  b. Repeat the word or phrase over and over in your heart.

  c. Let the word or words speak to you and resound in you rather than analyze its meaning.

Step 5: *Oratio.* **Respond.**

    a. In silence, you may find that you want to thank God for what you have received, or to praise God, or to ask for the promise that you hear in the passage.

    b. Pray to God in the way that seems right to you.

Step 6: *Contemplatio.* **Rest.**

    a. Remain in silence before God, asking nothing but to enjoy God's presence.

    b. Whenever thoughts enter your consciousness, return to the word in the passage that spoke most strongly to you.

Step 7. **Prayer.** At the end of the time, thank God for God's presence to you during this time together.[20]

---

20. Prepared for publication by Robert D. Hughes III, PhD. Adapted for the *EfM Reading and Reflection Guide.*

UNIT THREE

Developing a Sustaining Spirituality

Week Sixteen

Read

All years:

Essay by Holmes, "The Spiritual Person," provided in Part II pages 194–206

Lecture on "The Sanctification of Time and Life," provided in Part II, pages 207–19

Focus

Attend to the fundamentals presented in the two assigned essays, found at the end of this unit.

Especially note how Holmes's work defines spirituality and how prayer is understood within the framework of spirituality.

Identify how the people of God have sanctified their life and time through the ordering of worship by the development of liturgies. Key terms: cyclical liturgies; crisis liturgies; *chronos*; *kairos*; *the Apostolic Tradition*; *Didache*; "hours of prayer"; and "service of light"

Developing a Sustaining Spirituality

Begin with the premise that the purpose of life is to have loving, life-giving relationships with God, self, others, societies, and the global environment. The challenge of the times in which we live requires sustaining disciplines that deepen life-giving relationships with God, others, self, and creation. What responses do you make to those assertions?

The Education for Ministry curriculum, like other theological education initiatives, helps people learn how to have life-giving, loving relationships. The learning takes place within the context of Christian community while drawing on the Christian heritage. The establishing of such relationships calls for developing a sustaining spirituality.

Spirituality embraces individual and communal living. Relationships flow from value, meaning, and worth. Spiritual theology proclaims that the Spirit is the source of all relationships. Prayer and worship, as intentional acts of entering into a relationship with God, make concrete a person's spirituality.

Deepening one's spirituality means deciding how to structure daily life around prayer and worship. A broad understanding of the meaning of both prayer and worship grants access into the depth dimension within the specific contexts of a person's life. Entering the deep can feel threatening and dangerous whenever conventional patterns undergo change.

Three standards provide a safe environment for entering more fully into loving and life-giving relationships:

First, remember that the choice is always present to say "Yes" or "No" to any activity.

Second, all work within the depth dimension occurs within an increasing awareness of a person's context. Relationships with other persons (past or current); growing awareness of one's physical life; alertness to the surrounding societal realities; recalling life-shaping events; and acknowledgement of meaningful work organize a person's life context.

Third, a person moves progressively deeper one step at a time as she or he enters the realm of spirituality.

Unit Three guides the work of creating a sustaining spirituality by encouraging prayer and worship as spiritual disciplines. Along with study and theological reflection they form a sustaining spirituality.

Respond

Reflect on how Holmes's presentation illuminates your understanding of spirituality and prayer.

- What experiences have you had that parallel those of the earliest Christians?

- What stands out in contrast?

Practice

Reflection on a Sustaining Spirituality

Identify Beginning with the term "a sustaining spirituality," decide on an image or metaphor that reflects that concept.

Explore Considering the selected image/metaphor, identify which of the perspectives of sin, judgment, repentance, or redemption are addressed. That is, is your decided image one that reveals destructive qualities (sin), one that poses questions of direction (judgment), one that indicates a turning around in some way (repentance), or one that highlights a resolution of celebration (redemption)? Describe the image in terms of answers to the question(s) that applies.

What does your image reveal about God's nature?

Connect Write about how the exploration helps you connect to

- personal experiences;
- content from your EfM reading;
- contemporary culture;
- personal beliefs.

Apply What did you become aware of as you developed and reflected on the nature of "sustaining spirituality"? In light of the reflection, name some implications for ministry in your life.

Week Seventeen

YEAR ONE

Read

Psalms

Focus

Notice how the Psalms are grouped in the Bible and reflect on why they are arranged in that way.

Identify a psalm that illustrates each of the following categories:

• complaints;

• hymns of praise;

• royal psalms;

• thanksgivings

YEAR TWO

Read

Powell, Chapter 10, "New Testament Letters" and Chapter 11, "Paul," pages 215–53

Hyperlinks 10.1–10.4 at www.IntroducingNT.com

Focus

Information about New Testaments letters: Pastoral Epistles; Prison Letters; Catholic Epistles; *cuneiform; ostraca; papyrus;* amanuensis; structure of epistles; *chiasm*

Authenticity: pseudepigraphy; Muratorian fragment

Using the material in Powell's Chapter 11, construct a first-person spiritual autobiography of Paul's life. For example, identify ten to twelve events that cover his entire life: "I was born and raised as a member of the people of Israel within the tribe of Benjamin"; "I lived as a Pharisee observing the Jewish law"; "I studied and the feet of Gamaliel." Read through the events of Paul's life to get a sense of the flow of his life as a whole.

Note the different experiences Paul had that shaped his spirituality—how he prayed and worshiped; revelations and/or visions he reported; and other experiences that formed his relationship with God.

Key theological ideas of Paul's theology to know: gospel (*euangelion*); Jesus' death, resurrection, and ascension; life after death; being made right with God (justification); new age of God; nature of Jesus

YEAR THREE

Read

MacCulloch, Chapter 11, "The West: Universal Emperor or Universal Pope," pages 363–95

Focus

Recounting waves of renewal:
monastic revival in England; Cluny Abby's legacy; agrarian economy; pilgrimage piety; origin of purgatory; Peace of God movement

Power and authority:
universal monarchy; marriage as sacrament; rise of papacy—from Vicar of Peter to Vicar of Christ; clerical celibacy; dividing lay and clergy

YEAR FOUR

Read

Allen, Chapter 11, "The Temptations in the Wilderness," pages 107–16

Focus

Theological concepts and their significance to note:
biblical use of the number forty; Jesus' three temptations for ministry in daily life; misguided theology based on premise: faith in God means being protected from harm; Matthew 5:45b; felicity and joy in God's presence; self-limitation of Jesus; hiddenness of God

ALL YEARS

Ministry is supported by our spirituality and is about our relationships with God, with people we encounter, and with the world we inhabit; i.e., all creation.

Respond

Compare the way that people in the lesson understood God's actions with your understanding; for example, do they understand God as active in or removed from the world, as vindictive or caring? Explain the effect of those understandings on their/your relationship with God, each other, and society.

Describe how participating in prayer and worship influences your ministry.

Practice

Dean Holmes employed five features to develop a generic and experiential definition of spirituality. The first feature he explored was the capacity for relationship: "Spirituality is our openness to relationship, which is a universal capacity involving the whole person." Use the following to guide you in reflecting on spirituality and ministry in your life.

Identify Consider the various contexts of your life, e.g., work, friends, family, times of leisure, study, physical life. How have you experienced being open to relationship within those various contexts and other contexts you might name?

Explore An image or metaphor describes how one understands the circumstances of one's life and can be likened to a snapshot of creation, that is, the known world is like the image in some way. What metaphor or image expresses what it is like to be open to relationship in any of those contexts? What questions do you have for the image-world? What questions explore the "snapshot" from the standpoints of sin, judgment, repentance, or redemption?

Connect Make connections between the image and our Christian tradition and/or the EfM lessons; our society or the culture we inhabit; and personal values or beliefs about openness to relationship. Write belief/value statements.

Apply In terms of openness to relationship, what do you see that you have not seen before? What contributes to and has implications for ministry in your life and for developing a sustaining spirituality?

Week Eighteen

YEAR ONE

Read

Song of Songs
Collins, Chapter 23, "Psalms and Song of Songs," pages 236–47

Focus

Given the fact that the Song of Songs does not mention God, in what ways might it convey a theology? Make a case of why or why not the book conveys a theology.

Psalms tell of the kingship of God, the human situation, and the character of God. Name two or three features of the theology found in the Psalms.

YEAR TWO

Read

The Letter to the Romans

Focus

The Letter to the Romans likely contains familiar quotations. Be sure to place any you notice in the context of the letter. Note how the letter is structured and how Paul builds his case.

YEAR THREE

Read

MacCulloch, Chapter 12, "A Church for All People?" pages 396–423

Focus

Persons, events, terms, and writings to note:
King Robert II; Waldensians; Brethren of the Free Spirit; twelfth-century Renaissance; *scholae* educational method; Peter Abelard's *Theologia Christiana*; friars (*fratres*); Dominic and Dominicans (Blackfriars); Francis, Franciscans, and Francis's *Testament*; Carmelites; Fourth Lateran Council; transubstantiation (Real Presence); *inquisitor*; Juliana; Thomas Aquinas; *Summa Theologiae* (Sum Total of Theology); Anselm, Ablelard, Hildegard of Bingen; *The Cloud of Unknowing*; Meister Eckhart; Bridget of Sweden; Catherine of Siena

YEAR FOUR

Read

Allen, Chapter 12, "The Sacrifice of the Cross," pages 117–27

Focus

The chapter discussed teachings on atonement—the only doctrine that has no established consensus. Note different atonement theories: ransom, satisfaction/substitutionary. Key figures who expressed different theories: Paul, Anselm, and Abelard.

Images/metaphors of importance: distance; Suffering Servant

Important concepts: self-limitation of God; ancient meaning of passion; sin as life apart from God; biblical view of God's power, wisdom, and goodness; atonement as the restoration of the human capacity to know, love, and obey God

ALL YEARS

Respond

Each generation inherits social, political, economic, and technological arrangements that supposedly work for the common good. Whenever these patterns no longer serve individual and corporate needs, times are ripe for change. In unsettling times, reformation of fundamental thought and social patterns occurs. "Re-formation" literally means to create something anew out of that which has grown ineffectual, obsolete, and unfruitful.

In one way or another, readings assigned for this session deal with a reshaping of the conventional patterns. Deuteronomic reforms, how to communicate over great distances, the Christian's response to political and economic changes in the Latin West, or contemporary reinterpreting of basic theological themes each participate in re-forming.

What specific re-formations, great or small, do you find in your readings?

If past is prologue for the present, describe how what you have been reading connects with your daily life and ministry.

Practice

Take time to reflect on the theme of refashioning basic patterns so that learning can contribute to recognizing and responding to opportunities for ministry in your life.

Identify a focus:

Construct a "mind-map" by making associations with the centering theme "re-formations." For example, the mind map starts with a theme placed in the center of paper. As you make associations from your assigned reading over the past few weeks, write those associations around the theme and draw a line between the theme and each association. This link, http:// mindmap.nu/how-to-do-radiant-thinking-based-on-mindmapping/, provides for more information on "mind-mapping" or "radiant thinking." Find other sources of information on this process.

Reconstruct   **Confess**

"RE-FORMATIONS"

After making several associations, study the entire map.

- What images or metaphors express the nature of "re-forming?"

- Select one to explore.

Explore the world of the metaphor/image:

Identify a specific point from which to explore the chosen image. For example, if the image is "Jumping into an Abyss," then be sure to explore the image from a standpoint such as the person jumping into the abyss. Do not shift to other possible standpoints such as observing someone jump into the abyss or leading someone to the edge of an abyss.

Develop two or three questions and explore the image through those perspectives. For example, what questions would explore the destructive dimensions of the image (Sin)? What questions explore the nature of the world of the metaphor-image (Creation)? What questions bring in the Judgment dimensions of the metaphor? Or the Repentance and/or Redemption perspectives?

Connect with other areas of life:

Begin connecting with your life by briefly stating when you experienced the world depicted in the image/metaphor. Remember to work from the standpoint previously identified. For example, when have you metaphorically "jumped off into an abyss"?

Connect with other sources, such as contemporary culture and the Christian tradition. You may find that something from your reading over the past few weeks comes to mind.

Bring in your personal beliefs. What do you believe? What do you hold to be true?

Apply to your life going forward:

Notice how what you learn from the reflection applies to your life. For example, what light does this reflection shed on how you engage opportunities for ministry?

Week Nineteen

YEAR ONE

Read

Proverbs

Collins, Chapter 24, "Proverbs," 248–55

Focus

Cite four or five passages from Proverbs that appeal to you. Note the passages in Proverbs that do not appeal to you.

What significance does Proverbs 8 have for faith today?

The Psalms contain five smaller books with different kinds of psalms. As poetry, they are best read aloud or sung. They also give voice to the human experience. The Song of Songs is also largely composed of poetry. Proverbs mainly consists of ancient aphorisms.

Scan the Psalms, Song of Songs, and Proverbs and select four or five passages. Draw from what Collins wrote to guide your selection. Read the selections aloud, noticing what stirs in you. Reflect on how the passages you selected reveal something of your deeper self: your hopes, your concerns, your experience.

YEAR TWO

Read

Powell, Chapter 12, "Romans," pages 255–71

Focus

For Western Christianity, the Pauline teaching on justification is highly influential and formative. Powell presented on page 263 "Models for Understanding Justification." Which model or combination of models best clarify the "justification issue" for you?

YEAR THREE

Read

MacCulloch, Chapter 13, "Faith in a New Rome," pages 427–65

Focus

Hagia Sophia (pronunciation = **EYE**-yah so-**FEE**-yah)—sacred space shaping Eastern Orthodox Christianity
Describe three or four characteristics of Orthodoxy.

Byzantine Spirituality
Name distinctive qualities of Byzantine spirituality.

Iconoclastic controversy
What concerns motivated both sides of the iconoclastic controversy?
Name one or two reasons why understanding the controversy is important to you as you live in today's world.

Orthodox Missions to the West
In a nutshell, describe Photios's missionary strategy and the significance for Christianity in the twenty-first century.

YEAR FOUR

Read

Allen, Chapter 13, "The Resurrection of Jesus and Eternal Life," pages 131–46

Focus

Everlasting life or eternal life issues turn on the understanding one holds of life. *Bios* and *zoe* distinctions frame thinking about the nature and purpose of life. Think about how those distinctions affect your theology of ministry.

Allen used a painting analogy to support understanding the Good News found in the Gospels. Which of the resurrection "pictures" painted in the Gospels appeal to you?

All in all, what difference does a person's view of life after death have on daily ministry?

ALL YEARS

Respond

"God Save the Queen!" or "God Bless America!" or "Long Live (You Name It)!" What is meant by such statements? Is it a prayer, a hope, a conviction, a battle cry? The act of blessing, to borrow a phrase from David Ford and Daniel Hardy, "needs to be rescued from the magical and superstitious associations it has gathered." Such a rescue operation often begins with clarifying definitions and etymological investigations. Ford and Hardy provided such when they wrote:

> There is a comprehensive biblical term for the powerful yet respectful interaction between God and the world, in which the world is enhanced at all levels. It is that of "blessing." In being blessed a person, animal, plant, situation or thing is affirmed by God in the way most appropriate to its nature and future. There is no manipulation, but a combination of discernment and active enabling. "God rules creation by blessing," said the Jewish rabbis of the time of Jesus. . . .
>
> Blessing is the comprehensive praise and thanks that returns all reality to God, and so let's all be taken up into the fulfillment of creation. For the rabbis of Jesus' time, to use anything of creation without blessing God was to rob God. Only the person receiving with thanks really received from God, and if there is one summary expression of Jewish response to God it is the blessing of the divine name, which represents God's whole being. Jesus was in this tradition, and himself blessed God, food, children, and disciples. His whole work is summed up in Acts having been sent to bless, completing the history of the blessing of Israel through Abraham (Acts 3:25f). Jesus is seen as the concentration of the mutuality of blessing. God blessing people and people blessing God. This is the dynamic of both creation and reconciliation.[21]

Blessing occurs within the radical specifics of one's situation. For someone imagining the social, cultural, and intellectual contexts of a bygone era, the risk is always to rush to judgment, thereby projecting current mores into the lives of people of the past. Notice how the people you read about this week understood blessing and how their understanding shaped praying. How, if at all, was God active in their lives as One who blesses?

---

21. David F. Ford and Daniel W. Hardy, *Living in Praise: Worshipping and Knowing God* (Grand Rapids, MI: Baker Academic, 2005), 102–103.

Practice

Reflect theologically on how you have experienced blessing in your life.

Identify a focus

Recall how you have experienced and participated in blessing food, children, friends, crosses, pets, or God.

Notice what threads of commonality are present in the variety of experiences and list them for yourself.

Select one of the identified threads or themes to focus the reflection.

Explore the focus

Develop questions to explore the world of the theme. For example, what kind of world is assumed?

How is God present (or not) in that world?

Question the view of humanity assumed or actively present.

Examine what unexpected influences are present.

Connect to other sources

What stories from the biblical and historical heritage of Christians come to mind?

Identify what from society/contemporary culture connects with the reflection.

Express what beliefs, values, and/or positions you hold about the focus of the reflection.

Apply what is learned to daily life

Once a person takes a stance or affirms a position, implications for ministry begin to emerge.

What do you see for your ministry as you live day to day?

Close by composing a prayer adapting the structure of Jewish prayers:

Blessed are you, O Lord God, _____,

for you _____

and make us _____

through Jesus Christ our Lord. Amen.

Week Twenty

YEAR ONE

Read

Job
Ecclesiastes (Qoheleth)
Collins, Chapter 25, "Job and Qoheleth," pages 256–67

Focus

Job and Qoheleth (Ecclesiastes) provide literary classics from the world of the Hebrew Bible. They expose humanity's agony and glory. The giftedness of the main characters lay hidden amid the dramatic rubble of their lives.

YEAR TWO

Read

Hebrews
Powell, Chapter 23, "Hebrews," pages 427–43

Focus

Powell notes that "persistent Christians have found real substance in this [Hebrews] letter: teaching that not only reveals who Christ is but also discloses who they are (and can be) in relation to him." What significance does knowing who Christ is and who people are in relation to him have for sustaining one's spirituality? Notice especially the role faith plays in fostering spirituality.

YEAR THREE

Read

MacCulloch, Chapter 14, "Orthodoxy: More Than an Empire," pages 466–502

Focus

MacCulloch uses a sweep of eight centuries of history to show how Orthodoxy became more than an empire's religion. Describe the profile of Orthodoxy that comes through to you from the chapter. What key figures, ideas, and events contributed to what Orthodoxy became?

YEAR FOUR

Read

Allen, Chapter 14, "Jesus as Lord and Jesus as Servant," pages 147–68

Focus

Allen outlines a theology of Jesus as Servant-Lord that defines a Christian's relationship with God and with one another. Describe the essence of the doctrine of discipleship asserted and the importance for ministry in daily life.

ALL YEARS

Respond

Work and worship live in a symbiotic relationship. The Greek word for worship—*leitourgia* (let-oor-YEE-ah)—literally means work of the people done on behalf of all the people. Worship (that is, liturgy) expresses ultimate significances of the meaningful action a person takes on from day to day. While "work" in common usage refers to income-producing activity, a deeper understanding moves toward activity done creatively. The work of parenting, hosting a party, creating a painting, caring for the needs of a loved one are all activities done out of a deeper sense of meaning. They matter to the person, for the work shapes personal identity, builds belonging, contributes to the community, and draws the person beyond oneself.

Basic human yearning for intimacy, belonging, contributing, and transcendence motivate work. What work do the people in your readings engage? Look for what values underlie the work.

State four or five values held by the people in your assigned reading.

Reflect on how those values might have shaped worship.

Practice

In English, "worth" (in the sense of value) is closely related to worship. Worship is the response given to someone or something that is worthy of reverence, honor, and praise. Work—in the sense of meaningful action—is done out of a sense of worth. As a way to develop a connection between your meaningful work and your worship, use the worksheet "An Individual Theological Reflection Process" to reflect theologically on a specific work. For example, it might involve an incident from your income-producing activity. It might be the creation of a special meal. The sole criterion for selection an incident is that it involves some meaningful activity.

An Individual Theological Reflection Process

IDENTIFY A FOCUS	**RESPONSES**

Write a brief description of an incident for reflection.

For this reflection, use something related to "work" in a broad sense. Recording the experience aids in making the identification specific and concrete. Use the criteria of "a piece of your life story which challenged your feelings, values, or way of looking at things."

For instance: Describe one specific incident of parenting, or income-producing work, or hobby. The criterion is that the incident matter to you.

List the shifts in action in the incident you chose, and choose one shift for the focus.

"Shifts in action" can be physical, emotional, or cognitive movement. Conscious decisions as well as spontaneous responses are listed. Look over your list and choose one. Any of the shifts will serve as a point of departure. Therefore, choose one that holds a certain interest for you.

Example: A work-incident of creating a garden that was raided by deer might have shifts such as:

- *I walked out to enjoy coffee in my garden.*

- *I saw most of the plants eaten down to the ground.*

- *I saw deer prints.*

- *I sat down and cried.*

One of the shifts in your incident will have the most energy. Choose that one as the focus.

IDENTIFY A FOCUS	**RESPONSES**

Recapture the feelings and thoughts at the moment of focus.

List three or four feelings and thoughts you had *at the key moment of shift of focus identified above.* Often, there is the temptation to project feelings and thoughts into past situations. Recall as accurately as possible what you actually experienced at that moment specifically.

Thoughts	*Feelings*
Oh no!	Shock
I'm going to set a trap	Anger
All that work gone	Sorrow

Recall another time when you had the same combination of feelings and similar thoughts.

Identifying another time when you viewed life in the same way is important. Metaphors are generated best by comparing two or more incidents. When you recall a past experience, new insights often occur. Briefly record the similar incident, including any insights and awareness.

Similar Incident

Create a metaphor.

Think about both experiences. Allow them to become present again. Consider what they were like. How would you describe them using a single metaphor, image, or simile? List all that come to your mind. Then, choose one to explore further.

Example: At the moment of seeing the destroyed garden—Possible images/metaphors that capture what it's like in that kind of moment: "I feel like a wrung-out dishcloth"; "I feel like I've been hit in the stomach"; "I feel like a fallen soufflé."

What images/metaphors reflect what life is like when you had the thoughts and feeling you identified?

Write or draw your metaphor.

EXPLORE THE FOCUS	RESPONSES

Explore the "world of the metaphor."

Explore or question the metaphor from one or more perspectives such as:

"What is life like in the metaphor?" (CREATION)

"What temptations to destroy are there in the metaphor world?" (SIN)

"What brings those in that image up short, takes their breath away?" (JUDGEMENT)

"What changes would be called for?" (REPENTANCE)

"What would be an occasion for celebration?" (REDEMPTION)

These are some of the questions that can be used to develop your understanding of the "world of the metaphor." Don't attempt to give a full account of each question. When your energy begins to slow, take this as a sign that enough work may have been done. Sometimes insights will occur while exploring the metaphor. Write those down.

Example: In a world of being hit in the stomach—Creation—what the world/life is like: life is dangerous, needs caution, painful

Sin—what tempts those in this world to be destructive: tempted to seek revenge, to harm in return, to give up because of anger or fear

CONNECT TO OTHER SOURCES OF MEANING	RESPONSES

Bring in the Christian Tradition.

Consider the material that you have been studying as it relates to this reflection. Is there anything from the current reading chapter that comes to mind? Review several of the chapters you have read. Write a few sentences commenting on the part of the TRADITION that connects with the selected metaphor/image.

What stories from the Bible or hymns or prayers come to mind with this metaphor? Ex.: Where in the Bible would there be accounts where someone might feel/think "It was like being punched in the stomach"?

List possible stories and select one. Read it carefully.

Compare and contrast the perspectives of the metaphor and of the piece of Christian Tradition.

Write a short paragraph that compares and contrasts the Christian Tradition with the perspective contained in the "world of the metaphor."

How is the scripture story or hymn or prayer similar to and different from the metaphor perspectives?

Connect to Contemporary Culture/Society and Personal Beliefs.

What examples are there in our contemporary CULTURE of life being like the metaphor you chose? How is God present in those times?

Record your responses.

Include any statements or judgments that represent presently held positions or beliefs. How would you state the "truth of the matter" as you see it in this reflection (POSITION/BELIEF)? What does "the truth of the matter" contribute to the relationship of meaningful work and worship?

APPLY   **RESPONSES**

Identify insights and questions.

Record insights you now have. Do you have any new   *Record your responses.*
questions related to the matters that the reflection
brought up for you?

Decide on implications.

In light of your reflection, what might you do?   *Record your decisions.*
Are you aware of something you want to change,
or study more, or pray about, or talk to someone
about? You might want to choose a new way to
act out your ministry during the next few days.

Week Twenty-one

YEAR ONE

Read

Ruth
Jonah
Esther
Collins, Chapter 26, "The Hebrew Short Story," pages 268–77

Focus

Imagine Ruth, Jonah, and Esther as three stories in a volume of fictional
short stories. Now consider them as nonfiction stories that are to be taken
as literally and historically true.

Notice what happens to the stories when read as fictional prose or as history.
What contribution does each reading bring to developing a spirituality?

YEAR TWO

Read

1 Peter
2 Peter
Powell, Chapter 25, "1 Peter" and Chapter 26, "2 Peter," pages 463–91

Focus

As you read 1 and 2 Peter, notice what Powell had to say about them and
what each contributes to developing a spirituality.

YEAR THREE

Read

MacCulloch, Chapter 15, "Russia: The Third Rome," pages 503–47

Focus

Note how MacCulloch describes some of the markers of Orthodox spirituality that developed in this period: church architecture, kenotic emphasis on
Christ's example, the Holy Fool, monastic communities, hermits, Rublev's
icon of the Trinity, liturgy, popular piety.

YEAR FOUR

Read

Allen, Chapter 15, "Revelation and Faith," pages 155–68

Focus

Allen uses the metaphor of a flashlight to point to how theology functions. Theology illuminates our view of important questions and issues. How does the theology that Allen presented shed light on understanding humanity, the world, and God?

ALL YEARS

Respond

Human ingenuity has created varieties of ways to dispense resources. One way to think about the exchange of necessary resources is through economics. Etymologically, the origin of the word "economy" referred to the management of the household. Over time an economy was the system by which needed and wanted goods were distributed.

In most recent societies, economy is based on money. The currency of the nation measures the value of a specific item. Work, time, and products could all be measured by the cash value. Almost all economic conversation today assumes a monetary economy. During the Middle Ages of Western Europe, people lived under an economy of inherited privilege. The lord of the land distributed food, shelter, and clothing according to social rank. Society operated on the benevolence of the king who received his rank by divine action. The divine right of kings was an act of God and accepted as God's way of ordering life. Privilege was extended from God to king and then to whomever the monarch so desired. Another economic system moved goods through negotiated bartering; cow's milk was traded for some other produce. The barter system has time-honored roots likely springing from the earliest human communities.

Varieties of economic systems exist simultaneously within any society. Often economies live in peaceful coexistence. A credit-based economy includes money, bartering, and social privilege.

One economy that persists within every society—or so it seems—is the economy of violence. Fear of suffering, destruction, and death fuels the violent economy in which the darker motivation of human nature presides. Terror becomes the currency through which power and authority distribute goods and services. Street gangs live off this economic system. Some households run on the economy of violence. Nations trade with fear where suffering, destruction, and death keep order through the threat of warfare. A systematic deployment of an economy of violence requires participation. Such involvement occurs overtly. Other participation operates through passive complicity that covertly supports the violent dynamic.

How have the people, issues, and events presented in your reading assignment participated in an economy of violence? Describe how the doctrine of God as the Lord can be lived out in such an economy.

In addition, give thought as to how prayer, worship (liturgy), and spirituality address the destructive qualities of any economy, especially the economy of violence.

Practice

Theology touches on the whole person—mind, heart, and soul. Theological reflection should always have safeguards that provide a supportive, safe environment. Safeguards take the form of commitment to group standards. The following standards are basic to establishing a reflecting community:

- Participation is voluntary—a person can opt out of the discussion without judgment.

- A person speaks in the first person using the pronoun "I."

- What a person shares is selected from options (for example, someone might recall several different experiences and knows that only some might be comfortably shared).

- Confidentiality is essential—anything of a personal nature stays within the group.

Theology done experientially necessitates looking to personal experience as a continual source for God's self-disclosure. To think theologically about violence requires a method that guides the reflective process with care and precision. The following approach, adapted from methods developed by the EfM program, begins by collecting personal experiences of violence.

Violence here is defined broadly to include more than physical violence. Physical violence is easily identified—for the most part—however, other forms of destructive behavior often are less dramatic and noticeable. Emotional abuse covers a significant range of behavior. Verbal abuse, taunts, and bullying chip away at a person's well-being. Sometimes humor masks the destructive behavior, allowing it to be acceptable. Sarcasm, practical jokes, and ethnic-based jokes usually are not seen as destructive. However, abusive and violent behavior is determined not by the actor but by the effect the behavior has on the vulnerable person. Violence in the form of societal impact may be the chosen realm to consider. Or experience with war. Or any number of possibilities.

Identify a focus
Individual work:

Recall several times when you were the object of destructive behavior. It may be something like a practical joke, or being the subject of a playful trick. Or it may be something more physically dangerous like being mugged or robbed.

Make a list of the experiences for your eyes only.

Look for threads that run through that list. Do several of the experiences relate to the same person, or do some share a similar aspect? Write all the threads you can identify. Pick one as the focus and on which you would like to reflect further.

Explore the focus

Reflection around the focusing thread may produce an image (picture) or metaphor ("It's like this when I experienced the violence . . .") or an issue. Write or draw an image or issue suggested by the thread you selected. Whatever form it takes can be explored using theological perspective questions:

Develop questions to explore the world of the thread. For example, what kind of world does the image or issue assume?

What destroys in that world?

How is God disclosed (or not) in that world?

Consider the view of humanity assumed or actively present in the image world.

Examine what unexpected influences are present in that world.

Connect to other sources of meaning

Culture: Record what literary works, scenes from movies, or song lyrics come to mind.

What pieces from the Christian tradition feed the conversation? Especially look at Psalms, liturgies and prayers (cf. Book of Common Prayer), hymns, etc.

Ask, "What seems to be the truth about this reality?" Allow yourself to think deeply and write one or more beliefs you have around the ideas and images you surface in the reflection.

Apply learning to daily life and ministry

Sometimes a good reflection leads to better questions. What questions arise for you in light of the conversation?

How might your participation in prayer and worship be impacted?

Close with a collect:

O God who _____

We pray _____

So that _____

In Christ's name. Amen.

UNIT FOUR

Building a Theology: Integrating Belief, Behavior, and Doctrine in Everyday Life

Week Twenty-two

It is a continual theme of Christian theology that every new generation must take up the task of "faith in search of understanding" with fresh vigor and creativity. Over the centuries, this task has been undertaken by many, sometimes in the midst of enormous social crisis, sometimes in the stayed quiet of history's rare moments of peace. It is a task that has been embarked on when Christian theology has voiced the thoughts of the powerful and also in cases when only stifled whispers of a repressed and silenced faith could be heard. It is a task as hard as it is rewarding, as fraught with tensions as it is guided by grounding wisdoms, a task both invigorating and daunting, an enterprise filled with as many surprises as familiar truths.[22]

The purpose of Unit Four: "Building a Theology: Integrating Belief, Behavior, and Doctrine in Everyday Life," is the task of "faith in search of understanding." A person of faith continually seeks understanding of what that life of trust (faith) means to everyday life. Each generation has to make sense out of their social and intellectual situation in relation to Christianity. In short, each generation of Christians has the task of building a theology that supports and enlivens faithful living as a person of God. Theological books from the past can seem like dusty antiquated relics that have been stored in the attic and remembered only as nostalgic expressions of bygone eras. Christian theology—at its best—is a creative, invigorating process that draws people into the wonder and grace of the Holy. However, in the most recent past, theology has fallen on hard times because it became an intellectual puzzle rather than a vital, essential inquiry into the mystery and wonder of being human. Ellen Charry, a Princeton University professor, brought challenge and freshness to the meaning of theology when she wrote, "Theology is not a theological enterprise—a set of ideas that ought to fit together like pieces of a puzzle. Theology is about knowing and growing in the love of God and our neighbor so that we flourish in the destiny that God has in mind for us."[23] Theology for her is learning about God so that she knows God's love—a love that spills out into the lives of others. When theology embraces the intellectual, imaginative, affective, and sensory process of knowing, then a holistic understanding develops. Theologians may too often today seem to be people living apart in a rarified intellectual atmosphere. The first person to be known as a theologian was St. Gregory of Nazianzus for whom people coined the word "theologian," which literally meant a

---

22. Jones and Lakeland, *Constructive Theology*, 1.
23. Ellen Charry, "Growing into the Wisdom of God," *The Christian Century* (February 13–20, 2002): 22.

God-knower. Whenever people spent time with Gregory, they came away with the sense that they had experienced something of God. The first theologians, while being learned persons, were seen primarily as God-knowers.

The call is to "do theology" that merges one's mind, imagination, emotions, and senses into "knowing and growing in the love of God and our neighbor so that we flourish in the destiny that God has in mind for us." This lofty goal brings a person into an inquiry that (as expressed in the opening quotation): "It is a task as hard as it is rewarding, as fraught with tensions as it is guided by grounding wisdoms, a task both invigorating and daunting, an enterprise filled with as many surprises as familiar truths." The task seems like mission impossible. Facing such an enormous task may seem like trying to eat an elephant. How does one do that? The well-worn response is "one bite at a time."

This unit's six sessions initiate and encourage a lifelong process. Constructing your theology is a lifelong pilgrimage characterized by continual revisions in light of new information and experience. EfM participants accumulate a body of knowledge that comes from systematically studying scripture, Christian history, and theology. Reflecting on experience in light of the increased knowledge sets the stage for "doing theology."

Each person comes into EfM with a theology, often implicit and occasionally explicit. The process of building a theology is an ongoing conversation among one's beliefs and experiences along with acquiring additional knowledge gained though directed reading of the work of scholars. The process of becoming a theologian involves disciplined practices. Every discipline requires assimilating the vocabulary that supports the ongoing practices.

Vocabulary for Practicing Theology

Theology: Theology directs attention to knowing about God and knowing God through reason, imagination, behavior (deeds), and affect (emotion). Christianity over the centuries has expressed theology through each of these modes of knowing.

Reason: Theology's normative mode of expression consists of propositional statements. A common example of this form of theology is a catechism with a series of questions and answers concentrated on theological themes. Academic theology employs carefully reasoned propositions that answer fundamental questions. The theologian desires to have the teachings (doctrines) interconnect. The resulting writings describe the "interconnection of doctrines in what is variously called systematic theology, dogmatic theology, doctrinal theology, or constructive theology."[24] The primary mode of human consciousness employed in such theologies is reason. Examples of such

---

24. David Ford, *Theology: A Very Short Introduction* (New York: Oxford University Press, 2000), 105.

writings include Paul Tillich's three volumes of *Systematic Theology* or Robert Jenson's two volumes bearing the same title.

Imagination: Theology expressed in story, myth, picture, and symbol engages the imagination. For example, C. S. Lewis presented a comprehensive theology through his *Chronicles of Narnia.* Liturgy, especially as enacted in the Eastern Orthodox churches, expresses theology through worship's drama. Plays such as Archibald McLeish's *J.B.* present dramatically the theology found in Job. Myths, stories, symbols—religious or otherwise—express a deeper understanding about the nature of something; God, the world, human condition, to name a few. Christian symbols help express an attitude or knowledge about God. The imagination has continually played an important role in "doing theology."

T. S. Eliot's *Four Quartets* and *Ash Wednesday* employ imagination and affect to create theological meaning. Dante's *Divine Comedy* can be seen as Thomas Aquinas's theology expressed through poetry. Additionally, music is a prime example of theology expressed through emotion. Bach, Beethoven, and Handel are but three composers who "do theology" through music. Contemporary song and lyric writers continuously use feelings to create theological meaning.

Behavior/Deeds: Action, service, and dance communicate feelings and beliefs. South African Christians literally danced with joy at the end of apartheid. Church ceremony uses movement and gesture to "speak" theologically. Ministry that extends compassion to those who live in society's shadows—the poor, aged, and prisoners—communicates theological meaning not only to those served but also to those who hear of such service. Notice the impact Mother Teresa has had on theological discernment. Once again borrowing words of Ellen Charry, "The life of prayer and study will ring hollow unless illuminated by service. And in service to children, the elderly, the poor, the weak, the sick, and the imprisoned, one worships and glorifies God and comes to know the Lord and perhaps to touch his wounds, so that doubt is stilled."[25] Theology (God-knowing) frequently emanates through compassionate contact and action.

Affect/Emotion: Concepts and ideas, story and myth, music and poetry, actions and behavior frequently awaken emotional responses. The feelings can range from deep gladness to profound sadness, joyful alleluias to "depart-from-me" trepidations. Human affect, carefully guided, motivates the creation of meaning.

Knowing God draws on reason, imagination, action, and emotion that reenvisions and reforms theology into supporting life-giving faith.

---

25. Ellen T. Charry. *By the Renewing of Your Minds: The Pastoral Function of Christian Doctrine* (New York: Oxford University Press, 1997), 242.

Constructive, systematic, dogmatic, or doctrinal theology: Coherence drives the work of this approach to theology. The aim is to express theological knowledge into a coherent whole and in turn connect that whole to other fields of knowledge. Current systematic/constructive theologians encourage diversity and differences to be present in theological writing. Most recently, this has meant that theology is best done within a community that brings diverse cultural, ethnic, and gender voices to the table. Additionally, in this time of rapid and continual change, they see their work as an ongoing process that moves through various revisions and amendments. The desire is to understand and encourage a life-giving faith for all people in today's world.

Doctrines: Simply put, doctrines are the major themes or teachings of Christianity. They refer often to major topics such as the "doctrine of God" and "doctrine of human nature." In the Book of Common Prayer there is a section called "An Outline of the Faith—commonly called the Catechism." The document is structured around major topics. The topics (themes) are the doctrines held as important to the Episcopal Church in the United States. A question-answer format follows each topic and expands the basic beliefs of each doctrine. Taken together the "answers" form a summary of the teaching (doctrine) under consideration.

Dogmas: In the nineteenth century, people thought of dogmatic theologians as people who brought comfort through theologies of certainty and stability. Their dogmas grounded people and provided security of knowing truth. Dogmas, somewhere along the way, became taught by finger-pointing teachers whose fear mongering permeated their teaching. Students avoided dogmatic theologians and the dogmas they professed.

Salvaging the word "dogma" is relatively easy. Simply put, dogmas are "authorized doctrines," teachings that a community of believers hold through consensus. Dogmas carry more authority than thoughts conceived by a single individual. The reliability of the dogma in actuality rests on the trustworthiness of the community that commends the doctrine. Dogmas define essential teachings of a community.

Identifying dogmas for twenty-first-century churches is difficult. The difficulty lies in developing decisive definitions in complex, diverse, and pluralistic societies. Add to the mix the certainty of rapid change and instant communication, the development of well-stated dogmas is much like trying to nail Jell-O to the wall. Yet each community and communion has a network of dogmas that identifies essential elements necessary to their theology.

Confessional theology: In the Protestant Reformations of European Christianity, each fractured body of believers constructed an extensive statement of beliefs (their confession). The credal assertions helped establish a church's identity and made the particular church's ethos distinctive. Intellectual assent to beliefs became the measure of faith. One had faith whenever one professed specific beliefs. Conversely, if someone could not give intellectual assent to theological statements, then they did not have faith and were no longer considered to be members of the community.

It remains important that people know what they believe and why they believe it; however, any theology worth its salt understands intellectual beliefs as the means to living faithfully, not the end. Basic Christian beliefs give voice to what it means for a person to live faithfully through loving God, others, self, and creation.

Behavioral theology: Behavioral theology refers to the theology evident in examples, actions, and deeds. It can be instructive to examine the theology implied or expressed through behavior. What does one's behavior communicate about the doctrine of God, humanity, society, and the cosmos? When St. Francis of Assisi said, "Preach the Gospel at all times and when necessary use words," he was advocating the construction of a behavioral theology.

Hermeneutical skills: Hermeneutics is a word that basically means interpretation. It refers to the set of skills necessary to explain or interpret theological concepts, theories, experience, and beliefs. In EfM most of those skills are organized around theological reflection, especially within the movements of identifying, exploring, connecting, and applying. Moving through the four-fold process of theological reflection requires specific skills. Listening, critical thinking, expressing oneself, and drawing implications are crucial skills in reflecting theologically. Effectively constructing a life-giving theology depends on the principles and skill of hermeneutics.

Credo: This Latin word is usually translated as "I believe." Much is lost in translation for the word holds a much richer meaning than the usual translation into English. It also means "setting one's heart," "pledging allegiance," "to love intimately," "hold dear," "to commit one's life." All of these meanings get wrapped into the meaning communicated when someone says *credo*. A mark of a quality theology is less about intellectual integrity and more about bringing head, heart, gut, and body together into a continual commitment to love God, others, self, and creation.

The word "creed" derives from the same Latin word. Creeds are more than a series of theological propositions. Creeds point a person to realties which undergird meaning, love, fulfillment, and purpose. The sublime goal of reflecting theologically is realized as a person knows God as the source of love, fulfillment, meaning, and purpose.

Habitus: The concept of *habitus* finds clear definition in the following statement by Mark McIntosh in *Mysteries of Faith*:

> Learning to see the mystery of God's plan, to see in a way that illuminates the meaning of the world, requires you to develop some habits of mind and heart. The word "habit'" comes from the Latin *habitus*, meaning condition or character; it is a form of the Latin verb *habere*, meaning to have and to

hold. So when theology becomes a habit, it becomes part of your character, a fundamental having and holding of who you are. Or we could say that theology "inhabits" you, that God's Word comes to dwell within your heart by the power of the Spirit.[26]

The coming weeks will provide ways to construct a holistic theology that includes concepts (ideas), images/symbols, emotional energies, and behavior. The intent is to enter the constructive process of identifying and exploring basic elements of your theology. Constructing a theology is an ongoing dialogue between experience and Christian doctrines.

Christian doctrines often are organized around such categories as God, human nature, and the world (cosmos). Different qualities of God, humanity, and the cosmos can be found throughout scripture and Christian history. People utilize ideas (concepts), images (metaphors), emotion (feeling), and behavior (action) from the Bible, Christian literature, history, and the arts to develop their knowledge of God. Unexpected and unwanted events often shake a person's theological foundations. It is important to know the sources that shape personal theology.

For example, two people were very active in their church. Both of them demonstrated the same behavioral theology in how they participated in church. Both were injured in the bombing of the Alfred P. Murrah Federal Building in downtown Oklahoma City in 1995. After one year, one person, depressed and angry, stopped participating in any church activities and dropped out of almost all other activities as well. Her behavioral theology changed. She kept saying, "I was a faithful Christian. Why did God not protect me?"

Even while still recovering from wounds one year later, the other person continued and even increased her church activity, living with a profound sense of joy. She had never asked, "Why did God allow this to happen to me?" Since childhood she held the belief that no matter what happened, God was with her.

Both behaviors prior to the tragic event communicated similar theologies. The difference was in the image and concept of God that shaped behavior. One viewed God as Father-Protector who kept safe those who served him. The other imagined God as Emmanuel (God-with-us) and held that nothing could separate her from God's love.

Whenever a person recognizes the sources that shape beliefs and behavior, then in times of unrest and uncertainty these sources can be reexamined and either rejected or reaffirmed. Knowing the scriptural and theological basis for beliefs facilitates the affirmation process. Ignorance delays it.

---

26. Mark McIntosh, *Mysteries of Faith*, New Church Teaching Series (Cambridge, MA: Cowley Publications, 2000), 12.

Focus

Building a theology begins with identifying the ideas, images, feelings, and actions through which and by which a person knows God—and, for that matter, is known by God. "The eye through which I see God is the same eye through which God sees me; my eye and God's eye are one eye, one seeing, one knowing, one love."[27] Theology builds from awareness of the points where one knows and is known by God.

Constructing a theology starts with two axioms: God is ineffable, and "God knowing" begins as a response to God. Ineffability means that however we express our knowing God, we know the words, images, intuitive sense, and behavior are incomplete—there is always more. While what is expressed rings of truth, the expression also is not true. All statements about God contain the qualifying phrase, "It's as if. . . . " For example, it is one thing to say, "God is Father"; it is quite another thing to say, "It is *as if* God is Father." Communicating with God always falls short, for God is ineffable. Faith is always the person's response to God. Theology, understood as "faith seeking understanding," arises as human beings respond to God's initiatives. God acts and the person responds. The response may be done in an awareness of the presence of holiness. Or the response may be a dismissal of God as an illusion. Either way, the person makes a response.

Throughout the unit, the work will bring together perspectives and learning from the three previous units. This unit develops a three-step integration process of awareness, decision, and practice. Integrating belief and behavior starts with awareness of the theologies operating.

Once the gap between belief and behavior is identified, a decision-making process of exploring and connecting begins. Insights gained from the theological reflection are realized as they are put into practice. Awareness, decisions, and practice provide the essential ingredients for constructing theologies.

What did you learn about theology that you did not know and what was familiar?

What was difficult for you in the essay's discussion?

Respond

Review your spiritual autobiography and the assigned readings to identify and record ideas, images, emotions, and behavior you have experienced in response to God, self, others and the world.

---

27. Meister Eckhart, *Sermons of Meister Eckhart* (London: H. R. Allenson, Ltd), Kindle edition, location 199–212.

Practice

Theological awareness exercise:

The exercise provides a way to become more aware of individual capacities and preferences in using the faculties of reason, imagination, affect, and behavior through which each finds the holy. No one person would employ all four ways equally, but likely all will be present when we do theology in community.

1. List as many responses as possible to each of the following:

   a. Reason: What ideas or concepts of God do you currently hold? What ideas or concepts have matched what you have known of God?

   b. Imagination: What stories, songs, art, and so forth have best helped you to sense something of God?

   c. Behavior/Deeds: What actions, behaviors, and/or deeds help you experience something of God?

2. Sit quietly with your responses, recalling specifics of each. What emotions (affect) can you identify or recall in relation to your experience of reason, imagination, and behavior above? What emotions do you generally attribute to a sense of God's presence?

3. Based on what you discover, write a page on how you know and experience God and how God reaches you.

Week Twenty-three

YEAR ONE

Read

1 Samuel and 2 Samuel
Collins, Chapter 11, "First Samuel" and Chapter 12, "Second Samuel," pages 116–30

Focus

First and Second Samuel paint a sweeping picture of the formation of the Jewish faith. As you read, identify the concepts, ideas, images, and actions that expressed knowledge of God, human nature, and the world as the people of the time understood.

YEAR TWO

Read

Philemon
Jude
Powell, Chapter 27, "Philemon" and Chapter 28, "Jude," pages 415–25 and 509–17

Focus

Identify a common idea or theme in Philemon and Jude. Notice how Powell explored that idea. Analyze the idea or theme by asking two or three theological perspective questions of creation, sin, judgment, repentance, or redemption. For example: For repentance, a question of whatever theme or idea you identify could be "From what did someone in the scripture of Philemon or Jude turn?"; for the creation perspective, a question might be "What kind of world did the people in Philemon or Jude inhabit? What were the norms of that world?" In addition, consider contemporary views in our news media that connect with the identified idea. Decide what you believe to be true in relation to the idea you are using in your reflection and the implications for your ministry in daily life.

YEAR THREE

Read

MacCulloch, Chapter 16, "Perspectives on the True Church," pages 551–603

Focus

With this chapter, MacCulloch returns to Western Christianity. Events, especially tragic ones, impact how people think about and know God. Describe how the Black Death influenced behavior and belief.

YEAR FOUR

Read

Allen, Chapter 16, "The Holy Spirit, the Church, and the Sacraments," pages 169–82

Focus

Select an image Allen uses, for example, "the rush of a violent wind." Imagine what it is like to feel the wind's rush. Ask two or three other theological perspective questions of that image—from creation, sin, judgment, repentance, or redemption. Connect the reflection with something from literature or film. Finally, what do you believe about the matter under reflection? Recall a time when you experienced a gap between that belief and your behavior. Consider how Allen's chapter on sacraments addresses such a gap.

ALL YEARS

Respond

Incoherence between belief and behavior has a long history. In his Letter to the Romans, St. Paul confessed:

> I do not understand my own actions. For I do not do what I want, but I do the very thing I hate. Now if I do what I do not want, I agree that the law is good. But in fact it is no longer I that do it, but sin that dwells within me. For I know that nothing good dwells within me, that is, in my flesh. I can will what is right, but I cannot do it. For I do not do the good I want, but the evil I do not want is what I do. Now if I do what I do not want, it is no longer I that do it, but sin that dwells within me. —Romans 7:15–20

In congested traffic, drivers may demonstrate an inconsistency between claiming love of neighbor and words or gestures directed at another motorist that suggest a different belief. Patterns of consistency or disjuncture between behavior and belief point to what might be termed "behavior theology." Such theology is illustrated by the story about a fifth grade teacher who in the teachers' lounge made pronouncements using a graphic image: "Human beings are the scum on the cesspool of life," then among his students showed great patience, love, and commitment. His behavioral theology clashed with his professed theology. A Pauline-like confession or a blatant contradiction of behavior and his opinion represent the theology of professed beliefs and the theology of revealed actions and may cry out for reconciliation and agreement.

What is required to fashion a harmony between belief and behavior? Several factors must be kept in mind as one enters the integration process. First, theological positions and actions have fluidity. For example, in the early morning moments a person snuggling with a lover in a warm, comfortable bed will easily feel the poetry of praise. Later in the day, the same person being robbed in a dark recess of an urban skyscraper will voice a markedly different theology. Theological thoughts and actions morph within starkly different situations. Second, a person's theology develops as the spiritual journey proceeds. The slogan "Be patient with me, God isn't finished with me yet" encapsulates the reality of theological formation. Additionally, limitations imposed within the particularities of time and space necessitate partial knowing, which invites living by faith more than by certitude. Premature certitudes generate dangers that St. Gregory of Nyssa expressed well, "Concepts create idols; only wonder comprehends anything. People kill one another over concepts. Wonder makes us fall to our knees."

Recall three or four personal incidents that indicate a gap that existed for you between a personal belief and your behavior. Select one and write a short paragraph that describes the incident.

Practice

As a way to reflect theologically on belief and behavior, use the incidents you identified in the Respond section. The following "Wide-Angle Lens" reflection method is one possible avenue.

The Wide-Angle Lens Method

Why this title? The Wide-Angle Lens Method begins with a variety of perspectives and focuses on a thread/theme/idea/image that connects them. An individual would start by finding the threads or themes present in several personal incidents, a movie that one watched, weekly assigned EfM reading or the like. The key is that use of this method by an individual requires initiation from something that could produce several themes or ideas. In an EfM group, the beginning point can be themes from the spiritual autobiographies, themes from the week's reading, themes from any on-board time of the group, or some other starting point from which a variety of perspectives can be elicited. The key is to list themes and find a thread that runs through several of them.

Identify

FIND A COMMON THEME FROM EXPERIENCE

Begin with your incidents identified in the Respond section of this week's work.

What are the common themes or elements that emerge? Is there a burning question, struggle, or issue? These threads may be expressed as simple statements, as an image, as a metaphor, or as an issue.

Select *one thread* that connects various themes. For instance, a review of several incidents (either ones identified by an individual or those identified in a group) could yield themes of frustration, tiredness, hurry, and feeling overwhelmed. Those themes would have shown up in two or more of the incidents. Asking, "What ties some of those themes together?" yields a thread that may have run through some incidents; perhaps, "Having too much to do results in impatience with others" could be named as a thread that ties two or more incidents.

Explore

REFLECT ON SOME THEOLOGICAL PERSPECTIVES

What kind of an image could paint the picture of the example thread above or of your identified thread based on your incidents?

Draw that image. Examine the image for what's going on in it.

Write about what's going on in that image.

Which theological perspective (Creation, Sin, Judgment, Repentance, or Redemption) does it seem to indicate? What would Repentance look like in that image? Or Redemption?

Connect

This is the point at which one looks at the various sources in life to help find meaning in matters of daily life and ministry. The object is not to find the worst in the sources, but to find connections that teach us something; what gets taught could be either creative or destructive and sometimes it is difficult to distinguish which is which.

CONSIDER THE CONTEMPORARY CULTURE AND SOCIETY

Focus on **one or two** areas of your culture or society so that the reflection will not be too broad. These connections might come from your local community or the larger world; our work environment, our education system, our health care system, our grandmothers, movies, TV, literature, art, songs, artifacts, architecture, government, the press, to name a few. Just pick one area of our contemporary society with which to connect.

What does the world in which you live teach you about dealing with the identified theme? Where do you find evidence of people dealing with tiredness and anger in the world around you?

What have you learned from your culture that helps you or challenges you regarding the theme?

How do the areas of Culture/Society speak to or about this thread? For instance, what does the world of employment teach us about tiredness and anger?

What about our health care system? What about our advertising? Again, just use one aspect of our society.

CONSIDER THE CHRISTIAN TRADITION

1. Identify biblical passages or other elements from Christian Tradition in which this common thread is evoked or brought to mind. Provide time to find and read passages.

2. Select one text that seems to speak most clearly to the thread that was evoked.

3. Examine the passage with these questions:

    a. What do you know about the meaning of the text in its original setting?

    b. How have others interpreted this text?

    c. What does this text mean to you?

COMPARE AND CONTRAST CONTEMPORARY CULTURE AND CHRISTIAN TRADITION

From the perspectives of Culture and Tradition, what kind of a world emerges?

Where do these perspectives join or compete? Where do they clash or contrast?

Use the themes of creation, sin, judgment, repentance, redemption, celebration, the doctrine of God, or grace to shape your reflection. Likely, there is time to use only one or two of these themes during any one reflection unless there is time for more exhaustive exploration. As an example, if the New Testament passage about Jesus cleansing the temple were used for the Christian Tradition and the work environment for the Contemporary Culture connection, how do those two perspectives compare and contrast? What messages do we hear from either or both?

CONNECT TO BELIEFS, POSITIONS, AND AFFIRMATIONS

What do you do with the messages from our Christian Tradition and our Contemporary Culture?

What do you feel about where this reflection has led?

What do you think about it?

Where are you in the reflection?

What positions or affirmations do you hold about this reflection?

Apply

IDENTIFY INSIGHTS AND PERSONAL IMPLICATIONS

What have you learned about coherence of belief and behavior?

What moves or energizes you? What insights come to mind?

What are you personally called to do differently, to affirm, or to change?

What prayer do you want to offer?

DECIDE ON SOCIAL AND CIVIC CONSEQUENCES

What actions will you take to carry out the implications you have discovered?

What will you investigate further in your community in order to make a difference?

Whom can you contact to join you or inform you?

What action might you take?

Week Twenty-four

YEAR ONE

Read

1 Kings
2 Kings
Collins, Chapter 13, "First Kings 1–16: Solomon and the Divided Monarchy" and Chapter 14, "First Kings 17–Second Kings 25: Tales of Prophets and the End of the Kingdoms of Israel and Judah," pages 131–52

Focus

Prophets speak God's truth to those in power and generally have the most to lose in speaking. Difficulties arise when prophetic voices do not agree on what the "truth" is. Two possible responses to the contradiction are either to wait to see which was speaking truth or to decide, in the midst of the uncertainty, which is correct and act accordingly. Reflect on how uncertainty impacts the consistency of belief and behavior.

YEAR TWO

Read

Philippians
Colossians
Powell, Chapter 17, "Philippians" and Chapter 18, "Colossians," pages 343–69

Focus

Note what passages Powell highlights from Philippians and/or Colossians. Which passages did he not include in his discussion, but that you thought were important?

YEAR THREE

Read

MacCulloch, Chapter 17, "A House Divided," pages 604–54

Focus

Describe the values that drove the actions of reformers. Think about how those values shape doctrines of God, humanity, and creation. How do those values relate to your personal experience and values? How are those values reflected in our contemporary society? What challenges or support are there for you in living faithfully with your values in today's world?

YEAR FOUR

Read

Allen, Chapter 17, "Sin, Evil, and Hope for the Future" and the Epilogue, pages 183–99

Focus

Allen presents several key ideas in these two essays: for example, Julian of Norwich's comparison of knowledge of God to wounds; a "colony of heaven"; and "truth which is active in the soul [the whole person]" (Simone Weil). State key ideas you found in your reading. What significance, if any, do the ideas have to tensions between belief and behavior?

ALL YEARS

Respond

Rushmore Kidder, an ethicist, wrote *How Good People Make Tough Choices: Resolving the Dilemmas of Ethical Living*, in which he defined a dilemma as a choice between two "goods." The gap between a belief and behavior can be framed within the conflict between two values in a specific situation.

As in the preceding session, identify a incident or two in which you were in a dilemma of conflicting values, perhaps between two good choices; for instance, I planned to work on a necessary project one day and a neighbor suddenly appeared at the door needing help. What's the dilemma? What are my choices? What beliefs do I use to sift and decide among choices?

Practice

Reflecting theologically on dilemmas can move a person toward integrating beliefs and behaviors. Building a theology relies on the integration of beliefs with doctrines as experienced in the actions taken in everyday life.

Use the Dilemma Method for Theological Reflection work sheet overleaf to work with a belief/behavior dilemma. Either use one identified above or one from the preceding session. Set aside an hour or so if you can to work through the process and take your work to the seminar session.

Dilemma Method For Theological Reflection

Identify

1. DESCRIBE an incident for reflection

An experience in which you felt pulled in at least two directions over something, and for which there are no decisions pending. The incident is over.

Description of the incident
Ex.: I had looked forward to my best friend's wedding for months and had my plane ticket and my new outfit. We had plans to enjoy the sights and catch up and just have fun. And then my mother got sick, but told me I could go ahead with my plans. I felt so torn. There was no one else there for my mother

2. DECIDE AND NAME the turning point in the incident

What's the central moment of the incident? Where is the tension greatest? What was happening? What were you thinking and feeling at that moment?

Record the central moment in a short sentence.

3. STATE the dilemma

Try to state what's at stake or what the central issue is at the moment of greatest tension.

Record the primary pair of tension statements as "I wanted _____ and I wanted _____":

To help get to the dilemma, list declarative statements about what you wanted at that moment or what interests were at stake at that moment.

Ex.: I wanted to attend my best friend's wedding and I wanted to stay to take care of my ailing parent.

Select a pair of statements that best represent the central tension.

Record the central issue/what's at stake. Ex.: Personal fun conflicting with caring for another

Identify what's at issue or at stake in that tension.

4. IDENTIFY another time

Clarify the dilemma by recalling another time when you experienced a dilemma.

Record your additional identification by completing the sentence: "It was a time when. . . ."

Explore

5. EXPLORE the dilemma

What is it like to live in that issue/tension? Use Cost/Promise (Risk/Hope) or Perspective Questions of Creation, Sin, Judgment, Repentance, and Redemption.

Record your responses to the questions using either Cost/Promise or Perspectives:

Cost of each choice   *Promise of each choice*

Perspective example:

Judgment—What choices are there?

Repentance—What might require a change of heart?

Connect

6. TRADITION

Identify some stories from scripture or church history that relate to the dilemma. Or perhaps some prayers or hymns come to mind.

Responses:

7. DIALOGUE between tradition and the dilemma—

Compare and contrast what our Christian tradition has to say about that dilemma. What choices would the tradition support? Not support? Why?

Responses:

8. CULTURE and POSITION

Where is that dilemma experienced in our culture? Have there been news stories about it? Have you read a book or seen a movie that dealt with that dilemma? Is there a political dimension to that dilemma?

What do you believe about that dilemma? How was your belief in conflict in the issue? What do you hope for regarding the dilemma?

Responses

Apply

9. INSIGHTS and QUESTIONS

What do you see in a new way now? What have you learned from facing this dilemma? What questions do you have about the dilemma in your life?

Responses:

10. IMPLICATIONS

What do you want or need to do about this dilemma? Are there social implications? Are there actions you could take? Is there something more to learn? What support would help? Where will you find that support?

Responses:

Week Twenty-five

YEAR ONE

Read

Ezra
Nehemiah
Collins, Chapter 21, "Ezra and Nehemiah," pages 220–28

Focus

Sometimes a reform movement is tied to strengthening a community's sense of identity. Why would this be important to the returning exiles? Where today do you see reform movements aimed at establishing or setting boundaries around religious identity?

YEAR TWO

1 Timothy
2 Timothy
Titus
Powell, Chapter 21, "The Pastoral Letters: 1 Timothy, 2 Timothy, Titus," pages 397–413

Focus

Think about Paul's struggle against "false teachings" while advocating "sound doctrines." Compare how the same issues play out in the contemporary church.

YEAR THREE

Read

MacCulloch, Chapter 18, "Rome's Renewal," pages 655–88

Focus

Often, reforming produced examination and renewal among those to whom the protestations were leveled. As you read through the chapter of the catholic counterreformations, consider what was disclosed about God.

YEAR FOUR

Read

Sedgwick, *The Christian Moral Life: Practices of Piety*, Introduction, Chapter 1, "Describing the Christian Life," and Chapter 2, "An Anglican Perspective," pages vii–51

Focus

Given Sedgwick's presentation, reflect on how the study of ethics contributes to the formation of theology. What are the creative aspects of Sedgwick's views? What choices do his views present to you? Reflect on how his views of ethics relate to what you see in our advertising today, or in our school systems. Note what you believe about the study and practice of ethics. What do you view in a new way after reading this week's assignment? Note what implications that awareness has for what you will do any differently next week.

ALL YEARS

Respond

Christian theologians over the centuries have developed a long list of doctrines. The table of contents of most theological textbooks reflects an author's arrangement of important doctrines. Often an author devotes an entire chapter to a particular doctrine or doctrines.

Each historical period prioritizes doctrines in response to the social and intellectual environment. For example, in the nineteenth and early twentieth centuries, most theology began with the doctrine of God; the characteristics and actions of God. By the end of the twentieth century, Anglo-American theologians began by discussing the doctrine of human nature; what are the characteristics of humankind—how we act and who we are. John Macquarrie, a Scottish theologian who taught at Union Theological Seminary in New York City and at Oxford University, consistently asserted that contemporary theology must begin from the ground up. Thus, his *Principles of Christian Theology* began with theological anthropology (i.e., the doctrine of human nature).

As a way to build a theology, create a list of fifteen or more doctrines. A denominational catechism would be a good place to start. For example, the Episcopal Book of Common Prayer (1979) beginning on page 845 presents "An Outline of Faith." Each boldface heading names a doctrine.

Once you have collected a list of doctrines, arrange them in an order that reflects your interest in the doctrine, beginning with what interests you the most. Using the first three or four doctrines, review the reading assignments over the past few sessions, noting how the author dealt with one or two of the doctrines of interest.

Practice

Try to locate doctrinal statements of several denominations (Anglican, Methodist, Christian Science, or any others) or faith traditions (Judaism, Islam, and so forth). Constructive theology is essentially a conversation among Christian doctrines and an individual's beliefs and actions (behaviors). Select one doctrine from your list, for example, the doctrine of God. Find a statement from the Catechism of the 1979 Book of Common Prayer that addresses the doctrine. Then make your own statement of your belief relative to the chosen doctrine. Finally, recall your behavior that revealed a stance relative to the doctrine.

EXAMPLE:

Question from the Book of Common Prayer—What are we by nature?

Answer from the Book of Common Prayer—We are part of God's creation, made in the image of God.

An individual's statement—I believe that we are all equal.

Behavior (action) that reveals an understanding of human nature—I cheered for my high school basketball team, shouting "We're Number One!"

Write about how the three statements support, challenge, or contradict one another. Reflect on images, emotions, or concepts that contribute to the threefold conversation. What other doctrinal statements from the Christian tradition speak to the conversation? What other position statements have you said or heard? Describe how different actions contribute to the conversation.

Week Twenty-six

YEAR ONE

Read

1 Chronicles
2 Chronicles
Collins, Chapter 22, "The Books of Chronicles," pages 229–35

Focus

The two books of Chronicles tell the history of the kingdoms from a slightly different perspective from how that history is related in 1 and 2 Samuel and 1 and 2 Kings. Collins notes that David and Solomon are idealized as cultic figures in the Chronicles. Where do you see evidence of this? For those who have returned from exile, what does the chronicler have to say about their relationship to the past? What might God's promises to David and Solomon mean for them in their new life as a restored community?

YEAR TWO

Read

1 Thessalonians
2 Thessalonians
Powell, Chapter 19, "1 Thessalonians" and Chapter 20, "2 Thessalonians,"
  pages 371–95

Focus

Note which doctrines are either implicitly or explicitly mentioned in the two letters to the Thessalonians. What light does Powell shed on the doctrines?

YEAR THREE

Read

MacCulloch, Chapter 19, "A Worldwide Faith," pages 689–715

Focus

Well-crafted histories aid in understanding the social and intellectual period in which contemporary theology has developed. Name the primary factors that influence the building of theology for today's world.

YEAR FOUR

Read

Sedgwick, Chapter 3, "Incarnate Love" and Chapter 4, "Love and Justice," pages 53–101

Focus

In Chapter 3 Sedgwick uses sexuality, idolatry, and hospitality as elements to sketch a picture of incarnate love. Chapter 4 brings an important discussion of love and justice to the table. Note which of the themes contribute most to the theology you are building.

ALL YEARS

Respond

No theology worth its salt can neglect prayer and worship. Concepts alone limit what one knows and experiences. As St. Gregory is said to have noted, concepts create idols; only wonder comprehends anything. Wonder grounds prayer and worship and encourages (which literally places courage in one's heart) us to risk loving others, self, God, and God's creation.

By necessity, constructing a holistic theology includes prayer and worship. On one hand, prayer and worship should frame theological reflection. And on the other hand, study (one of the spiritual disciplines) opens the heart to God. A piece of scripture provides an archetypical touchstone.

> Jacob was left alone; and a man wrestled with him until daybreak. When the man saw that he did not prevail against Jacob, he struck him on the hip socket; and Jacob's hip was put out of joint as he wrestled with him. Then he said, "Let me go, for the day is breaking." But Jacob said, "I will not let you go, unless you bless me." So he said to him, "What is your name?" And he said, "Jacob." Then the man said, "You shall no longer be called Jacob, but Israel, for you have striven with God and with humans, and have prevailed." Then Jacob asked him, "Please tell me your name?" But he said, "Why is it that you ask my name?" And there he blessed him. So Jacob called the place Peniel, saying, "For I have seen God face to face, and yet my life is preserved." The sun rose upon him as he passed Penuel, limping because of his hip. —Genesis 32:24–31

Striving with God to know God describes how theology develops. St. Augustine of Hippo's *Confessions* was a written prayer through which he worked out his theology. St. Anselm also wrote his *Proslogion* as a prayer. Both classics presented their theology as prayer thereby demonstrating the importance of the relationship of theology and prayer. Swiss theologian Hans Urs von Balthazar succinctly made the point with the quotation "theology on one's knees" (*die betende theologie* or *la théologie à genoux*).[28] Prayer, indicated by genuflection, underscores the significance of doing theology within an attitude of wonder.

Liturgy as work—work of the people of God for all God's people—can provide incidents for reflection. Recall three or four experiences within the context of liturgy that moved you in some way. Worship includes the entire spectrum of emotion. Include both "positive" and "negative" experiences in your list.

Examples:

I was at camp and went to the front of the chapel to pray. I knelt for prayer with many other campers. I entered deep into prayer and lost track of time. When I became aware of where I was, I looked around and realized that all others had left. I had no sense of how long I had been there.

I remember the feeling of belonging that I experienced at the close of an Easter service when I was eleven years old. I felt that everyone there in the church was part of one group. It was a spiritual thing more than a social thing, like a family belonging together. I remember this closeness and I think of it as what religion should be. But it hasn't been.[29]

Singing *The Messiah* for the first time. Singing in a choral group is always a good experience for me, but that time it was more than music. I felt I discovered what religion is about. And I was glad I could sing it.[30]

Decide which one or two of your own experiences you are willing to consider as a beginning point for theological reflection. Again write out your experiences in a brief paragraph or two.

Practice

Reflecting Theologically on the Identified Events

Identify a common thread

After you describe your incidents, what common themes or threads do you notice?

Choose one thread (theme) as the focus for reflection.

---

28. Hans Urs von Balthasar, "Theology and Sanctity," in *Word and Redemption: Essays in Theology 2*, English trans. (New York: Herder, 1965), 49–86.

29. Ira Progoff, *The Practice of Process Meditation* (New York: Dialogue House Library, 1980), 147.

30. Ibid., 148.

Explore

List five or six adjectives that describe the theme's "world." Is it a world of joy and wonder, a world of anger and resistance, something in between?

Deepen your reflection on the theme using two or three perspective questions like

- What temptations or dangers are present in such a world?
- What, if anything, shocks or causes wonder?
- Consider what is shown about human nature.
- What is celebrated in this moment?
- How is God disclosed?

Connect

Notice when you connect to sources from culture and/or tradition. What doctrines surface in your reflection?

Select one or two specific pieces from the Christian tradition that relate to your reflection and proceed with closer examination. If the tradition piece is from scripture, find and read the passage to study it further. Perhaps a Christian doctrine is mentioned. If so, find how the doctrine is treated in the catechism in the Book of Common Prayer or the book of worship used in any denomination.

Note your personal positions or beliefs about the matter under consideration.

Apply

What have you seen that you had not seen before or that you are seeing in a new way?

Discuss what helps you understand better the relationship between prayer and theology.

What are the implications for ministry in daily life?

Week Twenty-seven

YEAR ONE

Read

Amos
Hosea
Collins, Chapter 15, "Amos and Hosea," pages 153–63

Focus

Identify and describe behaviors or actions that upset Amos and Hosea and what they said about them. What was destructive in those actions? What could cause people or the prophets to become aware of the destructive aspects? When have you behaved in the same kind of way? What was the cost of that behavior? Compare and contrast your experience with the experience you identified in one of those prophetic books. How or when have you heard a "word of the Lord" that caused you to think again about your behavior? What actions in our contemporary world are similar to the destructive elements you identified in one of this week's prophetic books? What do you believe about the matter under reflection? Draw some conclusions that can direct you in your daily ministry.

YEAR TWO

Read

James
Powell, Chapter 24, "James," pages 445–61

Focus

Notice what Powell has to say about the letter. What are the deep hungers of those to whom James writes?

YEAR THREE

Read

MacCulloch, Chapter 20, "Protestant Awakenings," pages 716–65

Focus

Describe how learning about the "Protestant Awakenings" MacCulloch describes (especially pietism, Methodism, and the American Great Awakenings) contributes to vocational development and building a theology of mission.

YEAR FOUR

Read

Sedgwick, Chapter 5, "The Practices of Faith" and Chapter 6, "The Call of God," and the Appendix, pages 103–58

Focus

Record four or five ways in which Sedgwick's writings contribute to building your theology. Take special notice of the way Schleiermacher has influenced contemporary theology.

ALL YEARS

Respond

Throughout this constructive theology unit, you have worked with various facets of building your own theology. Such work always is enriched when done within a learning community. Mark McIntosh, in *Mysteries of Faith*, noted three movements that a person or a community undergoes in building a life-giving theology: 1) seeing differently; 2) developing a habit of life; 3) ongoing conversation with God.[31]

Regularly practicing the discipline of theological reflection allows people to see things differently. Fresh visions, in turn, lead to developing a "habit of life." Thinking theologically becomes routine. In McIntosh's words, "Learning to see the mystery of God's plan, to see in a way that illuminates the meaning of the world, requires you to develop some habits of mind and heart."

EfM presents opportunities to develop habits of mind and heart—ways of seeing God's mystery and presence. He noted that "when theology becomes a habit, it becomes part of your character, a fundamental having and holding of who you are." Theology opens a person to knowing about God and knowing God, and at the same time allows people to know more *about* themselves and, more importantly, to *know* themselves. The two-fold practice of knowing God and knowing oneself embodies the incarnational process. It is an interactive, dynamic, dance-like reality in which a person intentionally develops a "God-knowing" habit and simultaneously develops a *habitus* of self-knowing.

Review the work you have done throughout the unit and note what you have learned about yourself and about God. Assess where you are in the theological practice of knowing God and yourself.

---

31. McIntosh, *Mysteries of Faith*, 5–20.

Practice

Imagine the three points of a triangle. Each location represents a focus-point for constructing a theological system. One point locates Christian tradition conveyed through the language of doctrines and dogmas. A second point gathers a person's basic beliefs and convictions. The third point focuses on behavior and practices. The following figure illustrates the three-fold relationship:

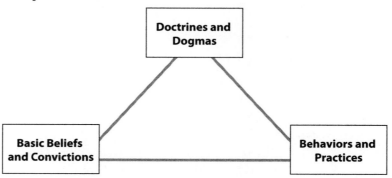

From the work you did in the Respond section of Week Twenty-five, select four doctrines that interest you, for example, the doctrines of human nature, mission (*aka* missiology), sacramental theology, and the doctrine of last things (eschatology). Select one, such as human nature—"humans beings are created in the image of God."

State in your own words what you believe about human nature, such as "I believe that people are innately good." As a way to assess the intensity of the belief, rate it on a scale from one to ten, one representing a lightly held opinion; ten a strongly held conviction. Using the example, a person might rate the belief as an eight. As a way to extend the rating, offer a rationale for that rating. For example, "I cannot rate it a 'ten' because my belief cannot account for people whose attitude is filled with evil intent."

Next, state a behavior and/or practice exemplifying the belief, such as, "Whenever I see a baby, I stop to talk with it and make silly faces to make the baby smile, but then I read an article about a parent deliberately harming a child and I feel pain at the nature of humankind."

Complete the process for three or four doctrines, beliefs, and behaviors.

When you have finished, prayerfully review all that you have done in this unit and write about what you see, hear, feel, worry about, or hope.

SECOND INTERLUDE UNIT

Ministry and Priesthood

Week Twenty-eight

But you are a chosen race, a royal priesthood, a holy nation, God's own people, in order that you may proclaim the mighty acts of him who called you out of darkness into his marvelous light. —1 Peter 2:9

Consider these questions from the Catechism in the Book of Common Prayer:

Q. Who are the ministers of the Church?
A. The ministers of the Church are lay persons, bishops, priests, and deacons.

Q. What is the ministry of the laity?
A. The ministry of lay persons is to represent Christ and his Church; to bear witness to him wherever they may be and, according to the gifts given them, to carry on Christ's work of reconciliation in the world; and to take their place in the life, worship, and governance of the Church.[32]

What is ministry? What images come to mind when you hear the word "minister"? The Episcopal Church teaches that we all are called into ministry through our baptism, yet how are we to understand the ministry of all in a church with ordained ministers, those who look to society around us like professionals, not unlike lawyers and physicians, whose occupation is "ministry"? It is frequently suggested that Education for Ministry should change its name because the term "ministry" has too clerical a connotation today in the United States. Some mistake the program for a course in preparation for ordained ministry. Lay persons may resist identifying themselves as ministers outside the boundaries of the church proper.

In cultures where professional classes are privileged, there is sometimes an implied hierarchy of ministers, with the ministry of the ordained set higher than that of the laity. This clericalism, as Fredrica Harris Thompsett notes, can be a mutual endeavor.

"Clericalism" exaggerates the status of clergy while devaluing and patronizing laity. In this mutually disabling relationship, distinction among church people is turned instead into divisions between them. Such separations in function and status raise questions about how we can be different but not alienated, neither domineering nor passive, patronizing nor lazy. Symptoms of clericalism include intimidation, hoarding educational resources, controlling so-called real theological language, congregational passivity, and renunciation of authority.

---

32. The Episcopal Church, The Book of Common Prayer (New York: Church Hymnal Corporation and Seabury Press, 1979), 855.

One clear example of clericalism is to describe a congregation that is searching for a new rector or vicar as "vacant." In clericalist language laity are often invisible, even in those moments when their energy is most in demand.

Yet clergy and laity both participate in clericalism. There are laity who expect clergy to be elitist and who sharply separate church from society; there are clergy who see part of their role as giving laity jobs to do in church, and whose own theology of authority places them somehow closer to God than to the people of God. Clericalism thrives on low expectations of lay people. Ultimately it inhibits the mission of the whole people of God.[33]

William Countryman suggests that one way to recover an appropriate understanding of the ministry of the whole people of God is to reexamine the concept of priesthood. There is, Countryman asserts, a fundamental human priesthood to which we belong, lay and ordained alike, a shared priesthood "forever in process of formation."[34]

Read

Countryman, Preface, Part I, "Rediscovering Priesthood," pages xi–78

Focus

Note how Countryman uses these terms:

Fundamental human priesthood; priesthood of religion; arcana; the borderlands; THE HOLY, TRUTH, etc.

Respond

Countryman says that "ministry" and "priesthood" should be understood as interchangeable terms. Do you agree or disagree? What challenges, if any, do you find with this assertion?

Practice

Identify

What images come to mind when you think of a priest? Choose one to explore.

Explore

What theological perspectives—the world, sin, judgment, repentance, redemption—come most immediately to mind as you consider this image?

---

33. Fredrica Harris Thompsett, *We Are Theologians: Strengthening the People of the Episcopal Church* (Cambridge, MA: Cowley, 1989), 97–98.
34. L. William Countryman, *Living on the Border of the Holy,* 30

Connect

How are priests depicted in your contemporary culture?

What are your personal beliefs about priesthood? Do you think of yourself as a priest?

Who are the priests in your life? How are you, or how have you been, a priest to others?

Apply

What new understandings of priesthood/ministry are forming for you now?

Where might you look for opportunities to exercise your own essential priesthood?

Week Twenty-nine

Read (All Years)

Countryman, Part Two, "Priesthood and the Church," "Priestly Spirituality," pages 81–195

Focus

Note how Countryman uses these terms:
Sacramental priesthood; the *laos*; the priest as icon

Note what Countryman names as some common misperceptions about the ordained (or sacramental) priesthood.

Respond

In a sermon at the ordination of a bishop, Verna Dozier reflected on the vocations of the two priesthoods in the church:

> The Church of God is all the people of God, lay and ordained, each order with its own unique vocation, the lay order to be the people of God in the world, to witness by their choices and their values, in the kingdoms of the world, in the systems of commerce and government, education and medicine, law and human relations, science and exploration, art and vision, to witness to all these worlds that there is another possibility for human life than the way of exploitation and domination; and the vocation of the ordained order is to serve the lay order, to refresh and restore the weary souls with the Body and the Blood, to maintain those islands, the institutional church, where life is lived differently but always in order that life may be lived differently everywhere.[35]

How is this congruent with Countryman's description of the relationship between the sacramental and fundamental priesthoods? How does it differ?

Practice

Countryman says that cultivating a spirituality of fundamental priesthood requires being attentive to where the borderland of the HOLY crosses our lives. Looking back over the work you have done this year so far, consider the following questions. Journal or make some notes as you wish.

What indications of life on the border of the HOLY do you find in your own spiritual autobiography?

---

35. Verna Dozier, sermon preached at the consecration of Jane Holmes Dixon as Bishop Suffragan of Washington on November 19, 1992, published in *Virginia Seminary Journal* (April 1993): 33–34.

What experiences of fundamental priesthood did you hear about in the spiritual autobiographies of others in your group?

How does theological reflection help us to be more attentive to recognizing borderland experiences? Name some specific instances where this has happened for you, if you can.

How would you describe a spirituality of fundamental priesthood? What spiritual practices might be helpful to you in living into your own priesthood in the world?

What images of the priesthood of Jesus come to mind?

Countryman names vocation as the question central to a life in priesthood that is fundamentally human and fundamentally collegial. When have others helped you to recognize God's call in your life?

What would you like to share in the seminar? What questions remain?

UNIT FIVE

Vocation: Hearing and Responding to God's Call

Week Thirty

Theological formation equips people to recognize the sacred in daily life by accessing concepts, images, stories, and actions drawn from the Christian tradition. By reflecting on knowledge and experience they can discover better how to contribute to God's dream (also known as participating in the *missio Dei*.)

Unit Five, "Vocation: Hearing and Responding to God's Call," fosters vocational development within the context of missiology (the theology of mission and ministry) so that participants more intentionally know and follow God in everyday life.

Goals:

• Understand and use vocational/call "bridge metaphor";

• Reflect theologically on Ephesians 4:1–16 passage;

• Use the microscope method to reflect theologically on a past experience with ministry discernment;

• Reflect theologically on vocation/call issue(s) using the TR dilemma method;

• Use the Johari Window to foster vocational discernment;

• Use the Integration Triangle presented in Week Twenty-seven to pull together the year's work.

Mission, Vocation, and Gifts[36]

The gifts he gave were that some would be apostles, some prophets, some evangelists, some pastors and teachers, to equip the saints for the work of ministry, for building up the body of Christ, until all of us come to the unity of the faith and of the knowledge of the Son of God, to maturity, to the measure of the full stature of Christ. —Ephesians 4:11–13

In order to do its work and find its true identity, the church is dependent on the gifts God gives its members. The apostle Paul associated God's gifts with the work of ministry, with the identity of the church as the body of Christ, and with the vocation of Christians to become the mature persons God calls them to be. Ministry is what the church does, Paul says, and the identity of Christians is found as members of Christ's body. The mission of the church is to share in Christ's work (restoring all people to unity with each other and with God) and find a mature identity (measured by Jesus' full humanity). As members carry out the mission of the church, they mature into full human beings, with Christ being the measure of that maturity.

This chapter explores what is meant by the mission of the church, the vocations of its members, and how the gifts God gives are key to discovering and exercising vocation and mission. Paul has more than one list of gifts and there seems no reason to limit our understanding of gifts to those appearing in them.[37] There is a wide variety of gifts, but in each gift God's Spirit is active, guiding the mission of the church and calling its members to respond to their vocations.[38]

Mission

The mission of the Church is to restore all people to unity with God and each other in Christ . . . through the ministry of all of its members . . . according to the gifts given them.[39]

---

36. The Common Reading was written by the Reverend Doctor John de Beer as the introductory chapter of his thesis *A Vocation Worthy of Our Calling: Gifts Discernment and Congregational Development.* It was submitted to the faculty of Seabury-Western Theological Seminary in partial fulfillment of the requirements for the degree of Doctor of Ministry in Congregation Development. In addition to serving for eight years as the EfM Director of Trainers, during which time he developed the training network, he coauthored with Patricia O'Connell Killen *The Art of Theological Reflection.* After leaving Sewanee, de Beer developed the Klesis Project, which offers an adult curriculum of Christian formation. Information about Klesis is found at http://www.saintmarksburlington.org/adulted.php. The essay has been modestly adapted for use in Unit Five with the permission of its author.

37. Romans 12:4–8; 1 Corinthians 12:8–11, 27–28.

38. 1 Corinthians 12:4.

39. The Episcopal Church, The Book of Common Prayer, 853.

The 1979 revision of the Book of Common Prayer explicitly links the gifts of the members with the mission of the church. This is very different from how mission was understood in the 1950s, when the church in North America assumed that the society in which it was located was itself Christian. Then the mission field was considered as being overseas, in cultures that were largely non-Christian. The role of most church members in mission was to support the overseas missionaries by praying for them and providing financial support. The revision of the Prayer Book in 1979 is linked to a changing understanding of the mission of the church and the role of its members. The growth of interest in identifying the vocation and gifts of church members is a result of this change.

In his book *Transforming Mission*, David Bosch described clearly and comprehensively how the understanding and practice of the church's mission shifted over the centuries.[40] Bosch was a New Testament scholar who grounded his thinking in the texts of the Bible. He argued that the scriptures witness to a God who is the source of all that is and whose loving purpose is to restore a broken world to wholeness in a new creation. Thus God's loving purpose, the *missio Dei,* is primarily directed at the world; the church consists of those who are called to consciously participate in and witness to this new creation. The church enunciates the good news that God's love embraces both church and world; the church is privileged to participate in that love. The church then is a sign to the world of the new creation that God intends. This way of considering mission emerged in the second half of the twentieth century. It functions as a paradigm that guides the missionary activity of a wide spectrum of denominations today. Bosch wrote, "We define [the church's] mission—with true humility—as participation in the *missio Dei*. Witnessing to the gospel of present salvation and future hope we then identify with the awesome birth pangs of God's new creation."[41]

This way of understanding the church's mission has had a huge impact on how the vocation of church members is understood. Here again, Bosch began with the Bible. He pointed out that the mission of those who follow Jesus is not defined in the New Testament, but expressed in images (e.g., salt of the earth, light of the world, city on a hill). Bosch developed his argument as follows: The images of salt, light, and city go to the heart of what it means to be disciples. To follow Jesus is to be in the world, not defined by the world, rather disclosing the true nature of the world.[42] Jesus begins his own mission by announcing that the reign of God is at hand. God's reign is both personal and universal; it has come in the person of Jesus, and it is intended for all humanity. Jesus' disciples are called to share in his mission as witnesses to what God is doing. Mission is integral to being the church; we are called out in order to share the good news. "But you are a chosen race, a royal priesthood, a holy nation, God's own people, in order that you

---

40. David J. Bosch, *Transforming Mission* (New York: Orbis Books, 1991).
41. Ibid., 510.
42. John 17:18–19.

may proclaim the mighty acts of him who called you out of darkness into his marvelous light."[43]

Bosch helps us to see that there has been a profound change in the church's understanding of its mission. Christ's mission is to the whole world, not to the church only. The church is not primarily called to increase its own membership, or even to maintain its own life, but to point the way to the reign of God that is coming and is already here. When members of the church are true to this calling, they do not say to others, "Come and join us," as though God's love is to be found only in the church. Rather they say, "Let us follow him together," as all share in the new world that God is creating. The vocation of church members becomes witnessing to and participating in the way God is changing the world.

An ecumenical group of scholars further developed the implications for the church in North America of this understanding of mission.[44] Their work, *Missional Church*, explored the challenges facing congregations in a society in the midst of rapid change, set in a culture that has lost confidence in the rational, objective, and managed world of the "modern" era. It is not yet clear what will replace the "modern" worldview; we are living between the times, in a "postmodern" condition. In the postmodern world we inhabit, values are seen as relative and religious beliefs are simply a matter of personal preference. This postmodern context presents an enormous challenge to the church. Members of the congregation, as well as those who are unchurched, are affected by the culture of relativism in which we all live. The loss of connection to a center of meaning can easily lead to anxiety and depression. Congregations have been structured to function in a modern, "Christian" society. As the Church comes to terms with our postmodern, largely post-Christian society, congregations discover the mission field is right on their doorstep.

The conclusion of *Missional Church* echoes many of the themes developed by Bosch. The rapid changes and dislocations of our time call for a fresh understanding of mission. The authors invite the church to reclaim a sense of being subject to God, to again find the New Testament vision of being witnesses to the power of God's love. Then, the authors say, "mission is founded on the mission of God in the world, rather than on the church's effort to extend itself."[45] The study defines a missional church as one called into being by an awareness of the reign of God; the response of a congregation to the reign of God defines the congregation's mission. This understanding is grounded in the New Testament. The central teaching of Jesus is the reign of God, characterized as the "full prosperity of the people of God,

---

43. 1 Peter 2:9.

44. Darrell L. Guder and Lois Barrett, *Missional Church: A Vision for the Sending of the Church in North America*, Gospel and Our Culture Series (Grand Rapids, MI: W.B. Eerdmans Publishing, 1998).

45. Ibid., 82.

living under God's demanding care and compassionate rule."[46] The reign of God is understood here not as something we create or extend, but rather receive and enter. The mission of the church, then, is to invite others to join us as we receive and enter the reign of God. We are to "speak boldly and often, so that the signs of the reign of God in the Scriptures, in the world's history, and in the present may be clearly seen."[47]

Thus the task of a missional congregation is to shape a people who demonstrate and announce God's intention for creation.[48] The authors of *The Missional Church* envisioned the congregation as God's pilgrim people in a particular context, drawn to enter into God's reign. The local congregation organizes itself as the pilgrim people of God, with a covenant community at the leading edge, pointing the way to those who are drawn to accompany them. This wider body is defined not by its boundaries, but by the attraction of its members to the direction in which the covenant leadership group is moving, that is, by its mission. Each congregation has its own part to play in God's drama of salvation. Each congregation is called to discern its particular mission, to proclaim the Gospel to particular people at a given time in a specific place.

What are the distinctive marks of a missional congregation? James Fowler approached congregational mission from his study of the stages of faith in the lives of individuals. Fowler proposed that in our postmodern society, adult faith is becoming less conventional and more individual and reflective. He attempted to imagine the nature of the church that God is calling into being, a church that will sustain the growth of individual faith in the emerging world of the twenty-first century.[49]

Fowler described three congregations that illustrated a missional congregation, though he used different words; "missional congregation" became "public church." The "reign of God" became the "commonwealth of love and justice." (Fowler assumed that all understanding is metaphorical, and further that the metaphor of God as a sovereign no longer functions well. Thus "kingdom of God" is freshly imaged as "the commonwealth of love and justice." This evocative image is consistent with the biblical tradition. God reigns where justice and mercy have kissed each other.) Fowler described seven characteristics of a "public church."[50]

1. A public church fosters a clear sense of Christian identity and commitment.

2. A public church manifests a diversity of membership.

3. A public church consciously prepares and supports members for vocation and witness in a pluralistic society.

---

46. Ibid., 9.
47. Ibid., 109.
48. Ibid., 188.
49. James Fowler, *Weaving the New Creation* (San Francisco: Harper, 1991).
50. Ibid., 155–62

4. A public church balances nurture and group solidarity with forming and accountability for public life beyond the walls of the church.

5. A public church evolves patterns of authority and governance that keep pastoral and lay leadership in a fruitful balance.

6. A public church offers its witness in publicly visible and publicly intelligible ways.

7. A public church shapes a pattern of formation for children, youth, and adults that works toward the combining of Christian commitment with vocation in public.

Fowler's description of "public church" expands and gives specificity to the notion of a "missional congregation." In doing so, he was clear that the vocational development of the members is a crucial element in this new paradigm of the mission of the church. The following section explores the meaning of vocation and argues that vocational development is a central component of the Gospel for people in a postmodern age.

Vocation

When God calls a congregation, we speak of mission. When God calls an individual, we speak of vocation. It is the reign of God, experienced on an individual level, that constitutes vocation, just as the reign of God, experienced on a congregational level, constitutes its mission. In Fowler's words, "To be in vocation is to find a purpose for one's life that is part of the purposes of God. Vocation is that response one makes with one's total life to the call of God to partnership."[51] It is possible to have a purpose for one's life that is part of the purposes of God. This is very good news to a postmodern people lost in a sea of relativity (harassed and helpless, like sheep without a shepherd).[52] God equips each person for a unique role in the drama of salvation. A person finds meaning in life by discovering and playing his or her part in God's purpose for the world. Vocation is not chiefly an external duty or obligation, but the key to a life of abundant purpose and fulfillment.

Fowler expanded and intensified the meaning of vocation with four paradoxical illustrations:

1. The paradox illustrated in Psalm 139, that the Creator of all knows each one of us by name, formed us in our mother's womb, and claims us as partners.

2. The paradox of Ephesians 4:1, that our freedom comes through choosing to be prisoners of the Lord. Our hearts are made to be captivated by God; only when we allow this to happen do we find our true vocation and live in a manner worthy of our calling.

---

51. Ibid., 120.
52. Mark 6:34.

3. We become true individuals only in community, in relation to God and neighbor. In community we discover our gifts and our call.

4. What we most deeply want for ourselves can guide us to what God wants for us.

What we most deeply want is often buried under layers of self-protection and false identity. Parker Palmer wrote of the connection between vocation and identity: "How much dissolving and shaking of ego must we endure before we discover our deep identity—the true self within every human being that is the seed of authentic vocation?"[53] Our vocation is to be our true self, to mature into the persons in whom God delights. Vocation, identity, gifts, ministry—these are all interconnected. The place God calls us to is the place where we feel truly ourselves, able to give the gifts we have in service to others.

The argument so far has been that vocational discernment is a core mission of the congregation in order to meet the deep need of individuals to find their identities in God's purpose for their lives and to share in Christ's work of reconciliation. How then do individuals know whom God is calling them to be? What can a congregation do to help?

Gifts

The Church of the Savior in Washington, DC, strongly influenced the vocational discernment work at St. Martin's-in-the-Field, Maryland. The Church of the Savior is an ecumenical congregation, founded after World War II by Gordon Cosby and his wife, Mary. Cosby was a Baptist minister whose experience in the war left him determined to gather a church that would genuinely transform its members.[54] The congregation was constituted by "mission groups" that provided innovative ministries in Washington, DC. These groups emphasized helping members discern their gifts for ministry. Although the membership was small, the congregation had a very large impact on struggling individuals and neighborhoods in the city.

Elizabeth O'Connor was drawn to the Church of the Savior and became active in its life. She wrote several books out of her experience with the congregation. One book in particular became the basis for the workshop at St. Martin's-in-the-Field.[55] Although she did not use the word, the following passage by O'Connor is all about vocation and how it is discerned.

When we talk about being true to ourselves—being the persons we are intended to be—we are talking about gifts. We cannot be ourselves unless we are true to

---

53. Parker J. Palmer, *Let Your Life Speak: Listening for the Voice of Vocation* (San Francisco: Jossey-Bass, 2000), 9.

54. Gordon Cosby, *Handbook for Mission Groups* (Waco, TX: Word Books, 1975).

55. Elizabeth O 'Connor, *Eighth Day of Creation: Gifts and Creativity* (Waco, TX: Word Books, 1971).

our gifts. . . . We ask to know the will of God without guessing that His will is written into our very beings. We perceive that will when we discern our gifts. Our obedience and surrender to God are in large part our obedience and surrender to our gifts . . . A primary purpose of the church is to help us discover our gifts, and in the face of our fears, to hold us accountable for them so we can enter into the joy of creating.[56]

This passage goes to the heart of how the Church of Our Savior organizes itself for mission and became the basis for the Gifts Discernment program at St. Martin's-in-the-Field.

Jacqueline McMakin drew on O'Connor's writing as she created her own work on ministry and gifts.[57] She asked six questions that develop the connection between gifts and individual vocation:

1. What are my unique, God-given gifts?

2. How can I be a patron of another's gifts?

3. Which piece of God's vision is mine?

4. What is God calling me to do?

5. Is there a corporate dimension for my vocation?

6. How do my unique gifts and calling tie me into the larger body of believers?

Our gifts form one pillar on which our vocation is based. God calls us through our gifts, those things that we do well and love to do. We are connected to the church not primarily for our own comfort, but so we can contribute what we have been given in a community of support and accountability.

There is a second pillar for our vocation, though, alluded to in McMakin's question, "Which piece of God's vision is mine?" When we see with God's eyes, we care about what God cares about. Jesus taught us to pray, "Your will be done, on earth as it is in heaven." God is bringing about God's reign, the commonwealth of love and justice, and each of us is called to be a part of what God is doing.

Frederick Buechner described how vocation arises from our gifts and what we care about. "The place God calls you is the place where your deep gladness and the world's deep hunger meet."[58] When we are doing what we love to do and do well, there is a good chance that we are exercising our gifts. However, if we use our gifts for a trivial or selfish purpose, we are likely to be missing God's call. Similarly, if we are spending our lives in the service

---

56. Ibid, 119.

57. Jacqueline McMakin and Rhoda Nary, *Doorways to Christian Growth* (Minneapolis, MN: Winston Press, 1984), 185.

58. Frederick Buechner, *Wishful Thinking: A Theological ABC* (New York: Harper & Row, 1973).

of others in a way that drains us, we are likely to be serving our own sense of duty rather than God's call. Vocation is discovered as the bridge between our gifts and the particular piece of the world's hunger that calls to us. Our culture does not normally associate the idea of *deep gladness* with either *the world's deep hunger* or the concept of *vocation*. To understand that vocation and ministry have a dimension of gladness is a revelation to most parishioners. Gifts discernment is about celebrating and enjoying each person's true vocation. This is a message that needs constant repetition because parishioners are programmed to expect that vocation means doing what is difficult and unpleasant. A further revelation is that the voice calling us resonates within us. True vocation is not experienced as simply doing what some outside authority desires or what the church needs. Just the opposite is true. Genuine vocation provides an authentic path that strengthens the sense of identity and freedom of those who respond to God's call.

A Vocational Paradigm

The illustration below depicts vocation arising from the twin pillars of our giftedness, which is the source of our deep gladness, and our passionate connection to the world's deep hunger.[59]

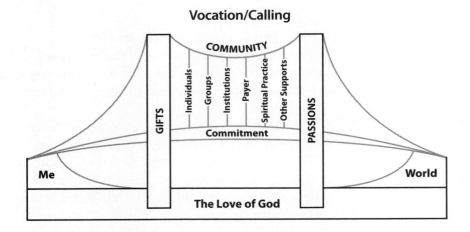

Vocation/Calling

The components of the bridge are drawn from a slightly modified and expanded version of James Fowler's model of vocation.[60]

1. **CHERISHED:** The Creator knows each one of you by name, formed you in your mother's womb, and calls you as partners. (Psalms 139)

2. **GIFTED:** What you do well and love doing are gifts from God. (1 Corinthians 12:1–12)

---

59. The illustration and following comments come from the *The Klesis Project: Hearing and Responding to God's Call* found at www. http://www.saintmarksburlington.org/adulted .php.

60. James Fowler, *Weaving the New Creation* (San Francisco: Harper, 1991).

3. **PASSIONATE**: Your passionate response to the needs of the world can guide you to what God wants for you. (Exodus 2:11–3:10)

4. **COMMITTED**: Your freedom comes through choosing to be prisoners of the Lord. Your hearts are made to be captivated by God; only when you allow this to happen do you find your true vocation and live in a manner worthy of your calling. (Ephesians 4:1–16)

5. **COMMUNAL**: You become true individuals only in community, in relation to God and neighbor. In community you discover your gifts and your call. (1 Corinthians 12:14–31)

Respond

The essay introduced participants to the discipline of missiology as the framework for vocation, call, and ministry. The more clearly one knows God's purpose and mission (*missio Dei*), answers to vocational concerns become easier. There is a direct correlation between God's mission and a person's vocation. Vocation operates on the universal level of God's activities with all of God's creation. It also operates on the societal level that finds expression in roles and responsibilities. For example, once a person becomes a parent that reality remains even after the children are grown. If a person takes on a specific profession that, too, becomes part of who the person is, even after retirement. Vocation also operates on a daily level, which is played out in the multiple exchanges a person has throughout a day.

An actual occurrence illustrates how the different vocational levels operate. An incident, described in a case-study format, serves to demonstrate how vocation operates out of a theology of mission.

> Early one morning the doorbell rang, which was highly unusual. The elderly neighbor had come to the door because he needed to use the restroom. Once he was in the house and attended to basic needs, he reported that he had locked himself out of his house and had slept all night in his car. The conversation continued, revealing that he was very confused and unable to remember things that had recently happened.
>
> Several decision points occurred during the next couple of hours. First, he could be sent on his way back to his own property to solve his own problem. Or we could set aside our work and attend to getting him the needed support. The decision was to talk with him, get names to contact, and keep him safe until family and church friends could provide long term help.

While a more detailed description is possible, a shortened summary serves to illustrate vocational levels. On the "immediate, everyday level" the incident's particularities presented several "mini-vocations." On a societal level, a missiology can answer the question as to what kind of community (neighborhood) God seeks to create. On the most expansive level the sweeping theological propositions point to the "big picture."

On the most comprehensive level as expressed in the Book of Common Prayer, God's mission is "to restore all people to unity with God and each other in Christ." The church is a primary, but not sole, instrument of the purpose.

On the societal level, the call is to participate with God in creating a "commonwealth of love and justice." What actions contribute to the vision and affect the quality of the community? Societal norms and conventions establish and support a quality of life. A "commonwealth of love and justice" grows out of customs that shape and protect just and loving relationships. Hospitality extended to a neighbor reinforces God's commonwealth.

A person faces several decisions in specific, concrete moments. The elderly neighbor in need presented those around him with multiple ethical and vocational dilemmas. For example, one issue is how best to aid him and also respect his dignity.

Reflect on how you have experienced and observed the operation of the three vocation levels—universal, societal, and individual.

Practice

Examine the bridge image presented in "A Vocational Paradigm," above. It functions as a metaphor that depicts the span between an individual and the world.

Explore the dynamics of the metaphor through some theological perspectives, such as: How do you describe the nature of the world shown in the metaphor? What dangers or difficulties are actually or potentially present? How is God disclosed in the metaphor's world? What characteristics of human nature come to mind? What is a cause for celebration in that image?

Extend the theological reflection by connecting the bridge metaphor to the four sources of Tradition (the Christian tradition), Culture (contemporary cultural attitudes), Action (personal experience), and Position (personal beliefs).

Record your position statements, noticing insights of what you see that you have not seen before or see again that you have seen before. Discuss how the reflection illuminates an understanding of vocation and call.

Consider how this reflection contributes to ministry in daily life. Notice especially what difference the reflection has for living out one's vocation and call.

Week Thirty-one

YEAR ONE

Read

Micah
Isaiah 1–39
Excerpt on Micah from Collins's *Introduction to the Hebrew Bible* found in
Part II, pages 220–23
Collins, Chapter 16, "Isaiah," pages 164–73

Focus

Micah and First Isaiah contain familiar passages that have been often
quoted. Identify key verses from both prophets that speak to vocation,
mission, and ministry.

YEAR TWO

Read

Galatians
Powell, Chapter 15, "Galatians," 307–22

Focus

Galatians, known as Paul's "angry" letter, brings emotion to center stage in
developing a theology. Consider how Paul's anger plays in the creation of
his theology. Explore what working with his anger led Paul to do. What light
might be shed on Paul's view of gifts for ministry?

YEAR THREE

Read

MacCulloch, Chapter 21, "Enlightenment: Ally or Enemy?" pages 769–816

Focus

The Enlightenment produced a sea change in Western Christianity that
continues well into the contemporary social and intellectual context. In
what ways has the Enlightenment revolutionized the understanding of
human nature? Think about the positive and negative impact the altered
views of humanity have had on understanding vocational development.

YEAR FOUR

Read

Peace, Rose, and Mobley, Foreword, Introduction, and "Part I: Encountering the Neighbor," pages xi–41

Focus

In the Foreword to *My Neighbor's Faith*, Joan Chittister aptly describes what the book intends and why: "In this book all the languages of God are spoken—Hindu, Buddhist, Jewish, Christian and Muslim—so that we can learn from one another."[61] Much is to be learned about God's "commonwealth of love and justice," also known as God's reign or the kingdom of God. Identify the ways the essays in "Part I: Encountering My Neighbor" contribute to developing a theology of mission and ministry in a pluralistic world. Also, what specific ideas, images, or stories foster vocational development?

ALL YEARS

Respond

The work done throughout this unit fosters vocational development within the context of a missiology that asserts that Christians are called to witness and participate in the way God is changing the world. To that end, review the work you have done this week and throughout the year. Identify key concepts, images (metaphors), stories, and actions that enhance your beliefs about what God is doing in the world, society, and individual lives. Particularly note how what you have learned and experienced enlivens the "Vocational Paradigm" (bridge metaphor) and how it (the metaphor) illuminates what you have read.

Practice

Christian vocational development must be grounded in scripture. One of the primary passages from the New Testament that has guided Christian formation comes from the Epistle to the Ephesians. The EfM theological reflection method that begins with a passage of scripture provides a way to thoroughly examine and understand the theological implications of a passage from scripture. You are invited to reflect on Ephesians 4:1–16 using this method.

> I therefore, the prisoner in the Lord, beg you to lead a life worthy of the calling to which you have been called, with all humility and gentleness, with patience, bearing with one another in love, making every effort to maintain the unity of the Spirit in the bond of peace. There is one body and one Spirit, just as you

---

61. Jennifer Howe Peace, Or N. Rose, and Gregory Mobley, eds., *My Neighbor's Faith: Stories of Interreligious Encounter, Growth, and Transformation* (Maryknoll, NY: Orbis Books, 2012), xii.

were called to the one hope of your calling, one Lord, one faith, one baptism, one God and Father of all, who is above all and through all and in all. But each of us was given grace according to the measure of Christ's gift. Therefore it is said, "When he ascended on high he made captivity itself a captive; he gave gifts to his people." (When it says, "He ascended," what does it mean but that he had also descended into the lower parts of the earth? He who descended is the same one who ascended far above all the heavens, so that he might fill all things.) The gifts he gave were that some would be apostles, some prophets, some evangelists, some pastors and teachers, to equip the saints for the work of ministry, for building up the body of Christ, until all of us come to the unity of the faith and of the knowledge of the Son of God, to maturity, to the measure of the full stature of Christ. We must no longer be children, tossed to and fro and blown about by every wind of doctrine, by people's trickery, by their craftiness in deceitful scheming. But speaking the truth in love, we must grow up in every way into him who is the head, into Christ, from whom the whole body, joined and knitted together by every ligament with which it is equipped, as each part is working properly, promotes the body's growth in building itself up in love. —Ephesians 4:1–16

The "Theological Reflection Beginning with Scripture" outline, found in Part II of the *Guide*, may be helpful for this reflection.

Additional questions to use in the **exploring** portion of the reflection on the Ephesians passage:

• How does God disclose God's self in this world?

• What deep need is exposed?

• What is shown about the "commonwealth of love and justice"?

When you reach the **connecting** phase of the reflection, focus on the following:

• An action/personal experience consideration around a time when you faced something related to the central idea of the scripture passage;

• A contemporary culture consideration around one area, such as what our world of employment says is important in relation to the central idea of the scripture passage; or what our government views as important regarding the subject of the passage;

• A personal position consideration around what you believe about the subject of the reflection.

When the reflection turns to **applying**, include questions such as:

• How do you understand vocation and call as the result of this reflection?

• Comment on implications for your vocational development.

Create a summary statement of what you have learned, especially with reference to vocational development.

Week Thirty-two

YEAR ONE

Read

Isaiah 40–66
Collins, Chapter 19, "The Additions to the Book of Isaiah," pages 197–208

Focus

The prophets studied in Collins's chapters are full of poetic imagery. Reflect on how the imagery has contributed to Christian theology and worship.

YEAR TWO

Read

1 Corinthians and 2 Corinthians
Powell, Chapter 13, "1 Corinthians" and Chapter 14, "2 Corinthians," pages 273–306

Focus

Review the opening essay of this unit (Week Thirty) to identify how passages from the Corinthians Letters were used to develop a theology of vocation. How does Powell's discussion of Paul's Corinthian Letters illuminate the theology of mission, ministry, and vocation?

YEAR THREE

Read

MacCulloch, Chapter 22, "Europe Re-enchanted or Disenchanted?" 817–65

Focus

This chapter laid out necessary components for setting the context of contemporary Anglo-American and European theology. Note what specific persons or ideas interest you, and how what you identify suggests about what gifts and passions you have.

YEAR FOUR

Read

Peace, Rose, and Mobley, "Part II: Viewing Home Anew" and "Part III: Redrawing Our Maps," pages 45–124

Focus

When someone crosses over to another culture and openly embraces the differences, upon returning the person sees home anew. Cultural dissonance sets in that requires redrawing of familiar boundaries. Which of the vignettes found in Parts II and III exemplified what de Beer described as "layers of self-protection and false identity"? Think about how their stories affect your sense of self.

ALL YEARS

Respond

Review these statements from this unit's opening essay by John de Beer:

> When God calls a congregation, we speak of mission. When God calls an individual, we speak of vocation. It is the Reign of God, experienced on an individual level, that constitutes vocation, just as the Reign of God, experienced on a congregational level, constitutes its mission.

> God equips each person for a unique role in the drama of salvation. A person finds meaning in life by discovering and playing his or her part in God's purpose for the world. Vocation is not chiefly an external duty or obligation, but the key to a life of abundant purpose and fulfillment.

Think through how your assigned reading supports and/or challenges the vocational development perspective contained in these statements.

Practice

The experiences a person has and how they are interpreted shape identity. Reinterpreting past experiences can uncover what a person most deeply wants. Reflecting theologically on selected experiences fosters new understandings in light of theological themes.

The discipline of theological reflection contributes to the formation of a person's vocation and how that call is lived out in everyday life. One of the elements of the discipline of theological reflection is the selection of incidents that begin the reflection process. While any experience can be used, selecting experiences of interest and energy enrich and focus theological reflection. Additionally, deeper reflection occurs when one chooses experiences that a person senses are about theological concerns, such as mission, vocation, gifts, and ministry.

Recall two or three past experiences that you believe might be about vocation or call. For example, the unexpected visit from an elderly neighbor described in Week Thirty likely holds much to be learned about vocation and ministry. Another would be how a person responded to someone in the grocery store who unexpectedly revealed her struggle with cancer.

Once you have recalled two or three experiences, choose one to describe in writing. Include sufficient detail to capture the experience. The description need not be more than a half page or so.

The description can initiate a reflection process using the worksheet for Individual Theological Reflection, located on page 233 in Part II of this guide. The method may also be used to start the reflection process in your EfM seminar. Whenever a theological reflection method is used to reflect on a particular theological theme, such as vocation or mission, the **exploring** questions can be adapted. For example, the "sin" question might be framed as "What inhibits or blocks responding to a call?" Or the redemption question asked as "What brings great joy in this world?" Another place where the theological reflection can be particularized is in the **applying** phase: "What implication does what you believe have for constructing a theology of vocation?"

Week Thirty-three

YEAR ONE

Read

Jeremiah
Lamentations
Collins, "Chapter 17, "The Babylonian Era: Jeremiah and Lamentations,"
pages 174–84

Focus

Identify and explore what doctrines are implicitly or explicitly present in the
prophetic traditions of Jeremiah.

YEAR TWO

Read

Ephesians
Powell, Chapter 16, "Ephesians," pages 323–41

Focus

Reflect especially in light of de Beer's comment, "What we most deeply
want is often buried under layers of self-protection and false identity. . . .
The place God calls us to is the place where we feel truly ourselves, able to
give the gifts we have in service to others."

YEAR THREE

Read

MacCulloch, Chapter 23, "To Make the World Protestant," pages 866–914

Focus

MacCulloch's chapter covers over two hundred years of history that is likely
familiar. As the historian's work comes closer to the present, the line between history and journalism blurs. Identify a thread that runs through the
chapter. In one or two sentences, describe it. Examine the thread using questions framed from the theological standpoints of human nature; creation,
sin, judgment, repentance, and redemption; the way God is disclosed; and
the kind of future desired. Develop associations with concepts, images, or
stories from current culture and society. Uncover what truths and beliefs you
hold. Consider what you have seen that you have not seen before. What do

you see that you have seen before? Describe what difference your reflection has for your day-to-day life as a Christian seeking to serve the world in Christ's name.

YEAR FOUR

Read

Peace, Rose, and Mobley, "Part IV: Unpacking Our Belongings" and "Part V: Stepping Across the Line," pages 127–203

Focus

"Interfaith encounter forces its practitioners to assume responsibility for both the actual and perceived histories of their groups."[62] Reflect on the significance of what the authors in Parts IV and V dealt with in such encounters. Recall what you have experienced whenever you have encountered "the hospitality of your neighbor's faith"?

ALL YEARS

Respond

As Elizabeth O'Conner so aptly observes, a person's identity, purpose, and vocation are communicated through gifts. She writes, "We ask to know the will of God without guessing that His will is written into our very beings. We perceive that will when we discern our gifts."[63] Often awareness of gifts comes unexpectedly and unseen and therefore arrives unexamined. O'Conner's observations grow out of a theology that takes very seriously that human beings are created in the image of God. Within this theology, vocational discernment is intertwined with who a person is as that person lives in community. Determining gifts is both individual and communal. In addition to self-knowledge, gift discernment involves seeing something of God's reflection. Whenever a person asks, "What are my gifts?" the person also asks, "What of God is specifically and uniquely being reflected through my gifts?" From the perspective of this theology, gift discernment is a sobering process. Therefore, it is to be entered into prayerfully.

Discerning gifts is somewhat like trying to see your face without the aid of another person or instrument. Others see a person's face directly, but the individual self cannot. Even the best mirror or camera only approximates the reality.

---

62. Peace, Rose, and Mobley, *My Neighbor's Faith*, 125.

63. Elizabeth O'Conner, *Journey Inward, Journey Outward* (New York: Harper & Row, 1968), 37.

Vocational discernment can happen only within community. The community may be intentional (like an EfM group) or unintentional like a chance conversation while standing in line to get a cup of coffee at Starbuck's. The community also includes those who have lived before us. Study of the Christian heritage can be approached as discerning one's mission, ministry, and vocation. Reading Job, the Johannine Letters, nineteenth-century Christian history, or encounters with people of different religions includes reading about identity, gifts, ministry, and vocation.

Review your reading for this and the last few weeks. Look at the material from the standpoint of gifts discernment. What do you notice about your interests, concerns, values—your gifts? Additionally, what gifts and passions of members of your group are reflected in what you have been studying?

Practice

In the early 1960s Joseph Luft and Harry Ingham together developed a deceptively simple model of self-awareness that became known as the Johari Window. It is a simple diagram that distinguishes four features of self-awareness: 1) Open and free: what is known to the person and known to others; 2) known to self, hidden to others; 3) known to others, closed to oneself; and 4) hidden to others, hidden to self. They arranged the four features into a four window diagram:

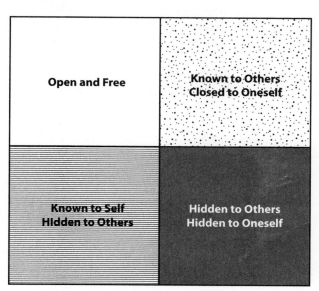

The four windows are not fixed, but depend on the specific context under consideration. What the diagram between two good friends looks like is different than that between two acquaintances. The Johari Window you would draw representing your work situation would be different than that representing family members around the dinner table.

Think through how this model of understanding human nature can be used in vocational discernment. For example, state one interest/passion you have that others in the EfM group know as well. Next, name an interest you have that you have not disclosed to them. Thirdly, if given an opportunity to ask what they have seen about your interests, what would you ask them? Lastly, reflect on thoughts and feelings things that are hidden from yourself and from others—those things known only to God.

Consider what light the Johari Window view of human nature throws on the prayer known as the Collect for Purity: [64]

Almighty God, to you all hearts are open, all desires known, and from you no secrets are hid: Cleanse the thoughts of our hearts by the inspiration of your Holy Spirit, that we may perfectly love you, and worthily magnify your holy Name; through Christ our Lord. Amen.

In the essay that opened this unit on vocation, de Beer writes:

What we most deeply want is often buried under layers of self-protection and false identity. Parker Palmer wrote of the connection between vocation and identity: "How much dissolving and shaking of ego must we endure before we discover our deep identity—the true self within every human being that is the seed of authentic vocation?" [65] Our vocation is to be our true self, to mature into the persons in whom God delights. Vocation, identity, gifts, ministry—these are all interconnected. The place God calls us to is the place where we feel truly ourselves, able to give the gifts we have in service to others.

How does work with the Johari Window support and clarify your sense of vocation, mission, and ministry?

---

64. The Book of Common Prayer, 355.
65. Palmer, *Let Your Life Speak*, 9.

Week Thirty-four

YEAR ONE

Read

The Book of Ezekiel
Collins, Chapter 18, "Ezekiel," pages 185–96

Focus

Identify a concept that runs through the readings. Write one or two descriptive sentences that capture the idea. Explore the dimensions of the topic, such as what is assumed and valued; name the destructive elements that are present in the topic; examine the explicit and implicit hopes for the future. Ask, "What light do ideas and voices from contemporary literature, television productions, or Internet blogs shed on the reflection?" Note what position or beliefs you hold in relation to the topic. Consider the importance and implications your thinking has for serving and ministering to those among whom you live and work.

YEAR TWO

Read

1 John, 2 John, and 3 John

Powell, Chapter 27, "The Johannine Letters: 1 John, 2 John, 3 John," pages 493–507

Focus

Reflect on how the theme of "God is love" relates to your interests and passions.

YEAR THREE

Read

MacCulloch, Chapter 24, "Not Peace but a Sword," pages 915–66

Focus

Look for the themes that interest you in the chapter and explore one using a couple of the theological perspective questions. Notice what connections you make with your experience and culture. What do you believe about the theme? Reflect on the implications your line of thought holds for living as a Christian in the various contexts of your life.

YEAR FOUR

Read

Peace, Rose, and Mobley, "Part VI: Finding Fellow Travelers," pages 205–40

Focus

Identify a theme that runs through the essays presented in Part VI. State the theme in writing. Examine the dimensions of the theme using the theological perspectives, such as how God discloses God's self; the quality and characteristics of humanity revealed in how the theme is developed in the essays; how the viewpoints of creation, sin, judgment, repentance, and/or redemption are discussed. Relate content from contemporary society and culture to the theme. Ask what you believe, value, and affirm as true. Draw out the significance for your ministry.

ALL YEARS

Respond

From time to time it is important to retrace the year's journey. This is particularly crucial when fostering vocational interests. Recall Frederick Buechner's descriptive definition of vocation: "The place God calls you is the place where your deep gladness and the world's deep hunger meet."[66]
Deep gladness fuels and sustains mission and motivates ministry.

Revisit your notes for the year and review some of the passages you have highlighted in your textbook(s) during the year. Notice what interested you and consider how those interests provide clues for your "deep gladness." Review your spiritual autobiography to see what has delighted you. Recall any discussions that suggest what you love doing. Call to mind experiences that you celebrate and enjoy.

Write a short paragraph describing the deep gladness you have within you. It may take several drafts to reach some clarity.

People often have issues that "push their buttons," causing them to jump on a "soap box" and rant in response to what they have heard or seen. Such rants can point toward what Buechner calls the "world's deep hunger." A rant usually grows out of a recognized profound need. Recall two or three of your "rants" and explore the yearning that provides the energy for the protestation. Describe the human and/or social need that often evokes your "soap box speeches."

Issues and concerns that you are passionate about, coupled with your joys, may reveal God's call. Name three or four contexts in which you experience the marriage of yearning and joy.

---

66. Buechner, *Wishful Thinking*, 119.

Practice

Identify when you experienced the tension of wanting two things simultaneously, such as a desire to try new things in life and a desire to remain where life is familiar. Choose an experience that has ended, i.e., there are no decisions pending. For example, "I had just begun to work on a project that I like doing when my phone rang showing that a friend was calling. I knew from an earlier conversation that he was living through a crisis. At that moment I had to decide whether to answer the phone or let it ring, hoping my friend would leave a message that I could respond to later."

Find the Dilemma Method for Theological Reflection work sheet in Week Twenty-four (page 112) of the *Guide*.

Use the outline to reflect theologically on the issue that you have identified.

After completing the worksheet, reflect on the ways in which the theological reflection sheds light on your vocation and ministry.

Week Thirty-five

YEAR ONE

Read

Collins, Chapter 20, "Postexilic Prophecy" and Chapter 29, "From Tradition to Canon," pages 209–19 and 302–6

Focus

Identify the story, image, and/or idea that affected you from your reading.

YEAR TWO

Read

The Revelation to John
Powell, Chapter 29, "Revelation," pages 519–37

Focus

State one new understanding and one thing that bothers you about the scripture's Book of the Revelation of John.

YEAR THREE

Read

MacCulloch, Chapter 25, "Cultural Wars," pages 967–1016

Focus

Reflect on how MacCulloch's context as an Oxford-trained British citizen shapes his understanding of history. How does his understanding compare with yours and the context from which you read history?

YEAR FOUR

Read

Peace, Rose, and Mobley, "Part VII: Repairing Our Shared World," pages 241–66

Focus

Describe one "deep gladness" and one "hunger of the world" that surfaced for you from reading the essays in Part VII.

ALL YEARS

Respond

Use the week's assigned reading to:

Identify the focus of what you read.

Explore the views of the world, sin, judgment, repentance, and/or redemption that may have been presented in your reading

Connect by

Noting how the author(s) drew on contemporary culture in writing the chapter;

Noting the beliefs that the author seemed to hold and how those intersect with your beliefs;

Recalling personal experiences related to the chapter's focus.

Apply by considering how the material of your text reflection relates to ministry you can offer in the world each day.

Practice

Keeping in mind the Integrative Triangle, consider the following questions.

Integrative Triangle

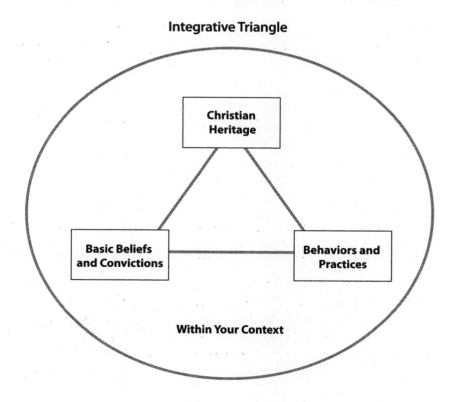

Christianity has multiple voices expressing varieties of theologies. Invest time and energy to identify how your beliefs resonate with theologies voiced throughout this year in EfM.

How have your behavior, practices, and attitudes been affected by your experience in EfM?

Imagine you have only two minutes to answer the question, "What is your ministry and how do you determine you are following God's call?" [Okay, you have five minutes.] Write a response.

Ending the Year

Week Thirty-six

Worship

TRADITION

Without a coming there can be no leaving, and without a presence absence
is only emptiness. There is a ministry in which our leaving creates space for
God's spirit and in which, by our absence, God can become present in a new
way. The great mystery of the divine revelation is that God entered into intimacy with us not only by Christ's coming, but also by his leaving. Indeed, it is
in Christ's absence that our intimacy with him is so profound that we can say
he dwells in us, call him our food and drink, and experience him as the center
of our being.[67] —Henri Nouwen

Prayer of One Who Is Moving On

Guardian, guide, no pillar of cloud by day nor fire by night,
Yet we sense your presence with us, God of the journey.
You are walking with us into a new land.
You are guarding us in our vulnerable moment.
You are dwelling within us as we depart from here.
You are promising to be our peace as we face the struggles
of distance from friends and security,
the planting of feet and heart in a strange place.

Renew in us a deep trust in you. Calm our anxiousness.
As we reflect on our lives we can clearly see
how you have been there in all of our leavings,
You have been there in all of our comings.
You will always be with us in everything.
We do not know how we are being resettled,
but we place our lives into the welcoming arms of your love.
Encircle our hearts with your peace.
May your powerful presence run like a strong thread
through the fibers of our being. Amen.[68]
—*Joyce Rupp*

---

67. Henri Nouwen, *Bread for the Journey: A Daybook of Wisdom and Faith* (San Francisco:
Harper San Francisco, 1977), 77.
68. Rupp, *Praying Our Goodbyes*, 144–45.

Check-in

Take a few minutes to consider and note in silence, then share as you choose:

What events during the year have especially affected you? **ACTION**

What for you is the essence of EfM? **POSITION**

Celebration

TRADITION

The poet Rilke asks the question "When can **we** be real?" I propose that we are **on the way** to being real when we pay attention to non-action, that is to the **via positiva** (awe) and the **via negativa** (darkness) in our lives. But we don't actually **become** real until we abandon ourselves to creativity, until the Spirit that made the heavens and the Earth can flow through us and effect its New Creation through us. We become real when our work joins the Great Work. We become real when our inner work becomes work in the world; when our creativity, born of deep attention to both enchantment and nothingness, serves the cause of transformation, healing, and celebrating. In other words, we become real when our work becomes compassion expressed in creative ways that surprise and that effect change. This can only happen to the extent that we act out of non-action. That is when the Divine "pours the earth, the stars, into us." [69] —*Matthew Fox*

Wonder is to the cure of the soul what medicine is to the cure of the body.

Personal Reflection

ACTION

Wonder, Call, Freedom, Gift, Discernment, Ministry, Vocation:

Reflect on how each of these aspects of God's love arises in your life and in the life of the EfM seminar. Share what you would like to celebrate.

Only that work can be truly sacramental which flows from the heart to the heart, which comes from an inner place, which makes common cause with both light and darkness, enchantment and suffering. If we are engaged in our work at a deep heart level, then our work is truly sacrament: it accomplished what it signifies. One's work will be judged by what one gives birth to, not only by what one lets go of. [70] —*Matthew Fox*

---

69. Matthew Fox, *The Reinvention of Work: A New Vision of Livelihood for Our Time* (New York: HarperCollins, 1995), 113–14.

70. Ibid, 300.

A Litany of Farewell

Fellow Christian ministers, let us pray for the saving presence of our living God.

> In this world:
> *He is risen.*

> In this community:
> *He is risen.*

> In our Diocesan Family:
> *He is risen.*

> In this gathering:
> *He is risen.*

> In the hearts of all faithful people:
> *He is risen.*

> But especially we pray and give thanks now for _____
> who is leaving our community.

> For expectations not met:
> *Lord have mercy.*
> For grievances not resolved:
> *Lord have mercy.*
> For wounds not healed:
> *Lord have mercy.*
> For anger not dissolved:
> *Lord have mercy.*
> For gifts not given:
> *Lord have mercy.*
> For promises not kept:
> *Lord have mercy.*

> And, also, for this portion of your lifelong pilgrimage which you have made with us in this place:
> *Thanks be to God.*
> For friendships made, celebrations enjoyed, and for moments of nurture:
> *Thanks be to God.*
> For wounds healed, expectations met, gifts given, promises kept:
> *Thanks be to God.*
> For trust and confidence shared; times of good humor and moments of gentle leadership:
> *Thanks be to God.*

For bread and wine, body and blood:
Thanks be to God.
And so, to establish a home in _____ with other members
of the family of Christ:
Go in peace.
To continue the journey with new friends and new adventures, new gifts
to give and receive:
Go in peace.
To offer wisdom and experience, competence and compassion, in the
ministry to which you are called:
Go in peace.
With whatever fears, whatever sadness, whatever excitement may be
yours:
Go in peace.
With our faith in you, our hope for you, our love of you:
Go in peace.

Offer intercessions, petitions, and thanksgivings.

Together:
Now, we pray, be with the one who leaves and with those who stay; and
grant that all of us, by drawing ever nearer to you, may always be close to
each other in the communion of your saints. All this we ask for the sake
of Jesus Christ, our Savior.   Amen.

Worship

TRADITION

We sustain each other in the constant interplay between absence and presence. A sustaining ministry asks ministers to be not only creatively present
but creatively absent. A creative absence challenges ministers to develop an
ever growing intimacy with God in prayer and to make that the source of their
entire ministry. [71] *—Henri Nouwen*

CULTURE

When you part from your friend, you grieve not
For that which you love most in him may be clearer in his absence,
As the mountain to the climber is clearer from the plain.[72]
—K. Gibran

---

71. Nouwen, *Bread for the Journey,* 77.
72. Kahlil Gibran, *The Prophet.*

Prayer for One Going to a New Ministry   TRADITION

"You shall go out in joy, and be led back in peace." (Isaiah 55:12)

Yahweh, God of the journey, you went with the Israelites in the form of a pillar of cloud by day to show them the way and by night in the form of a pillar of fire to give them light for their journey (Ex 13:21–22). We long for that kind of assuredness of your presence on our new roads, too. We fear the unknown and we wonder what the future will hold for us. A part of us wants to hold onto the blessings we have known and to rest in the security that is ours.

Remind us often that we are to bring the good news, that we are your servants, heralds of justice and peace (Is 52:7). May we be so open to your word and your way as we travel on that people will "take us by the sleeve" and say: "We want to go with you since we have learnt that God is with you" (Zec 8:23). Encourage us with a deepened awareness of our calling when we want to look back or when we experience feelings of loneliness, doubt or homelessness. Take us to your people and shine through our lives. Amen.[73] —Joyce Rupp

---

73. Rupp, *Praying Our Goodbyes*, 168.

PART II

Resources

Overview of the Year: Reading Assignments for Volume A

Notes

1. Common readings at the beginning of each unit are read by all years.

2. Assignments for Years One and Two marked with an asterisk are readings in the Bible. Chapters in the survey texts are numbered. Please note that chapters are sometimes read out of sequence. When both are assigned, it is suggested that the Bible be read before the survey text chapters.

3. Readings in the each of the three texts for Year Four are indicated by name of the author(s).

WEEK	UNIT	YEAR ONE	YEAR TWO	YEAR THREE	YEAR FOUR
		Collins	Powell	MacCulloch	Allen, Sedgwick, Peace
1	Introductory Meeting	Norms, Books, Housekeeping, Orientation, and Planning	Norms, Books, Housekeeping, Orientation, and Planning	Norms, Books, Housekeeping, Orientation, and Planning	Norms, Books, Housekeeping, Orientation, and Planning
2	Unit One Spiritual Autobiography and Listening	Common Readings: Listening as Ministry Spiritual Autobiography	Common Readings: Listening as Ministry Spiritual Autobiography	Common Readings: Listening as Ministry Spiritual Autobiography	Common Readings: Listening as Ministry Spiritual Autobiography
3		Preface, Introduction 1 The Near Eastern Context 2 The Nature of the Pentateuchal Narrative	Preface 1 The New Testament World 2 The New Testament Writings	Acknowledgements, Introduction 1 Greece and Rome	Allen: Preface Introduction: What Is Theology?
4		* Genesis 1–11 3 The Primeval History	3 Jesus 4 The Gospels	2 Israel	Allen: 1 The Holy One of Israel
5		The Priestly Creation Story	* Matthew	3 A Crucified Messiah	Allen: 2 Holiness for Today
6		* Genesis 12–50 4 The Patriarchs	5 Matthew	4 Boundaries Defined	Allen: 3 The Maker of Heaven and Earth 4 Limits of Science
7		* Exodus 1–15 5 The Exodus from Egypt	* Mark 6 Mark	5 The Prince: Ally or Enemy?	Allen: 5 What Is Meant by "God"?

WEEK	UNIT	YEAR ONE	YEAR TWO	YEAR THREE	YEAR FOUR
8	Unit Two Theological Reflection as a Life Skill	Common Reading: Theological Reflection as a Life Skill	Common Reading: Theological Reflection as a Life Skill	Common Reading: Theological Reflection as a Life Skill	Common Reading: Theological Reflection as a Life Skill
9		* Exodus 16–40 6 Revelation at Sinai	* Luke	6 The Imperial Church	Allen: 6 Nature as Witness and Innocent Suffering
10		* Leviticus * Numbers 7 Priestly Theology: Exodus 25–40, Leviticus and Numbers	7 Luke	7 Defying Chalcedon: Asia and Africa	Allen: 7 Innocent Suffering and Life beyond Death
11		* Deuteronomy 8 Deuteronomy	* John	8 Islam: The Great Realignment	Allen: 8 Suffering from Nature and Extreme Human Cruelty
12		* Joshua * Judges	8 John	9 The Making of Latin Christianity	Allen: 9 The Sacrifice in Creation Essay: DuBose on the Trinity
13		9 Joshua 10 Judges	* The Acts of the Apostles 9 Acts	10 Latin Christendom: New Frontiers	Allen: 10 The Incarnation as Sacrifice
14	Interlude 1	Common Reading: Bryan, Part I	Common Reading: Bryan, Part I	Common Reading: Bryan, Part I	Common Reading: Bryan, Part I
15	Interlude 1	Common Readings: Bryan, Part II	Common Readings: Bryan, Part II	Common Readings: Bryan, Part II	Common Readings: Bryan, Part II
16	Unit Three Developing a Sustaining Spirituality	Common Readings: The Spiritual Person The Sanctification of Time and Life	Common Readings: The Spiritual Person The Sanctification of Time and Life	Common Readings: The Spiritual Person The Sanctification of Time and Life	Common Readings: The Spiritual Person: The Sanctification of Time and Life
17		* Psalms	10 New Testament Letters 11 Paul	11 The West: Universal Emperor or Universal Pope?	Allen: 11 The Temptation in the Wilderness
18		* Song of Songs 23 Psalms and Song of Songs	* Romans	12 A Church for All People?	Allen: 12 The Sacrifice of the Cross
19		* Proverbs 24 Proverbs	12 Romans	13 Faith in a New Rome	Allen: 13 The Resurrection of Jesus and Eternal Life
20		* Job * Ecclesiastes (Qoheleth) 25 Job and Qoheleth	* Hebrews 23 Hebrews	14 Orthodoxy: More Than an Empire	Allen: 14 Jesus as Lord and Jesus as Servant
21		*Ruth * Jonah * Esther 26 The Hebrew Short Story	* 1 Peter * 2 Peter 25 1 Peter 26 2 Peter	15 Russia: The Third Rome	Allen: 15 Revelation and Faith

WEEK	UNIT	YEAR ONE	YEAR TWO	YEAR THREE	YEAR FOUR
22	Unit Four Building Theology: Integrating Belief, Behavior, and Doctrine in Everyday Life	Common Reading: Building a Theology: Integrating Belief, Behavior, and Doctrine in Everyday Life	Common Reading: Building a Theology: Integrating Belief, Behavior, and Doctrine in Everyday Life	Common Reading: Building a Theology: Integrating Belief, Behavior, and Doctrine in Everyday Life	Common Reading: Building a Theology: Integrating Belief, Behavior, and Doctrine in Everyday Life
23		* 1 Samuel * 2 Samuel 11 First Samuel 12 Second Samuel	* Philemon * Jude 22 Philemon 28 Jude	16 Perspectives on the True Church	Allen: 16 The Holy Spirit, the Church, and the Sacraments
24		* 1 Kings * 2 Kings 13 First Kings 1–16 14 First Kings 17–2 Kings 25	* Philippians * Colossians 17 Philippians 18 Colossians	17 A House Divided	Allen: 17 Sin, Evil, and Hope for the Future
25		* Ezra * Nehemiah 21 Ezra and Nehemiah	* 1 Timothy * 2 Timothy * Titus 21 The Pastoral Letters	18 Rome's Renewal	Sedgwick: Preface, Introduction, 1 Describing the Christian Life 2 An Anglican Perspective Epilogue
26		* 1 Chronicles * 2 Chronicles 22 The Books of Chronicles	* 1 Thessalonians * 2 Thessalonians 19 1 Thessalonians 20 2 Thessalonians	19 A Worldwide Faith	Sedgwick: 3 Incarnate Love 4 Love and Justice
27		* Amos * Hosea 15 Amos and Hosea	* James 24 James	20 Protestant Awakenings	Sedgwick: 5 The Practices of Faith 6 The Call of God Appendix
28	Interlude 2	Common Reading: Countryman: Preface Part I	Common Reading: Countryman: Preface Part I	Common Reading: Countryman: Preface Part I	Common Reading: Countryman: Preface Part I
29	Interlude 2	Common Reading: Countryman: Preface Part II	Common Reading: Countryman: Preface Part II	Common Reading: Countryman: Preface Part II	Common Reading: Countryman: Preface Part II
30	Unit Five Vocation: Hearing and Responding to God's Call	Common Reading: Mission, Vocation, and Gifts	Common Reading: Mission, Vocation, and Gifts	Common Reading: Mission, Vocation, and Gifts	Common Reading: Mission, Vocation, and Gifts
31		* Micah * Isaiah 1–39 Excerpt: Collins on Micah 16 Isaiah	* Galatians 15 Galatians	21 Enlightenment: Ally or Enemy?	Peace, Rose, Mobley: Foreword Introduction 1 Encountering the Neighbor
32		* Isaiah 40–66 19 Additions to the Book of Isaiah	* 1 Corinthians * 2 Corinthians 13 1 Corinthians 14 2 Corinthians	22 Europe Re-enchanted or Disenchanted?	Peace, Rose, Mobley: 2 Viewing Home Anew 3 Redrawing Our Maps

WEEK	UNIT	YEAR ONE	YEAR TWO	YEAR THREE	YEAR FOUR
33		* Jeremiah * Lamentations 17 The Babylonian Era	* Ephesians 16 Ephesians	23 To Make the World Protestant	Peace, Rose, Mobley: 4 Unpacking Our Belongings 5 Stepping Across the Line
34		* Ezekiel 18 Ezekiel	* 1 John * 2 John * 3 John 27 Johannine Letters	24 Not Peace but a Sword	Peace, Rose, Mobley: 6 Finding Fellow Travelers
35		20 Postexilic Prophecy 29 From Tradition to Canon	* The Revelation to John 29 Revelation	25 Culture Wars	Peace, Rose, Mobley: 7 Repairing Our Shared World
36	Final Meeting	Celebration	Celebration	Celebration	Celebration

Terms

Common Reading

A common reading is assigned to all year levels. Each unit begins with an introductory essay read by all participants. Interlude texts are also assigned for common reading.

Identify, Explore, Connect, Apply

Theological reflection is described in four movements: *Identify, Explore, Connect, Apply.* This pattern also underlies the *Read, Focus, Respond, Practice* pattern of the *Reading and Reflection Guide.*

Interlude

An interlude is a two-week session in which all participants in a group read and respond to a common text chosen in relation to the theme of the *Reading and Reflection Guide.* There are two interludes in each program year.

Interlude Text

The text assigned to an interlude session is called an interlude text or interlude book. Two interlude books are read each year. The books address special topics that reinforce the theme of the *Reading and Reflection Guide* for that program year.

Participants

Those enrolled in a seminar group are generally referred to as participants or group members.

Program Year

The approximately nine-month period (thirty-six sessions) during which the group seminar meets is its program year.

Read, Focus, Respond, Practice

The guide for each session follows the sequence of *Read* (assigned reading), *Focus* (questions or terms specific to the assigned reading), *Respond* (connects the reading to the unit theme), and *Practice* (suggested application for individual and/or group work). This sequence provides a four-fold discipline for the practice of ministry.

Reading and Reflection Guides

These guides outline what is needed for participants to prepare for each of the thirty-six seminar meetings in a program year, including individual reading assignments and suggested ways to focus, respond, and practice what is being learned. There will be four volumes, A–D, used in a cycle. All groups will use the same *Reading and Reflection Guide* volume in a program year.

Readings in the Christian Tradition

The textbooks that replace previous chapters in the red notebooks provide participants with their weekly readings in the Christian tradition: the Hebrew Bible in Year One; the New Testament in Year Two; church history in Year Three; and theology, ethics, and interfaith encounters in Year Four.

Theme

Each volume of the *Reading and Reflection Guide* has a central theme that is carried through each of the units and interludes. Volume A's theme is ministry in your own particular context. Themes for the subsequent volumes are (B) ministry in an intercultural and interfaith context, (C) growth into Christian maturity, and (D) the journey into a deepening relationship with God.

Expectations

The Participants

You, the participants in an EfM seminar group, are all adults. You set your own learning goals and need the latitude to learn as each individual does best. This requires a certain commitment to the program, but every participant does not need to work in the same way or with the same intensity. EfM has the flexibility for each of you to work in his or her own way.

There are some basic expectations of each participant:

- Attend the seminar sessions or at least maintain the community by letting others know when you will be absent.

- Read the materials and complete the work assigned to the best of your ability.

- Participate in the discussions, reflections, and worship of your seminar group.

The Mentor

The role of the mentor is crucial to the life of the group. The term "mentor" originates in Greek mythology. Mentor was a friend of Odysseus who remained in charge of his household while he was away. "Wisdom" in the form of Athena took shape in Mentor to be the guide and teacher of Telemachus. A teacher who guides is a description of an EfM mentor.

The EfM mentor brings skills in working effectively with small groups of people. The responsibility for the life of the group belongs to everyone, but the mentor is the initial convener. The mentor works to allow everyone an opportunity to learn, to share, to discover. At the same time, the mentor is also a member of the group. The mentor is also there to learn, to share, and to discover. The mentor has a second role, that of administrator for the group. The mentor handles registrations, receives and distributes materials, files reports, and acts as the contact for the group with the administrative staff in Sewanee.

The mentor serves the group neither as a teacher whose most important task is to provide information nor as a therapist. The mentor is a guide in a journey of discovery. Some groups have co-mentors who work together as a team. This can be very helpful to the process since it can be very difficult to lead and participate simultaneously.

Mentor training and accreditation by an EfM trainer is required. It is an important component of the EfM program. Mentors must renew their accreditation within eighteen months.

The Seminar Group

The EfM seminar group is the crucible for learning in the EfM program. Each seminar group usually contains no fewer than six and no more than twelve participants and a mentor (or two co-mentors). The group provides an environment that supports the exploration and expression of ideas so that discovery and learning occur. It is a place of trust and confidentiality as participants in the seminar reflect upon ways to pursue a life of faith on a daily basis.

Seminars usually meet for two and a half to three hours once a week over a period of thirty-six weeks during the academic cycle. For many of us this cycle begins in September and ends in June, but the group may decide to meet more frequently for shorter periods of time or less frequently for longer periods of time. Less frequent meetings can be very helpful when participants are scattered or they live in a region where bad weather can make travel difficult for extended periods. Some seminar groups meet online.

EfM seminars regularly engage in three different aspects of learning. These may not all be done in any one session, but attention needs to be given to all three aspects.

- There is time for social and spiritual needs to be addressed. This is a way to build trust, friendship, and community. It is an opportunity to support each other and maintain the freedom we all need to express our thoughts and feelings.

- There is time to discuss the materials which participants read in the texts. It is not a time for classroom presentations, rather an occasion to raise questions, wrestle with the materials, obtain clarifications, and generally share impressions about what has been read.

- There is an opportunity to engage in reflective activity. This may come in the form of a spiritual autobiography, one of many forms of theological reflections, studying and following a spiritual discipline, or exploring the meaning of the ministries we have.

The Program

The EfM Program expects participants, mentors, and trainers to remain faithful to the program. EfM is a program for adults and one expectation of the program is that adults take responsibility for their lives, set their own goals, and seek the support necessary to move forward. The program asks participants and mentors to provide an arena in which learning can take place on a mature adult level.

The relationship of EfM and The University of the South to the local church and to the judicatory/diocese is one of collaboration. Together we join to provide a program of theological education for the laity that carries a number of benefits.

- Portability–Participants can begin in one location and continue their work in another one.

- Accreditation–EfM grants Continuing Education Units to indicate completion of the work.

- Access to an international network

- A training opportunity for the laity

- Connection with The University of the South and its School of Theology

- Basic theological education to support the laity in responding to the call to ministry in daily life. For some, the theological groundwork in EfM may be supplemented with additional opportunities to prepare for ecclesial roles such as that of lay reader, vocational deacon, or educator.

Providing the program is something in which various agencies participate. The local church provides a setting and may offer some financial assistance to participants. The diocese may contract with EfM, which lowers the tuition for participants. When there is a contract with the local jurisdiction, a function of that contract is the appointment of a coordinator who maintains a liaison with the EfM program in Sewanee, arranges for mentor training locally, acts as a communicator for EfM, and promotes the program.

What EfM Is NOT

- *EfM is not only Bible study.*
  EfM participants study what the Bible says, but they also learn how to understand the Bible within its historical context and literary setting. Biblical studies form the primary work of the first two years. EfM is more than a Bible study in which one reads the Bible, seeks to understand it, and then applies it to daily life. EfM takes seriously God's revelation through all of Christian tradition, from the earliest biblical messages, through the development of liturgy and theology, and even in the context of the challenges we face in our own times.

- *EfM is not a program in personal therapy or problem solving.*
  While EfM groups develop a close community in order to delve deeply into matters of faith and theology, the group does not exist as a problem-solving agency or as a setting for analyzing or addressing personal and social problems. In an EfM group members may wish to share various aspects of their lives, but EfM is not a place to probe or press individuals to talk about those things they would prefer to leave unexamined.

- *EfM is not a closed community.*
  The content of EfM materials and the processes we use for reflection are not secrets. A group may invite a guest such as someone who brings some special information or someone who would like to participate for a session in order to decide if he or she might like to join. On the other

hand, we do respect one another's privacy. This means that we expect the group to maintain confidentiality about personal matters. The rule of thumb is: secrets—no; privacy—yes. Participants may share with others what they have learned and how that was learned, but they are expected to retain in confidence specific personal aspects of their colleagues' lives that may have been shared during the course of the program.

- *EfM is not an academic program leading to a degree or an ordination program.* Local arrangements may permit EfM to become part of the work leading to a degree or to ordination, but the School of Theology of The University of the South makes no recommendations about ordination nor does it grant course credit for completing the Education for Ministry program.

Purpose Statements for the Five Units

Unit One, Spiritual Autobiography and Listening: to develop the theme of ministry in personal context through creating a spiritual autobiography using contextual lenses and to approach listening as a fundamental skill for ministry.

Unit Two, Theological Reflection as a Life Skill: to learn how to use theological reflection models and methods as a means for integrating experience and content and to develop the discipline of theological reflection as a life skill for ministry in daily life.

Unit Three, Developing a Sustaining Spirituality: to guide the work of developing a personal spirituality through prayer and worship which, when combined with study and theological reflection, offer a four-fold spiritual discipline that can help sustain us in the practice of ministry.

Unit Four, Building a Theology: Integrating Belief, Behavior, and Doctrine in Everyday Life: to provide means by which a person can examine and build a personal theology through the integration of belief, behavior, and doctrine.

Unit Five, Vocation: Hearing and Responding to God's Call: to offer a Vocational Development Model for use in discerning and responding to God's call; and, second, to provide a framework for reviewing the year's work.

Supplemental Readings in the Christian Tradition

Week Five, Reading Assignment for Year One

The Priestly Creation Story

The Priestly creation story in Genesis 1–2:4a is one of the shortest and yet most tightly packed theological statements in the Bible. In its present form it dates from the time of the Restoration in the fifth century BCE. It had developed, however, over a much longer period and had been polished smooth by the time P gave it its final working. We must study it line by line in order to unpack the many levels of meaning in it.

Let us go over the main points.

First read **Genesis 1–2:4a.**

Then read again the biblical reference for each point in conjunction with the discussion.

1. God alone is the creator of all, with no divine helpers. The world is not simply shaped by God. (1:1)

2. God creates by speaking; God simply says, "Let there be . . . ," and what is spoken comes to be. (1:3, 6, 9, etc.)

3. God creates light; it is not the gift of the sun, which shines only with the light God has given it. (1:3)

4. God keeps the waters of chaos in their place by calling for a firm dome to keep out the waters that are above and by gathering the waters below into the seas so that the dry land appears. (1:6–10)

5. The heavenly bodies—sun, moon, planets, and stars—which were thought to be gods by many cultures in the ancient Near East, are only creatures of God. (1:14–18)

6. The earth shares in the task of creation, though only at God's command: the earth brings forth vegetation. The waters also bring forth sea creatures and the earth, animal life, but not in the same way as the earth brings forth vegetation. God creates the higher forms of life. (1:11, 20–21, 24–25)

7. God creates humankind in God's own image and gives it dominion over all the creation. (1:26)

8. God creates humankind male and female, and this fact is connected closely with humankind's creation in the divine image. (1:27)

9. God blesses humankind with sexuality and the gift of children. (1:28)

10. The final work of creation is God's rest on the seventh day. (2:2)

Even from this brief outline we can see some of the things that were on the mind of the author. First, one important aspect of this story cannot be seen in most English translations. Grammatically, the Hebrew begins in the middle of a sentence. What could this mean? Is it a mistake? Was the first corner of a manuscript lost? No, there is a theological meaning. Beginning a sentence in the middle is a way of saying, "We do not know what God was doing before our world came into being. Our knowledge cannot pry before the beginning of our world; God's beginning is unknowable to us."

Next, it is important to say, above all else, that God is completely different from everything else. Other religions may have said that there were all sorts of divine beings: animal monsters, heavenly bodies, the seas, storms—anything that seemed powerful or mysterious. For the P writer, nothing in the world is divine. Rather, the whole universe is God's creation. Some religions may have thought of at least part of the universe as being made out of the substance of the divine, flowing forth out of the god. For P, nothing of God flows into the universe; God is God, and all else that exists is not God and is not divine.

Third, there is no need to look to lesser gods for the fertility of the earth. Vegetable crops and animals are included in God's design for the world, and the earth brings forth her increase at God's command. The worship of Baals (fertility gods), with all the gross practices that went with it, is not necessary; indeed to worship them would be to deny the power of the one Creator.

Fourth, the whole creation leads up to the creation of humanity. Life has not been created in order to provide playthings for the gods nor to act as slave-servants to the gods. Humanity, man and woman, is created to be God's representative in governing creation. It is a position of great dignity and worth.

Each of these points was important in the life of Israel. She had been chosen to be God's people; God had made a covenant with her and had promised that, through Israel, all the nations of the earth would be blessed. The covenant was the basis for all of Israel's religious faith. After the Israelites had settled in Canaan, they were tempted and led away from God to the worship of the Baals and the *astral deities*—the sun, moon, planets, and stars—which the other nations worshiped. The prophets constantly tried to overcome the worship of these false gods so that Israel would be faithful to the covenant. When the northern kingdom was destroyed and the leaders of Judah (the southern kingdom) were carried into exile, the warnings of the prophets were shown to have been correct. Thus we can see the P writer—in the circumstance of exile—expressing in this story the true dignity of humankind and the complete sovereignty of God as these facts had been learned in Israel's life and taught by the prophets. All of what Israel stood for was expressed by the covenant. This was how Israel knew God; God was the God who had made the covenant with Abraham, Isaac, and Jacob and who had sealed it at Sinai through Moses. This God, and this God alone, had created the nation of Israel, and this God alone had created the heavens and the earth and all things.

The creation story expresses the faith of Israel learned by her experience as the people of God's covenant. Just as God had made Israel God's people at Sinai, so also God had made all of humanity in God's own image at creation. Both the covenant story and the creation story say the same thing: God has given humanity dignity and worth and dominion; therefore, the creation story reaches its climax in the creation of humankind.

The P author does not end the story with the creation of humanity. The final day of creation is not the sixth, on which human beings are created, but the seventh, on which God rests. This rest does not mean only a mere recuperation from the exhaustion of creation. Rather it is a cessation of regular work in order to enjoy the fruits of that labor. God rests in order to enjoy creation. The P author, with special interest in the *cult*—the practices of worship—leads us to the practice of the Sabbath. This is not, however, a contradiction of what we have just said about the creation of humanity as the climax. The covenant, the basis of Israel's faith in the dignity of all people, is what the Sabbath is all about. The Sabbath is the celebration of the covenant. Therefore, the story leads to two ends, both of which refer to the same central point of Israel's faith: (1) God's gift of life and authority—a people under God—and (2) the Sabbath, which is the celebration of this people under God through the covenant.

You are not expected at this point in your studies to be able to feel all that is involved in the covenant. The point you should be able to grasp at this stage is that the P creation story sums up the experience of Israel and is not a simple childish story. You will come back to this story again and again, and the more you become familiar with the rest of the Old Testament, the more you will feel the power of it. Now look back again to the beginning of the story, and we will go over it more closely.

This verse, which looks so simple in the English translation, is very strange in the Hebrew because it begins mid-sentence. The text can be translated, carrying it on through verse three, in several ways. (1) "In the beginning God created the heavens and the earth. The earth was without form and void, and darkness. . . ." (2) "When God began to create the heavens and the earth, the earth was without form and void, and darkness. . . ." (3) "In the beginning of God's creating of the heavens and the earth—(when) the earth was without form and void, and darkness was upon the face of the deep, and the wind of God was moving over the face of the waters—God said, 'Let there be. . . .'" None of these translations really fits the text as we have it, but each one is possible. Somewhat closer might be to start with an ellipsis ". . . " and then use the wording of option 3 above.

What difference would it make which translation we pick? Some people have argued that if we use the first one, there is nothing before God creates. God creates the heavens and the earth, and they are formless and empty until God then shapes and fills them. While it is fine theology to believe God created from nothing—*ex nihilo* is the Latin phrase that is used—Genesis 1 does not make such a claim. If we take the second or third translation, there is already a formless empty abyss and God begins to create; God shapes and fills a chaos that already existed.

Later theology, especially Christian theology, has insisted that God created out of nothing not simply as a way of choosing one of these translations over the other. Theologians have been trying to oppose a point of view which was very common in the world of the first few centuries of the Christian era and is still very much with us. This point of view is called dualism. It says that there are two aspects of the world: the material and the nonmaterial, sometimes called the "spiritual." The material is usually regarded as less good, sometimes evil. Theologians have not wanted to say that there was something, anything, already existing when God began creation, because this already existing something, chaos, could be used by the dualists to refer to matter, the material stuff, which God shaped. They could then say that this matter is the source of evil. So the theologians said that God created *ex nihilo,* out of nothing; anything and everything that is, matter included, is created by God and is good. You can begin to see here that many beliefs, many truths, are not stated explicitly by every biblical passage on a similar theme.

Dualism had a great effect on the thinking of the early church. It came from eastern roots. In Persia the religion of Zoroastrianism taught that there were two gods, one evil and one good. The good god was the god of light; the evil god, the god of darkness. (The name of the god of light, Mazda, is known to many people although they may not know where it originated.) A man named Mani, who was greatly influenced by Zoroastrianism, developed a religion, dualistic in nature, that prescribed ways of combating the power of the material world and escaping into the world of spirit and light. His religion, usually called Manichaeism, flourished in the third and fourth centuries, especially in North Africa, and influenced many Christians. St. Augustine, one of the greatest theologians of the church, was a Manichee before he converted to Christianity.

The teachings of the great pre-Christian philosopher Plato have also led to dualistic conclusions. Plato taught that, although individual things in this world come and go—they are born and they die, they come into being and they decay—there lie behind the individual things the *ideas* of them. There are many individual trees, each different to some degree from the others and each destined to die and decay, but each is a partial representation of the idea Tree. The idea contains all that it is possible for a tree to be; it is complete and single, not needing many separate examples of itself to express its completeness; it lasts forever, eternally existing while the individual representations of it come and go. Why Plato said this, what problems he was trying to understand, we shall look at later. The fact that he said it, however, allowed people of a later time—during the third through the fifth centuries CE—to develop a religion that was dualistic in a much more subtle and sophisticated way than was Manichaeism. The Neo-Platonists taught that the ultimate One lies beyond all things, and it is impossible to speak of that One at all. The *via negativa* is all that is possible. From the One all the rest of the universe emanates as light emanates, flows, or shines from a light bulb or a candle. The farther away from the source, the less like the One a thing becomes, until finally, at the farthest remove, there is matter. A human being, according to Neo-Platonism, is really spirit, akin to the One, but the spirit is trapped in a material body. Below humanity there is no spirit; all is merely material. Only by mystical exercises can humankind rise above the material body and reach union with the One. This point of view has influenced much of Christian piety. Augustine was also a Neo-Platonist before becoming a Christian.

Whatever the correct translation of this verse may be, theologians were right in thinking that the Old Testament opposed dualism. The Hebrews did *not* make a distinction between matter and "spirit." As we see in the JE (Yahwist-Elohist) creation story, the first human being is made from the dust of the earth and has life breathed into him so that he becomes "a living being." The entire creature, without division into body and spirit, is a living being. When the Christian church said that Jesus is the word of God made flesh, it also spoke against any kind of dualism.

This is why many theologians prefer the reading of verse one that says, "In the beginning God created the heavens and the earth." But there is no way to decide on the basis of the text itself. The P writer has other ways of dealing with the problem of dualism.

Whichever way you translate the first verse, when the earth appears it is without form and void—that is, it is chaotic, empty of all form, design, or meaning—and darkness is upon the face of "the deep." "The deep" is a translation of the Hebrew word *tehom*. Behind this word there lies a whole mythic tradition. In the ancient world of the Mesopotamian basin there existed a story of the creation of the world by means of a great battle between a warrior god and a dragon, a sea-monster, who represented watery chaos. To many peoples who lived in desert lands far from the sea, the sea was fearsome. Its great storms were powerful and destroyed ships and houses built close to the shores. Stories of sea monsters were told by returning sailors. So "the deep," the waters of the sea with its monsters, was a symbol of chaos to the ancient people.

The Babylonian creation myth is a long story about the birth of various gods and about the eventual conflict between the god Marduk and the goddess Tiamat. In the course of the conflict, Tiamat is slain, and it is from her body that the firmament, the great dome of heaven, is made. It is worth noting here that the name Tiamat is closely related linguistically to *tehom*. By slaying Tiamat, the chaos monster, the monster of the deep, Marduk makes it possible for order to reign.

Much has been made of the common background out of which the Babylonian and the Hebrew creation stories come. The differences between the stories are more important—and more instructive—than their similarities. The Babylonian myth is an involved story of the birth of the gods and of the struggles among them for supremacy. Human beings are created almost as an afterthought, to serve as slaves for the gods, tending the earth so that the gods might have leisure. In the P story, the reference to "the deep" is virtually the sole remnant of this older myth. There is no birth of God; God is there before the story begins. Only by taking a broad meaning of myth as we have done can the P story be called a myth at all. P has stripped the narrative of all features of a "story about the gods" and has reduced it to a statement of doctrine, using the older myth as a framework only. By using an older framework with which people were familiar, the writer is also able to "start where they are" and show them greater truth.

Week Twelve, Reading Assignment for Year Four

The Trinity[74]

The truth takes its own forms and expresses itself in its own ways. Our efforts at defining, proving, or establishing it are all acts after the event. It is what it is, and not what we make it. Christianity prevails in the world in a fact which we have called Trinity, and which is Trinity, however inadequate and unsatisfactory our explanations of the term or our analyses of the thing may be. I would describe Christianity in its largest sense to be the fulfilment of God in the world through the fulfilment of the world in God. This assumes that the world is completed in man, in whom also God is completed in the world. And so, God, the world, and man are at once completed in Jesus Christ who, as He was the *logos* or thought of all in the divine foreknowledge of the past, so also is He the *telos* or end of all in the predestination of the future. That is to say, the perfect psychical, moral, and spiritual manhood of which Jesus Christ is to us the realization and the expression is the end of God in creation, or in evolution. I hold that neither science, philosophy, nor religion can come to any higher or other, either conjecture or conclusion, than that. But now, when we come to the actual terms or elements of God's self-realization in us and ours in Him, we cannot think or express the process otherwise than in the threefold form of the divine love, the divine grace, and the divine fellowship, in operation or action. Putting it into scriptural phrase, we speak as exactly as popularly in defining the matter of the Gospel to be, The love of the Father, the grace of the Son, and the fellowship of the Spirit. As our spiritual life is dependent upon each and all of these three constituents, so we can know God at all only as we know Him in the actual threefold relation to us of Father, Son, and Spirit.

The first element in the essential constitution of the Gospel is the fact in itself that God is love. That God is love means that He is so not only in Himself but in every activity that proceeds from Him. The very phrase the love of the Father expresses the whole principle of the universe. That God is Father means that it is His nature, or His essential activity, to reproduce Himself, to produce in all other that which He Himself is. That God in Himself is love carries with it the truth that from the beginning all things

---

74. This essay concludes *The Gospel in the Gospels* published in 1906 by William Porcher DuBose, the first dean of The School of Theology of The University of the South, Sewanee, Tennessee. You will find more information about him at http://liturgyandmusic .wordpress.com/2010/08/18/august-18-william-porcher-dubose-priest-1918/.

else mean, and are destined to come to, love in the end. The mystery on the way that somehow light must come out of darkness, that love must needs conquer hate, and that in everything good seems to be only the final and far off goal of ill, may puzzle us but it does not disturb the principle itself. When we come to enter fairly upon the evolution of the future, the higher not merely psychical or social or moral but spiritual life and destiny of man, all the truth gradually dawns upon us in the following discoveries, which are already established facts of spiritual experience: The truth of all spirit is love; the matter of all law is goodness; God is not creator or cause only, nor lord or lawgiver only, but Father of all things, since all things through man are destined to share His spirit, to be partakers of His nature, and to reproduce Himself as Father in themselves as children. In order to be sons of God through actual participation in the divine nature there stands in the way indeed the need of a mighty redemption from sin and an as yet far off completion in holiness; but no matter how unredeemed or incomplete, we know beyond further question that all our salvation lies in redemption and completion, and that we shall be ourselves and the world will come to its meaning only when the self-realization of God as Father shall have accomplished itself in our self-realization as His children. If we knew the fact only that God in Himself is love, it would be to us a gospel indeed of great joy, because it would carry in it the assurance of the highest good, whatever that might be. But it would be but a partial gospel, and in fact only a gospel at all through its certainty of proceeding further.

The phrase Grace of the Son expresses that which perfectly complements and completes all that is meant by the Love of the Father. What is Father-hood without a correlative Sonship? And what is all love even in God as its subject apart from its actuality and activity as grace in man as its object? The divine propriety of the terms Father and Son as applied to God cannot be too much magnified. The distinction between God as He is in Himself and God as He is in all possible expressions of Himself is one that we cannot think Him at all without making. The most perfect expression of love is contained in the statement, that Love loves love. Its nature is to produce, to reproduce, to multiply itself. Itself is forever the true object of itself, at the same time that it is ever a going forth from itself into that which is not itself. This essential principle of love or self-reproduction is what makes God eternally Father. But the eternal Fatherhood is actualized only in an eternal Sonship. Nothing proceeds from the Father which is not reproduction of the Father, and is not therefore Son. Man sees himself now in nature and destinature son of God. He feels his call and obligation to fulfil God in him as Father by realizing himself in God as son. His spiritual end and impulse is to know as also he is known, to love in return as he is first loved, to apprehend that for which he is apprehended of God in Christ. In proportion as he finds the meaning and truth of his own being in the reproduction of God, in being son of God, he finds the meaning and truth of the whole creation realized and expressed in his own sonship as heir of all and end of all. And in proportion again as he thus finds all things meaning and ending in sonship, he comes at last to see God Himself as realized in the universal sonship Himself therein realized as Eternal Father. So it is that in Jesus Christ we see everything expressed, because everything realized or fulfilled. He is all truth, because He is the truth of all things God, Creation, Man. And because He is thus truth and expression of all, He is Logos of all. What else could the Logos of all be but Son, or the Son but Logos? What could perfectly express God but that which is the perfect reproduction of Himself, or what is perfect sonship but perfect likeness?

The Grace of the Son is the divine gift of sonship. How could we have known God only in Himself? How could God have been actually our Father without the actuality of our sonship to Him? And could we have known, could we have wanted, could we have willed, could we have accomplished or attained our sonship without the gift or grace of sonship in Jesus Christ? God, we are told, predestinated us unto sonship through Jesus Christ unto himself. He predestinated us to be conformed to the image of His Son, that He might be the first born among many brethren. In bringing many sons to glory, He gave to us a Captain of our salvation, an Author and Finisher of the faith of sonship and so of the sonship of faith, who was Himself perfected as Son through the sufferings that are necessary to the perfecting of sonship in us. We see in Jesus Christ all that is meant, involved, or implied, in the fact that He is the divine Fatherhood realized and expressed in human sonship.

If that fact, viewed in its totality, signifies not only a human act, nor only a divine act, but a divine-human act, an act of God in man which is equally an act of man in God, then we say that Jesus Christ is not only as well the humanity as the divinity in that act, but He is the divinity as well as the humanity. He is not only the *gratia gratiata* in it but the *gratia gratians*—not only the manhood infinitely graced but the Godhead infinitely gracing.

Jesus Christ is therefore to us no mere sample or example of divine sonship. He is no mere one man who more successfully than others has grasped and expressed the ideal of a divine sonship. Neither is He a single individual of our race whom God has elected from among equally possible others, in whom as mere revelation or example to all others to manifest the truth of God in man and man in God. On the contrary, Jesus Christ is Himself the reality of all that is manifested or expressed in Him. He is as God the grace communicating and as man the grace communicated. He is both Generator and generated with reference to the life incarnate in Him both the sonship eternally in God to be begotten and the sonship actually begotten in man. As He was in the beginning with God and was God, so is He universally with man and is universal man.

When we have thus adequately conceived Christ as the universal truth and reality of ourselves, and in ourselves of all creation, and in creation and ourselves of God, then we are prepared for the conclusion that we know God at all, or are sons to Him as our Father, or are capable in that relation of partaking of His nature or entering into His Spirit or living His life, only in and through Jesus Christ; because Jesus Christ is the incarnation or human expression to us of the whole Logos of God that is to say, of God Himself as in any way whatever knowable or communicable. We cannot get at God to know or possess Him otherwise than as He reveals and imparts Himself; and He reveals Himself through His own Word and imparts Himself in His own Son. There and there alone is He to be known, and there He is all our own. The Logos who is the eternal Self-revelation of God manifests Himself as ideal principle, first and final cause, meaning and end, of creation; and the end of the whole creation which manifests God is realized through spiritual humanity in the imparted sonship of the Everlasting Son of the Father.

There is yet one other condition of truly knowing or really possessing God as wholly our God. As God is unknowable and incommunicable but through Christ, so is Christ, however perfectly He is in Himself the self-revelation and self-communication of God, not so to us but through the coequal action of the Holy Ghost. There is no knowledge of God in Himself only, there is no knowledge of God in creation only, or in others, or even in Christ only, without the answering knowledge of God in ourselves also. It is only like that answers to like. The deep that answers to deep must be the same deep. Jesus Christ expected in every son of man not only the answer of the man in him to Himself as eternal and universal Son of man, but the answer of the God in him to the perfect God head in Himself. Ye cannot see God in me, He says, because ye have not God in you. No man cometh unto me except the Father draw Him. I do not wish to urge the mere conventional language of Christianity, true as I believe it and helpful as I may find it to myself. I would if possible speak in the common language of common experience. When we speak of knowing God, and having God, it must mean knowing Him where He is to be known and having Him as He is to be had. Now, whatever God is in Himself, He is knowable to us only in Jesus Christ, and He can be our God only as He is conceived in us by the operation of the Spirit of God and born of the want which He implants and the faith which He generates.

The doctrine of the Trinity is ordinarily thought of as the very extreme of speculative reasoning upon the nature of God. But let us remember that practical faith in the Trinity antedated any speculative thought or doctrine of the Trinity. And behind that faith the fact itself of the Trinity is all that makes God knowable by us or us capable of knowing God. Before there was the word Trinity, the new world of Christianity had come to know God in Christ, and to know Christ in itself. The entire doctrine developed out of that actual experience was nothing but a positive affirmation and a determined defence of the fulness of the truth of God in Christ and Christ in us. We can do no better than conclude this entire exposition of the Gospel with an interpretation of it in the only terms in which it is expressible, viz.: in terms of the Trinity.

We have to do now with the Trinity, not as matter of doctrine nor as object of faith, but as fact in itself. But at the same time we neither forget nor minimize the essential Christian conviction that the fact of the Trinity through the actual operation of God's Word and Spirit has been so made matter of spiritual observation and experience as to be legitimate object of faith and material for doctrine. Our object at present, however, is not to define God but to define the Gospel, and our contention is that the Gospel is definable in facts that taken together make up the truth of the Trinity.

The first condition and constituent of the Gospel is the fact that God in Himself is love. How do we know that God is love? I believe that actually or historically we know it in Christ in whom the fact of the divine love is consummated and manifested. But in the light now of Christianity I believe that it is also philosophically demonstrable that goodness or love is the essential principle and the ultimate end of the universe. How God is love, not only in antecedent nature but in the actuality of self-fulfilment in the world, may be readable too in nature, after the light thrown upon it by Christianity, but in fact it is known in its reality only in Christ. Love is no more in God than in us an abstract disposition or affection. All the love we know is in concrete relations and the forms of affection determined by the character of those relations. Human love is marital, parental, filial, etc. out to the wider and widest forms of national, racial, and human affinity and affection. The concrete form in which alone we can know God as love is expressed by our designation of Him as eternal Father. That gives shape and definiteness to not only our conception, but the reality itself of His relation to us and ours to Him, and no less of how that relation is to be fulfilled. The full reality of fatherhood comes about in actuality only in the full realization of sonship, and that therefore must be God's meaning and end for all that is in the universe of His self-expression. We begin so to anticipate the truth that is to be expressed in such statements as that God has foreordained or predestined us to sonship through Jesus Christ unto Himself, that God has foreordained us to be conformed to the image of His Son, and many others to the same effect. But before we come to these unfoldings of the divine nature and purpose, let us reflect upon the following antecedent truth.

The beginning of all distinction between a pantheistic and a theistic conception of the world lies in recognizing the world as the expression, not of God Himself or, as we say, "of His substance," but of His Logos, His Thought, Will, Word. The Logos of God, then, is not God (*a theos*); we distinguish Him. And yet certainly the Logos is God (*theos*); we identify Him. Moreover, when once we have conceived and accepted God as eternal Father, we are in position to assume that the Logos, not merely as the principle of the divine self-expression but as God Himself self-expressed, must manifest Himself universally as Son or in sonship; since universal and everlasting Sonship is the only self-expression of eternal and essential Fatherhood.

The first constituent, therefore, of the Gospel is the fact in itself of the divine Love in Fatherhood. The second is, the equal fact in itself of the actualization of the divine Fatherhood in creature—or, definitely, in human—Sonship. The love of the Father fulfills and manifests itself in the grace of the Son. Love is grace *potentiâ*; Grace is love *actu*,—just as Fatherhood itself is Sonship potential, and Sonship is Fatherhood actualized. When we have once seen all humanity perfected as son in Jesus Christ, it is not hard to see in Him the whole creation so perfected in man as its head and as heir of its destiny. And then still less hard is it to see how we could never have known God as Father if He had not so fulfilled and manifested Himself as Son.

The hesitation and reluctance to see all God, and highest God, not only in the humanity but in the deepest human humiliation of Jesus Christ, is part of the disposition to measure exaltation by outward circumstance and condition instead of by inward quality and character. We find it impossible to recognize or acknowledge God in the highest act of His highest attribute. We cannot listen to the thought that it is with God as it is with us, that it only is with us because it is with God, that self-humiliation is self-exaltation. Not only in this way do we refuse to know God Himself as love, but we refuse to understand the universe as love. If we would but surrender our reason as well as our heart and will to God in Christ, we should cease to prate as we do of the mystery and the incomprehensibility of things. We could see how our Lord could say of the cross itself, Father, the hour is come. Glorify thy Son, that the Son may glorify thee. We lose thus the supreme lesson of human experience: Not merely to conjecture that somehow good is the final goal of ill; but to know by actual trial just how the supremest ills are the necessary steps to the highest goods. As St. Paul says, the cross of Christ is foolishness and a stumbling block only to the earthly wise and the self-righteous. To them that are saved, or are ever so little being saved, it is the wisdom of God and the power of God. To know God in Jesus Christ is to know the divine Logos, through whom alone God is knowable. It is to know him, not in His inferior activities of physical creation, nor yet in His higher capacity of lawgiver and law in a world of intelligent reason and free will. Rather is it to know Him in the act and process of that self-communication of love, grace, and fellowship, which is the basis and condition of the only real knowledge.

The third constituent of the Gospel is the fact in itself of the fellowship of the Spirit. Truly, our fellowship is with the Father and with His Son Jesus Christ. The possibility or potentiality of such a real unity and community with God must exist somehow beforehand in our nature as spirit, or in the natural relation of our finite spirits to the Father of spirits. But the actuality of spiritual relation or intercommunication which we call fellowship is no fact of nature but an act or interaction of spirits. It is not for us to say how, theoretically, spirit can act upon spirit; all that we can do is to understand how, practically and actually, spirit does act upon spirit. The most perfect expression of the actual action of the divine upon the human spirit is contained in the words, The Spirit beareth witness with our spirit, that we are the sons of God. Let us assume the objectivity or truth in itself of the eternal Fatherhood that is to say, not only Father-relation but Father-spirit, love, will, purpose or predestination, etc. of God in Himself. Let us also assume the objective reality as matter of fact of all that we have claimed to have happened in Jesus Christ: viz., that in Him as Logos God revealed Himself in the universe, and that in Him as Son God fulfilled Himself in humanity. In other words, let us assume that all that God is in Himself as Father has evolved itself through nature and man in the universal and everlasting Son-ship realized in Jesus Christ; God in Christ as Son is *actu* all that He is *potentia* in Himself as Father. When we have assumed all that body of objective truth the truth in itself of the Father and the Son what remains still to make it the Gospel to ourselves? Undoubtedly something remains. All the reality in the universe can be no Gospel to us so long as it remains objective, or until it enters into living relation with ourselves. Of course, it can never so enter unless there is in us the natural potentiality of entering into relation with it. But equally certainly that potentiality can only be actualized by ourselves. What is necessary within ourselves to give effect to all that is true without us is a corresponding response, or a response of correspondence, on our part. That correspondence is, I repeat, not a fact of natural relationship, but an act of spiritual communication or self-impartation. When the Spirit bears witness with our spirit, that we are sons of God, it is not only God who communicates the gracious fact, but it is God who awakens the humble and grateful response, and puts it into our heart to say, Abba, Father. If we cannot thus know God subjectively in ourselves, we cannot know God objectively in Jesus Christ. And if we cannot know Him in His Word and by His Spirit, we cannot know Him at all.

As we can know the eternal and universal Sonship incarnate in Jesus Christ only in the perfection of the human sonship realized in Him in other words, as we can know the Word or Son of God only in the man Christ Jesus, so we can know the Spirit of God only in ourselves or in our own spirit. We cannot know any spirit other than our own otherwise than through a certain oneness or identity of it with our own. There must be both an inter-penetration of the two as distinct and the identification of them as one. Hence the common demand upon men to be of one spirit. What a subject of reflection then, and of realization or actualization, is there for us in the fact of our fellowship, our participation, with the Father and the Son in the unity and identity of a common Spirit. It is in this eternal Spirit that God Himself is God and is Love. It was in this eternal Spirit that the whole creation in humanity offered itself without spot to God in the person of Jesus Christ; and in that consummate act fulfilled His relation to it through realizing its own relation with Him. It is through this eternal Spirit, which is God's and Christ's and ours, that we pass from ourselves into Christ and through Christ into God.

We have seen that there could have been no Gospel of God to us except one of objective Word and subjective Spirit. All life is defined as internal correspondence with external environment. We saw, I think, long ago that as it is the function of the divine Word aptare *Deum homini*, so is it that of the divine Spirit *aptare hominem Deo*. On the same line we may say, that as eternal life is given to us in Jesus Christ to be received, so is it given to us by the Holy Ghost to receive the life. Our Lord said of the promised Spirit, that its function should be to bring us to Him. There would be nothing to which to come if there were no objective fact and gift of life, there would be no coming to the life if there were no subjective preparing for and drawing to the life. How then finally does the Spirit fit us for Christ and fit us to Christ? It is the act and operation of the Spirit, first, that from the beginning, though yet a very far off, we can already know Christ as our own. That is the power of faith, which lives by God's Word and takes what that says as though it were. To faith Jesus Christ is the divine, not only revelation but reality of itself from the beginning of the foreknowledge of God in the eternity of the past to the end of the predestination of God in the eternity of the future. To faith Jesus Christ is all the eternal love, the all-sufficient grace, the perfect fellowship or oneness-with-it of God, which is salvation *ex parte Dei* or *salvailo salvans*; and no less in Jesus Christ the perfection of our own faith, hope, and love, our own holiness, righteousness, and life, our own death to sin, and our own life to God, which is salvation *ex parte hominis* or *salvatio salvata*. The Spirit thus brings us first to a perfect correspondence of faith with the fact of our life of God in Christ. But just because faith means life, that is, knows, desires, wills, and intends it therefore it is it. God already imputes, as He will impart, and faith already appropriates, as it will possess, the life which is so believed in. So believing in it we have it already in faith, and as surely shall have it at last in fact. Attuned to Christ by the anticipatory spell of faith, hope, and love, we shall be by a natural process of spiritual assimilation transformed into His likeness in act, character, and life, until coming to see Him perfectly as He is we shall be wholly what He is.

It has not been my object to add to the solution of the speculative problem of the Trinity. I have only aimed to show practically and spiritually that if at all we are to know and worship God in reality as our God, we must do so as Christianity has always done in Trinity. We must worship God in the Father, and the Son, and the Holy Ghost. Because God is, and is operative for us, not alone in one but in all these. We cannot but distinguish the Three; it is only in the completeness of their threefold operation that we can perfectly know the One.

Week Sixteen, Reading Assignment for All Years

The first step in creating a sustaining spirituality is to understand, as best as we can, the human dimension to which the word "spirituality" directs our attention. Urban T. Homes, III (aka Terry Holmes) served as dean of The School of Theology at Sewanee when the Education for Ministry Program began. While serving as dean, he went on a sabbatical leave during which time he wrote what became, after his death, Spirituality for Ministry. *The beginning essay of his last book serves us well in laying a foundation for developing a spirituality that supports, nurtures, and encourages ministry in daily life.*

The Spiritual Person[75]

It has been my experience that one does not drop the word "spiritual" into a conversation lightly. "How is your spiritual life?," I unwittingly asked a minister in the presence of some others. There was a sudden, discernible tension in the air, as if I had inquired into the intimate details of his sex life. Someone coughed and the person of whom I inquired, obviously sharing the embarrassment, felt he had to say something to me. After all, I was a fellow pastor. "Great," he said with an enthusiasm tinged with condescension. "I've really gotten it all together." Somehow "getting it together"–the tired jargon of humanistic psychology—was not what I had in mind, but now aware that I was treading on forbidden territory I let it pass.

Later on in a conversation with several of the same people, a colleague of mine who had the irritating habit of never rebuking me directly but always through intermediaries remarked, "Why are we asking people about their spiritual life?" Since I was the only one who asked, the "we" obviously meant me. "After all," he averred, "all of life is spiritual!" As I walked away somewhat chastened, I wondered why, if all of life is spiritual and my question had been pointless and unanswerable, the mention of the word so perceptibly heightened the anxiety of those gathered there.

This scenario has been repeated several times due to a stubborn streak that makes me keep asking questions in search of answers. After one such conversation I inquired of someone with whom I felt some rapport why the word "spiritual" evoked so much feeling. He replied, "I don't think we realized that you are charismatic. You know most of us have been pretty active

---

75. Urban T. Holmes, "The Spiritual Person," in *Spirituality for Ministry*, The Library of Episcopalian Classics (Harrisburg, PA: Morehouse, 2002), 3–19.

in the civil rights movement and protesting the Vietnam War." I am not sure he spoke for anyone but himself, but for him "spiritual" did not mean everything, "all of life"; it was something very specific. It was synonymous with "baptism in the Holy Spirit," speaking in tongues, prayer meetings, and opposition to the church's social action. It was the escape from the confrontations of the 1960s. It was the enemy. I explained that I could hardly count myself charismatic, and he looked puzzled. Obviously wishing to get off the subject, he said, "Whatever it is, we don't do it."

I responded to his sensitivities, but something else came clear to me at that moment. There is judgment connected with the word "spirituality," particularly when used by clergy of a certain generation. I remembered a classmate in seminary many years ago telling me why he had transferred from another institution. In the former school during his first year he had chosen a course entitled "The Life of Prayer." After three weeks of faithful attendance, he had not heard the word "prayer" mentioned. That day after class he asked the instructor when they would begin to discuss the subject of the course. With some anger the instructor glared at this poor bumpkin. "Young man," he said, "a hot bath will do you more good than all the prayer in the world."

Why the tension? Why the anxiety? Why the ferocity? Is it possible that a whole generation of clergy rejected something they understood to be spirituality, without totally removing from the conscience an inchoate, lingering suspicion that this is precisely what they are to be about? Mention of spirituality provoked guilt, anger, and defensiveness in them.

Then came the renewed interest in spirituality in the church and the tragedy was compounded. For almost a generation clergy have pursued little classical education in spirituality and have had few models for its practice. Caught in an enthusiasm that has touched the lives of many church people, the word "spirituality" came to mean whatever anyone wanted it to mean. Because of their ignorance—culpable or not—there has been a serious lack among the church's leadership of the knowledge that gives substance and direction to a contemporary form of the authentic spiritual renewal of the church. Not infrequently they fall back on the worst kind of hick piety.

Devoid of clear meaning, spirituality has become a catchword for whatever one favors or opposes. I have discovered that passing mention of spirituality can bring immediate acceptance by some or can evoke intellectual skepticism in others. The cynicism of its detractors is only reinforced.

In truth we use the word far too loosely. In my interviews with persons considered spiritually mature it was clear that there was no consensus as to what spirituality meant. "Spirituality" has too little intellectual substance. It has to be more than a name for warm feelings, which in our search for assurance we attribute to God. These feelings may very well be an intimation of our awareness of God's presence, but until we can distinguish spirituality from what it is not—an initial criterion for a definition—then we do not know what it is. It cannot be everything and have any meaning. The word needs to point to a discrete, identifiable something before we can talk about it intelligently.

Defining Spirituality

The classical definition begins with certain dogmatic and religious presuppositions. For example, prior to recent times spiritual theology was divided into ascetical or ordinary spirituality and mystical or extraordinary spirituality. The assumption was that the latter was reserved for those particularly gifted. There has also been the assumption that there are specific tests of an authentic spiritual life by certain manifestations that accompany it. For example, there are the fruits of the Spirit, such as love, joy, and peace. Or some have insisted that various spiritual epiphenomena must be present, such as speaking in tongues.

The definition of spirituality in this study is generic and experiential. Inasmuch as spirituality is a theological discipline, it reflects the conviction that theology moves from humanity to God and not from God to humanity. This is often described as doing theology "from below." The distinction becomes clear when a generic and experiential definition of spirituality is contrasted with a classical definition.

I have no desire necessarily to pass a negative judgment on the classical definition of spirituality, whatever it may be; but there is a value in beginning with a generic and experiential definition. It permits the widest possible ground for dialogue, since it seeks to begin with the observable data. Furthermore, this definition permits the development of a correspondence with the human sciences although it will quickly move beyond the capabilities of those sciences. In other words, a generic and experiential definition is consistent with a foundational theology that argues for a continuity between nature and supernature.

With this in mind, I am defining spirituality as (1) a human capacity for relationship (2) with that which transcends sense phenomena; this relationship (3) is perceived by the subject as an expanded or heightened consciousness independent of the subject's efforts, (4) is given substance in the historical setting, and (5) exhibits itself in creative action in the world.

First, there are not two classes of people: those who are spiritual and those who are not. Spirituality is our openness to relationship, which is a universal human capacity involving the whole person. One priest spoke of this very directly:

> Spirituality is a total part of my life. I am a person who is concerned with realities and spirituality is as much a part of that as my right hand and my feelings and my perceptions. It is an appetite which I need to feed.

Plato said that to be is to be in relation and Aristotle defined the human being as a political animal, *zoe politike*. This term is sometimes translated "social animal," but it literally means a creature who lives in a city (*polis*). In other words, for us to be we must exist in a community, in which our identity does not stop with our skin, but extends into the corporate reality. We are our community or the multiple communities of which we are a part.

In the evolutionary process there is a movement from creatures whose behavior is totally intra-specific (i.e., the result of genetic coding), as in an amoeba, to those whose behavior is a reflection of an acquired memory overlaying biology, as in human beings. Culture is the carrier of this memory, and the individual appropriates the cultural memory by socialization within the immediate family and the society as a whole. The supreme example of cultural memory is language, which enables us to be self-conscious and consequently human. This is to say that Homo sapiens is a creature with the capacity to think about thinking, to transcend himself or herself, which is made possible by the ability to represent and retain the memory of experience by means of language and to reflect upon that representation with more language.

There is an abiding legend in the folklore of some cultures of the child abandoned by its parents and brought up by wild animals. For some reason the favorite animals are wolves, perhaps harking back to the story of the founders of Rome, Romulus and Remus, who were supposedly suckled by a wolf. Despite romantic speculations to the contrary, the "wolf child" is subhuman because it has not had a relationship with other humans. As a matter of fact, even if such a creature returned to the company of its own kind after a period of years, it would not be able to recapture its lost previous relationships. It would be forever less than human. The evidence in the human sciences that this would be so is overwhelming.

Spirituality begins with this fact that the human being is by nature a creature requiring relationship. It operates from the postulate that to be a person is to be open to the other and goes on to say that there is within each of us an innate longing for union with the other. This urge is known as eros, from which we get the word "erotic." But this desire is far more profound than a spicy feeling. It is the fundamental need we have for one another and ultimately for God. It is an energy within us, which, while perhaps deflected in its true end (what the doctrine of original sin seeks to say), is nonetheless a grounding for humanity's spiritual longing.

The human need for relationship is not satisfied by external proximity alone; it is not enough to touch. We must compenetrate, which is to say enter into the internal reality of the other, which requires that we share our inner self. This is the nature of intimacy: to come to know one another as we truly are—or come as close as we can. To put it more graphically, there is a desire to get inside each other's skin, of which sexual intercourse is the most profound symbol.

Yet we never do finally comprehend the other! In every relationship we must eventually come face to face with the mystery of the other person. There is no "solution" to the inquiry, Who are you? For we do not even know who we ourselves are. If we chose to answer the inquirer, we could not. Every human personality is rooted in the mystery of God, and attempts to "explain" humankind ultimately founder because they are inevitably reductions. Most of the self is hidden beneath the surface, reaching into the depths, of God's infinite purpose.

It is only an incredibly vapid culture, like our own, that could permit a theory of human nature to prevail that does not understand this mystery of being. A person is far more than the vortex of his or her material conditioning. Behaviorism, the theory that people can be explained in terms of conditioned reflexes, then, is a reductionism so patently contrary to our everyday experience of the mystery of the being of the other that it is difficult to see how anyone can take it seriously.

This leads, second, to the expectation of spirituality for relationship with that which transcends sense phenomena. If anything characterizes modernity, it is the loss of faith in transcendence, that reality that not only encompasses but surpasses our daily affairs. We have been seduced by our socialization into thinking that all truth is susceptible to scientific analysis (as in the natural sciences). Such analysis reduces all experience to numbers, which are then manipulated in the service of objectivity, prediction, and control. But these three values are incapable of explaining the mystery of human relationship. The fact of the matter is that scientific methodology does not describe reality or any part of it; it only builds models, which are subject to constant revision and are occasionally contradictory to one another.

Spirituality's experience of transcendence is one of being addressed from beyond the material world by that which is greater than anything we on our own can conceive. In the quest of eros for the knowledge of the other we become aware of the fact that the more we know, the more there is to be known. Every answer generates another question or series of questions. There is an infinite presence of the not-yet-known that engages the horizon of our knowing and yet recedes before our inquiry into infinite mystery. The very limits of our language in describing experience leave the questioning person with a sense that "of what we cannot speak we must remain silent"—to quote the philosopher Ludwig Wittgenstein (1889–1951)—and yet in expectant awe.

The transcendence that addresses us is an energy that takes certain forms. In other words, we do not know God in himself, but only as his transcendent being confronts our finite minds. God is the ultimate source of our intrinsic and normative values, but we perceive this as his energy moves in our world. The purpose of life is that final cause embedded in this transcendent presence, always calling us out of where we are to where we might be. It gives global and personal meaning, but that meaning is still penultimate. The transcendent presence imparts to life its quality, as opposed to its quantity. Numbers may point to what lies beyond, but they never encompass this mystery that overcomes the banality of brute facts. It is the character of the spiritual life to be open to this transcendent energy in all its forms.

The notion of transcendence subverts the idea, of course, that all of reality is reducible to the phenomena or the appearances of things. In fact, when science understands itself, there is every indication that its own methodology becomes spiritual (i.e., open to a relationship with what transcends the phenomena). This is to say that the explanation of the methodology of the natural sciences requires that it draw on that which addresses us from outside the material world. There is good evidence that the data resulting from our observations cannot find a coherent and unified resolution in relation to data themselves, but only by reference to a point beyond the data. If seeing alone were believing, as we sometimes suggest, then the world of natural science would be a hopeless morass of contradictions. Transcendence is the hope for meaning we cannot otherwise have, and spirituality is our capacity for a relationship to that meaning: the mind of God.

Third, the key to the identification of the spiritual experience is a heightened or expanded consciousness. This has been the notion guiding much of the research in recent decades in transcendental experience among sociologists of religion, and it is confirmed by the comments among the members of the research sample for this study. For example, one pastor spoke of spiritual awareness as "anything that builds and holds a sense of meaning in life." Another described a new "consciousness" as "something God did for me. It was there and [I] opened up to it. God did it." Still further, a priest spoke of a spiritual turning point as the "clarity of one's call." One pastor's spiritual journey was highlighted by a book, a person, and therapy, which gave his life and discipline "a whole new sense of meaning and purpose."

This sense of a new awareness is at the heart of the Christian spiritual tradition. Teresa of Avila (1515–1582) says of her own mystical experience, which she calls rapture, "What I know in this case is that the soul was never so awake to the things of God nor did it have such a deep enlightenment and knowledge of his Majesty." Among the early church fathers the sacraments, particularly Baptism, are spoken of as the illumination.

David Bohm, a theoretical physicist teaching at the University of London, in a book called *Wholeness and the Implicate Order*, advances the theory that reality is essentially energy, which surrounds us in a flux and flow. This energy, he argues, takes two forms: material reality and consciousness. Consequently, the stuff of creation possesses an implicate or enfolded order that is consciousness. Theological reflection upon this hypothesis suggests that God is present in his creation supremely as one to be known. If we are related to the living God our initial realization of this relationship is in the form of knowledge.

Coming to knowledge, awakening, and illumination are all words or phrases that indicate ourselves as passive recipients. Spirituality is not acquisitive. This is why, in one sense, it is not something we "do." There is nothing that we can possess by "being spiritual." It is receptivity, a waiting, a trusting. Whatever knowledge may come does so as a given, over which we have no power or control. It is not a form of problem solving, which is why some may think of it as antithetical to social action. The reason for this passivity is that we have no leverage on the knowledge. We cannot get behind it to grasp it; we have to be open and wait for it. But it is an active passivity, by which I mean that we actually seek to allow the possibility of God's illumination of our heart and minds.

We are aware of the divine energy in perceiving new knowledge. This is what John of the Cross (1542–1591) means when he says that the Word of God is the effect upon the soul. The soul possesses, of course, the mind or what I have described as the capability for the un-contingent process of knowing. When we know God, when the relationship with the transcendent is occurring, the perceivable effect is a heightened or expanded consciousness. In this sense God speaks and we hear his Word.

This approach follows from the understanding that spirituality is rooted in the dynamic of knowing and being known. The participation of the finite subject in the infinite God is in terms of the process of coming into knowledge. But the awareness of that process means it must become incarnate; it must be the form of concrete knowledge, however that may manifest itself. This is analogous to the creative process, which is not recognizable except in works of art, music, sculpture, poetry, and the like. Of course, just as the profundity of the creative process is measured by the quality of what it creates, so is our spirituality evaluated by the quality of the awareness that arises.

Fourth, this leads to the substance of that knowledge and the fact that it is always historical. By "historical" is meant that the shape of the content of knowledge is a function of a particular time and place. The Old Testament notion of God, for example, reflects the memory and language of the Hebrew people. The task of Paul was to translate the preaching of Jesus into the culture of the Roman Empire. This inevitably and appropriately gave our knowledge of God revealed in Christ a distinctive shape.

Generally speaking, Baptists do not have visions of the Blessed Virgin, Norwegians do not think of Christ as black, and Muslims do not quote Buddha. We frame our experience of God in those representations that are not only available to us, but particularly deeply ingrained in our memory. The deeper we draw from our memory the greater the power of our knowledge. If I can evoke the Christ of my childhood to help me understand God's presence, it will have far more impact on my life than what I may read about Christ in the latest book.

All this has a great deal to say, of course, about the understanding of spirituality in general in relation to specifically Christian spirituality. God transcends history. He is not in himself a Jew or Christian, any more than he is male or female. The God revealed in Christ is not, as he is to himself, a first-century Jew. The truth that the Christian holds as distinct from other forms of spirituality lies beyond the historical manifestation of God in Christ. For example, God is personal, loving, and forgiving. Even those concepts have a historical quality but certainly reach beyond a temporal and geographical provincialism.

A distinction of Christian spirituality is its willingness to affirm the historical nature of the knowledge of God as something positive. The belief in the Incarnation frees the Christian from the attempt to escape history. There is in Christianity the scandal of particularity, a catch phrase that calls to mind that the identification of God in a moment in history is an invitation to see God in all history. In the historical Jesus we have that supreme moment, the proleptic event of universal history; but it is still history. Human beings are spiritual creatures, therefore, who realize their spirituality in a historical setting.

Fifth, the making of decisions and the action that grows out of those decisions is a product of the knowledge to which we have come. One cannot play tennis unless he first knows there is a game of tennis and is familiar with its rules. A person cannot travel from New York to San Francisco unless she first knows there is a San Francisco and where it lies in relation to New York.

Every action, by which I mean anything we do in which we have a degree of choice (salivation is not an action but a reaction; writing this book is an action), is a projection into the future of what we know about the world. If in the spiritual quest it is true that God expands our consciousness and we know as we did not know before, then inevitably it shows itself in our actions. This is why it is contradictory to say that authentic spirituality is an escape from social action, if in truth God intends that his Kingdom come on this earth as it is in heaven.

For this reason a prophet is a mystic in action. His vision of what should be, if it is of God, can only come from God. It is our spiritual nature that enables us to see and know the world as it is in God's mind and as he intended it to be. Therefore, the fulfillment of a person's spirituality is measured by his or her action on behalf of the Kingdom. By their fruits, Jesus told us, we shall know them.

Ignatius Loyola (1491–1556), the father of modern spiritual theology, speaks to this fifth point. He explains that the purpose of contemplation is to attain the love of God, and then calls attention to two points:

1. Love ought to manifest itself in deeds rather than in words.

2. Love consists in the mutual sharing of goods, for example, the lover gives and shares with the beloved what he possesses, or something of that which he is able to give; and vice versa, the beloved shares with the lover. Hence, if one has knowledge, he shares it with the one who does not possess it; and so also if one has honors, or riches. Thus, one always gives to the other.

[Ignatius Loyola, *Spiritual Exercises,* (trans. Louis J. Puhl, SJ), 230–31.]

Spiritual theology is, therefore, logically prior to moral theology. Yet it is also a consequence of a moral conversion, the willingness to ask questions of value and to be open to a transcendent vision of the world.

Prayer as Spiritual Action

Prayer is often used as a synonym for spirituality. People who ask how your spirituality is mean to inquire about the state of your prayer life. It is necessary for this discussion to make a distinction between prayer and spirituality, to define prayer, and to explore kinds of prayer. There is no final authority to which to appeal in arriving at these distinctions. They must be drawn selectively from the tradition and our contemporary experience.

In my judgment prayer is to spirituality as eating is to hunger. Spirituality is an inner disposition toward a relation with him who transcends the appearances, and prayer is the action this begets. We pray because we are spiritual beings. Those people who do not pray are not "aspiritual"; they choose not to exercise their spirituality and could be said to be spiritually undernourished.

In turn, the desire for God is fed by the act of prayer. We become aware of our spiritual selves as we actively seek to enter into relationship with God. It is like someone who has not eaten for a long time. She may remark after her first bite or two that she did not know how hungry she was until she started to eat. In a similar vein, another may remark that he did not know how much he longed for his wife until he experienced their marriage. Prayer awakens our spirituality.

But this is not to say what prayer is. Our understanding of the meaning of prayer has very much to do with our understanding of God. The New Testament common verbs for prayer, *euchomai* and more especially *proseuchomai*, mean to pray as to wish for something. The implication is that God is the source of what we might desire and prayer consists largely of a "wish list." Such an understanding of prayer raises all kinds of questions about God, if we understand him as he who foreordains all things and knows all that shall come to pass. It is as if one prayed each day for the sun to rise the next. It is almost presumptuous, unless we assume that God chooses for the sun to rise each day by some capricious whim.

Prayer obviously means more than filing our wishes with God. In his treatise *On Prayer*, Origen, one of the greatest minds of the early church, struggles with this question. He believes that to be rational, we have to be free to make choices, but the freedom of humankind operates at a different level than the providence of God. One might say he defines God's providence as the divine vision for his creation. God is no capricious deity and prayer is more than the uplifting of a wish list to him. It is in prayer that the freedom of humankind meets the vision of God. In this act of meeting, humanity is drawn up into the divine purpose. One priest with whom I spoke said, "Prayer is a part of myself and the way I relate to things around me." This points to prayer as a way of seeing creation with God as our eyes.

Prayer is the movement of God to humanity and humanity to God, the act of meeting. It is no less nor is it anything different from that. In whatever manner this meeting is realized it is an act of prayer. In other words, prayer is communication within the relationship between humankind and God and flows both ways. Benedict of Nursia (c.480–550), in his reform of the religious life of the Western church, sought to dignify manual labor as worthy of the monk. He pointed out that to labor is to pray. This makes sense of Paul's injunction that we pray without ceasing (I Thess. 5:17), for it vastly broadens the context of relationship with God. Prayer is the act of making whatever we do a cause for meeting and knowing God.

Clearly prayer in this sense has as its primary goal not the favorable reply to our requests but the establishment of a relationship. We miss the point of those passages in the Gospels that assure us of the power of prayer if we do not see that they point first of all to the relationship that the follower of Christ has with God. Luke writes, "Even if he will not provide for him out of friendship, the very shamelessness of the request will make him get up and give him all he needs" (Luke 11:8).[76] But God is not only our friend, Luke tells us, he is to us as a loving father. He will give us his Holy Spirit (Luke 11:13): God present, disclosing himself to us and fulfilling our inchoate longing for him.

Not all forms of prayer, however, are the same. For centuries there have been efforts to distinguish different ways in which we pray, if for no other reason than to provide some standard by which to examine our own prayer life. Traditionally the distinction has been made between mental prayer and vocal prayer. The difference here lies in the focused articulation of words, sentences, and paragraphs directed toward God as opposed to the absence of such focus. A meditation on the Annunciation would be mental prayer. A prayer for the return of Aunt Susie's health would be vocal prayer.

It is better to distinguish forms of prayer by a less mechanical means that would allow for a less arbitrary or artificial division. I would suggest that the different kinds of prayer fall along a continuum of focused intentionality on the part of the person who prays. At one end of this continuum is prayer that intends to intend nothing at all; at the other end of the continuum there is prayer that intends a specific answer from God, for example, the healing of Aunt Susie, the safe return from a journey, the forgiveness of our sins.

It is apparent that as persons mature spiritually their prayers move from a more to a less focused intentionality. Classically this has been described as a movement toward contemplation and union with God. Richard of St. Victor defines contemplation as "the free, more penetrating gaze of a mind, suspended with wonder concerning manifestations of wisdom." There is nothing so extraordinary in what he means. An analogy might be the quiet communion that can take place between persons in a close, longstanding marriage. For example, my youngest child has, since his older siblings left home, complained of the silence in our home. My wife and I sometimes sit or drive together, saying nothing for hours. Our son will interrupt when he can bear it no longer and ask if we are angry with one another. When we reply in the negative, he then asks what we were thinking about. Often we have to say, "Nothing." Yet there is a specific desire to be with one another and the quality of silence together is indeed different from the quality of silence alone.

There are forms of prayer that have as their purpose the inducement of this state. They work on the principle that by means of simplicity and

---

76. Holmes quotes from the New English Bible.

repetition the mind is emptied of worldly concerns and becomes open to the transcendent Word. The Jesus prayer—"Jesus Christ, Son of God, Savior, have mercy upon me"—repeated over and over in rhythm with our breathing is an example. It has an honored history of over fifteen hundred years, but it is only one example of a genre of prayer, both Christian and non-Christian, that has the purpose of enabling us to intend nothing at all in the act of prayer. Any such prayer whose purpose is to empty the mind of images is called apophatic prayer.

Physical exercise, manual labor or jogging, for example, can also have an apophatic effect in prayer. There is an unfocused openness that can occur in this kind of activity that, when we consciously direct the experience, can allow for an awareness of God's presence to emerge. The same thing can happen in any routine task, such as driving on an interstate highway, that engages the more automatic level of consciousness and leaves the higher brain functions relatively free.

Prayer that lies at the less focused end of the continuum is in a listening mode. The aim is not to tell God what we wish, much less to inform him of the weather, world events, or of the little crises at home. In that curious mixture of sensory metaphors common to spiritual theology, we listen that we might see. A spiritual friend of mine describes sitting on a high place in a field and listening to the wind until it forms an image in her mind. This is a way of saying that prayer for her is an imaginative attending to what is beyond mere sense data.

Contemplation is not the same thing as meditation. Meditation is more focused in its intention than contemplation, although it still seeks to listen. The early Benedictines spoke of the *lectio divina*, "divine reading." There is nothing esoteric about this. What they meant was that we ought to read the Scriptures and books of spiritual merit in a slow and deliberate fashion, chewing over each sentence and paragraph for whatever message may be there. Later a whole methodology of meditation was built upon this and made popular by Ignatius Loyola and, even more, by the French spiritual masters of the seventeenth century such as Francis de Sales (1567–1622) and Jean-Jacques Olier (1608–1657).

Meditation that customarily draws upon scriptural imagery to be a "carrier" of the divine message in prayer is a kataphatic form of prayer. By this I mean that it requires an overt and imaginative retention of certain images. The one who prays plays with them, much as one might play with a kaleidoscope. There is no expectation of a given pattern that might emerge, but attention is paid to whatever pattern appears. It becomes a source of spiritual listening in order, to mix the metaphor one more, that one might see.

A number of the clergy interviewed in this research center their prayer in a meditative reading of Scripture.[77] Certainly this conforms to the Reforma-

---

77. In the Introduction of his book, Holmes described the research project he developed to prepare for the writing of *Spirituality and Ministry*. The reference to interviewing clergy alludes to the research project.

tion principle that if the individual comes to the Bible prayerfully, the Holy Spirit will illumine his or her understanding of what is read. There is nothing so formal as the principles of Jesuit or French methodology, but the intent is very much the same.

At the more focused end of the continuum of prayer is what has customarily been called verbal prayer. The Lord's Prayer is verbal prayer, as are the *Gloria in excelsis* and the Hail Mary. The one who prays is telling God what he or she has in mind. Such prayer has been divided into a number of classes of telling and these in themselves are of varying focus. For our purposes here, moving from the lesser to greater focus, I will list five classes of prayer: adoration, thanksgiving, confession, intercession, and petition.

Adoration is an act of love and praise. It is like telling a spouse, "You are the most wonderful man (or woman) in the world." It is akin to a football cheer. Obviously, what we expect in return is a like feeling. *Thanksgiving* is a recognition of the source of our blessings, and *confession* is an awareness of our failure to love as we claim to love. These three classes of prayer are clearly relational in nature and differ from contemplation and meditation only in the concerted activity of the one who would pray.

Intercession and *petition* are different. They have an end result in mind. It is in reference to such prayer that we struggle with the issue of "unanswered prayer." The great amount of energy spent on the problem of intercession and petition is symptomatic of a failure to appreciate the vast continuum of prayer and its fundamental goal of relationship with God. While there is no doubt some legitimacy to the problem of unanswered prayer in general, most effort has been expended on it vis-à-vis intercession and petition because of their sharply focused intentionality.

Many years ago I was listening to a radio preacher while driving across the country. He was explaining the cause of unanswered prayer in some very down-home imagery. As he said, the other day he had tried to call his old grandma, and all he got was static on the telephone. He complained to the telephone company, who explained that a cat had climbed the power pole, been electrocuted, and fallen on the telephone lines between him and his grandma. "If we expect our prayer to be answered," he suggested, "we have to get the 'dead cat' off the lines."

There is a sense in which this anecdote is misleading and another in which it is legitimate. The problem of unanswered prayer is not the result of technological failure. Yet prayer is primarily an act of communication that deepens our relationship with God. If we intend too much, want too much, want our own goals and desires too much, these intensions can become the "dead cat" on the lines. We cannot listen and see, because we lack the purity of heart of which Matthew spoke (5:8). Purity of heart is an uncluttered intention to know the will of God. The "dead cats" can be our notions of what ought to be which stand in the way of God's intentions.

Prayer that is not primarily listening always runs the risk of getting in the way of the ultimate purpose of prayer, a deepened sharing in God's vision for his world. This is the supreme lesson of Jesus' prayer on the Mount of

Olives: "Father, if it be thy will, take this cup away from me. Yet not my will but thine be done!" (Luke 22:42). In doing God's will we come into relationship with him, which is the ultimate goal of the spiritual life.

This is undoubtedly the reason why growth in the Spirit involves a movement toward a less focused intentionality in prayer, while not requiring a total abrogation of intercession and petition. The surrender of the ego becomes a very real part of prayer and, perhaps, a reason why prayer itself can be frightening—it is built upon trust.

Conclusion

The fundamental assumption of this study is that God created human beings with the capacity for relationship with himself. Spirituality is a disposition and a potentiality for that relationship. It is not a part or piece of humanity, it is a character that cuts through the totality of the human, involving all of the individual; but it points to a particular posture of the person, which is distinguishable from emotional well-being, physical health, or intellectual activity. The key to spirituality is the awareness of a transcendent gift of knowledge.

Whereas spirituality needs to be understood specifically and experientially, prayer requires a broader definition than we often give it. It is the intentional act of entering into a relationship with God. That intention does not have to be focused, however, in any specific way. The key to prayer is the conscious direction of the self to the subject that lies behind and beyond the world as it appears.

In Christian prayer the conscious intention has within it certain symbols, principally the symbol of Christ. This is what it means to pray in the name of Jesus. The manner of our reaching out to God is moved and shaped by our image of our Lord and the infusion of God's Word within our consciousness is substantially Christ like.

Week Sixteen, Reading Assignment for All Years

The Sanctification of Time and Life[78]

Cyclical Liturgies

The yearly cycle of seasons is a natural phenomenon in temperate climates. The constant repetition of spring, summer, autumn, and winter has always served agricultural peoples as a reminder of their dependence on nature. The liturgies of nature religions express this dependence in a symbolic way: with each important change in the seasons, the people cultically identify themselves with the gods who produce the crops, hoping to ensure abundant harvests by imitating them in fertility rites.

Israel developed its own interpretation to the experience of time. Time still moves in cycles, but it also points in a definite direction. Yahweh is the Lord of history who created the world which had a beginning, and has been directing it toward a meaningful fulfillment. Time, by the Israelite interpretation, is more than a repetition of moments or of seasons; it is a series of significant moments in which Yahweh has performed mighty acts by which to further his purpose of redemption and fulfillment. The difference is clear in the two Greek words for time: *chronos,* regular, measured time, with no particular moment having more value or significance than any other, and *kairos,* a significant moment, a "pregnant moment," the "fullness of time." Israel paid attention to certain *kairoi* (plural) within the passage of *chronos.* She took the ancient agricultural liturgies, which were observances of "chronological" time, and turned them into celebrations of the meaningful—"kairotic"—moments of her history.

The *Torah* commanded the observance of three festivals each year: Passover, Pentecost, and Tabernacles. Each of these probably originated in an agricultural event—the first lambing, the barley harvest, and the harvest of grapes for wine. By Yahwism, these festivals became annual remembrances of the exodus from Egypt (Passover), the giving of the Law at Sinai (Pentecost), and the life in the wilderness (Tabernacles). Thus, the foundation-myth of Israel was rehearsed each year. By *anamnesis* (recollection), each generation of Israelites relived the events in which the covenant was established.

For the Christian church, Jesus' crucifixion and resurrection during the time of the Passover festival made that feast especially important. In most languages except English, the annual celebration of the resurrection is called

---

78. From Education for Ministry, *Common Lessons and Supporting Materials* (2005), 7-1-1 to 7-1-14.

by a derivative of the Hebrew *pesah,* Passover ("paschal" is the adjective). The festivals of Pentecost and Tabernacles as such had no specific significance for Christianity. The "paschal" celebration of the resurrection, however, soon came to be extended throughout the approximately seven weeks from Passover to Pentecost. The Luke-Acts narrative possibly reveals liturgical influence in claiming the Jewish celebration of the giving of the Law as the Christian "Pentecost," the celebration of the sending of the Holy Spirit—a fitting climax to the "seven times seven" days of Easter.

The "Great Fifty Days," the period from Easter to Pentecost, extended the time of the Easter festivities, during which fasting was prohibited and joy reigned. Soon it became the custom for baptisms to be administered on the eve of Easter, so the candidates could begin their new lives at the feast of the New Life. A time of preparation for baptism—with instruction, prayer, and fasting—then extended the season of Easter backward. The season of Lent (the forty days before Easter) developed from this.

The Christian "foundation-myth," centering in the resurrection of Jesus, was rehearsed each year. The cycles of *chronos* were punctuated by the supreme *kairos*—the fullness of time in which God brought salvation-history to its climax. Eventually, all the major events of the Christian foundation-myth would be liturgically remembered, from the preparation for Jesus' birth through the sending of the Holy Spirit. But during the period we are studying, it was Easter, with the period of preparation before it and the season of festivities following, that dominated the yearly cycle.

Another kind of annual observance also began to emerge, as persecutions took their toll of martyrs. As Christian communities began to observe the anniversaries of the deaths of their sons and daughters, local "calendars of saints" developed alongside the cyclical observance of the foundational events in the life of Christ. (Paul used "saints" to refer to all Christians. The special honor paid to martyrs for their heroic witness marks the first stage in the process by which the word came to be reserved for extraordinary Christians.)

The seven-day week was the basic unit of time in ancient Israel. Since the phases of the moon recur in a regular pattern every twenty-eight days, many ancient cultures found it convenient to measure time by the four seven-day periods into which the lunar month neatly divides. The Priestly creation story, however, used the week as more than a timekeeping device—there, it is a liturgical cycle culminating in the Sabbath. The Sabbath was the day on which the covenant was celebrated. On the Sabbath, the Jew looks back to creation itself—especially the creation of Israel by the covenant with Yahweh—and forward to the great "Sabbath rest" when the kingdom of God is fulfilled.

Each week in the life of the Jew reaches its climax in the Sabbath meal, a liturgy centered in the home. "Home" then implied what is now called the "extended family": several generations, including any servants the family might have. A group, such as Jesus and his disciples, was bound together as a fellowship (a *chaburah*); it also functioned as an extended family in which the Sabbath meal was observed.

Early Christians retained the pattern of the seven-day week, but they moved the high point from the seventh day to the first. They celebrated the day of the Lord's resurrection, not the Sabbath. It was the first day of the new creation; it was also, figuratively, the "eighth day"—the eschatological "day of the Lord."

On "the Lord's day," the members of the Christian "family" gathered for their sacred meal. It was a "fellowship meal," like the *chaburah* meals the disciples had with Jesus, a family meal, such as Jews had always observed. Above all, it was the weekly celebration of a covenant, like the Jewish Sabbath.

On the Sabbath, Jews looked backward to creation and forward to the eschaton—the Day of Yahweh. Christians also looked in two directions as they observed the Lord's day in the sacred meal. For them, both directions pointed to the eschaton. The "paschal mystery"—the death and resurrection of Jesus—was remembered, and by this *anamnesis* the past event was made present. Although it was in the past, the event itself was eschatological. All of salvation-history from creation onward came to its fulfillment in the events of the paschal mystery. At the last supper the disciples participated in the "messianic banquet." Now, as the Christian family eats its sacred meal, the messianic banquet is experienced again. The host at the meal is the risen Jesus, now "Lord and Messiah."

There was still a future to look to. Although the eschatological age had begun, it would not be consummated until Jesus returned in glory. So the meal was still, like the Jewish Sabbath meal, an occasion for anticipation. In the present—a period "between the times" of resurrection and *parousia* (the return of Christ)—Christians participated in the reality of the *parousia* by sharing the food and drink of the messianic banquet, remembering the paschal mystery and anticipating the *parousia* itself.

While the Temple remained standing, morning and evening sacrifices were offered daily, and services of psalms and prayers were held in mid-morning and mid-afternoon. Most people, however, could not attend the Temple—it was available only to those who lived in Jerusalem or who visited as pilgrims. Indeed, the building itself was not designed for large congregations. Many could be accommodated within its grounds in the various courtyards, but the central part was intended for the priests and their attendants, not as a gathering place for the people. The sacrifices were performed *for* the people *by* the priests.

Most Jews worshiped in the synagogues. By the first century, services with the reading of scripture, preaching, psalmody, and prayers were held on at least some week days, with the major gathering on Friday evening immediately before the Sabbath meal.

Important as the synagogue services were, not every synagogue could muster a congregation each day. The day was sanctified primarily by the prayers of individuals. Every Jew was expected to pray three times a day— mid-morning, noon, and mid-afternoon.

At first, Christians too attended the Temple (Acts 2:46, 3:1), but they did so as Jews. Acts makes it clear that the specifically Christian assemblies took place in people's homes and consisted of teaching, fellowship, the breaking of bread, and prayers (Acts 2:42). It was not long before Christians realized that the Temple could form no part of their lives. The Epistle to the Hebrews makes this point, as does Paul's insistence that the cultic obligations of the Law no longer applied to Christians. What the priesthood had been appointed to do for the people was completely fulfilled in Jesus.

Synagogue worship, however, formed the basis for Christian weekday observances. As long as it was possible, Christians attended the synagogues. After Jamnia, in the face of growing animosity from the rabbis, they adapted the synagogue service to their own use. They added Christian writings and prayer in the name of Jesus, and interpreted the scriptures as fulfilled in Christ. They continued to hold this "service of the word" on weekdays, the sacred meal being reserved for the Lord's day. As in Judaism the Friday evening synagogue service had been followed by the Sabbath meal in the homes, so also on the Lord's day the service of the word preceded the celebration of the eucharist.

Crisis Liturgies—The Sanctification of Life

Any society, as time goes by, experiences events that alter its configurations. New members come into the group, by birth or marriage or some other process. Former members drop out; they resign, or they die, or are expelled from the group. Leadership changes hands. Relationships within the society itself change as people once single decide to marry. In each of these events, individuals are obviously involved. It is the individual who acts in all that happens. The events also have an effect on the community. In each instance, the community has to reorder its life in some way because of what has happened to the individual. Liturgies develop to respond to these circumstances, to enable the society to reorganize itself around the new conditions. Society pauses to observe the changes, names them, and then derives strength to go in new directions.

Most Jews, of course, became Jews by birth. Male children were circumcised on the eighth day after birth, and by the time of Jesus there was apparently some kind of ceremony marking puberty and the assumption of the duties of the Torah. But it was also possible for a Gentile to become a Jew.

Judaism did not actively seek converts; indeed, Roman law forbade such a practice. Converts to Judaism, therefore, had usually been "God-fearers" for some time. They had attended the synagogue and knew enough about Judaism to want to become Jews themselves. A prospective candidate had to respond appropriately to intense questioning about his motives; only those who seemed sincerely willing to undertake the burden of the Torah were accepted.

The next step was thorough instruction in the traditions of Judaism. A born Jew would have grown up with the words of the Torah, and a new candidate had to become equally well acquainted with them.

Circumcision was required of all males. For a born Jew, this external sign of the covenant was sufficient. But for Gentiles, an additional rite was imposed on both men and women candidates, to erase the taint of their former condition. A ceremony of cleansing was necessary, not only to remove the defilement associated with the low moral level of much Gentile culture but also to wash away the stigma of ritual pollution acquired simply by being a Gentile.

After publicly renouncing the old life, the candidate pledged loyalty to the Torah, and was led into a river or pool, for a momentary total immersion. On emerging, he or she was marked on the forehead with the Hebrew letter "Taw," the first letter of "Torah." (Christians should not picture this letter as a "T," similar in shape to the cross with which Christians are signed.) Obviously, immersion in water signified cleansing from the Gentile life. But it also symbolized participation in the crossing of the Sea of Reeds and the pilgrimage to the promised land.

Christian baptism was almost certainly an adaptation of the Jewish rite of initiation. Circumcision dropped out of practice, thanks to Paul's successful campaign against it, and out with it went the last cultic implication that women were not full members of the covenant. All the rest of the Jewish rite found its counterparts in the Christian initiation rites.

If the candidate were a Jew, very little instruction was required. The scriptures and the story of salvation-history were familiar settings in which the Christian message could be learned. A Gentile convert, however—unless a "God-fearer"—would need a protracted period of instruction. (Paul's relatively rapid success in winning Gentile converts and establishing congregations that could carry on after he left them was due to his appeal to the "God-fearers." Conceivably, the gross misunderstanding he worked so hard to correct at Corinth stemmed from converts who were accepted from paganism too quickly to be given adequate instruction.)

Early forms of baptismal liturgy required the candidate, after instruction, to renounce the present age of Satan and to profess faith in Jesus. Renunciation of the old life is necessary if one is to enter the new—death precedes resurrection.

As time went on, the original profession of faith in Jesus assumed a trinitarian form. The candidate was asked if he or she believed in God the Father; if the answer was yes, the person was immersed. Similarly, affirmations of belief in Jesus and in the Holy Spirit were each followed by immersions. The person had thus been baptized into "the name" of the Trinity; it was the triple confession of faith that was intended in Matthew 28:19, rather than a trinitarian formula, "I baptize you in the name of the Father, and of the Son, and of the Spirit."

In Jewish society, a person could be excluded from the community for moral offenses or for ritual pollution. For certain offenses, principally murder and adultery, "exclusion" took the form of death. For offenses less serious but grave enough to violate standards of acceptable behavior, the Torah prescribed specific penalties. When these had been paid and the penitent had expressed repentance and remorse, a suitable person—the head of the family, the chief elder of the community, or the rabbi—could grant restoration, usually symbolizing it by the laying-on-of-hands.

Ritual pollution would exclude a person as effectively as serious moral delinquency, though for quite different reasons. Any Jew was considered "taboo"—not to be touched or approached—as a result of contact with either a profane or a holy thing. (Tax-collectors were "sinners" because they came in close contact with Gentiles; women were quarantined after giving birth to a child. The "impurity" of new mothers was probably because of the new life they had borne, since life was considered holy.) Ritual pollution required only purification, not penance.

In Christian practice, as we have seen, the sin of apostasy was added to the unforgivable sins of murder and adultery. The punishment, however, was not death, but excommunication—expulsion from the community. In the view of the earliest Christians, it came to the same thing—to be outside the realm of salvation was equivalent to death. From Hermas through the events that produced the Novatian schism, the church moved to soften its stance against these "mortal" sins. The way to restitution, however, for those sins that could be forgiven, was similar to that practiced in Judaism: to express repentance and remorse to the community, and acknowledge restoration at the hands of the head of the Christian community—the bishop.

When we examine the nature of liturgies that express the relations of social groups with their leadership, the distinction between "communities" and "institutions" becomes very significant. As we are using the term, a "community" is a relatively small group established on the basis of natural relationships—a family, for example, or a group of friends. In a "community," the leader is usually clearly recognized and no liturgy is required. In a patriarchal culture, the father would be the head of the family; in a matriarchal culture, the mother. The biological relationship automatically establishes the official leadership, even if in fact someone else in the family exerts more effective control. In communities not related by blood, leadership may be established on the basis of aggressiveness—like the pecking order among birds—or some obvious talent. The "charismatic" leaders in Israel before the monarchy were accepted by virtue of their display of spiritual gifts.

In an "institution," however, people are linked together by more complex and less obvious ties. The leadership office is not as readily discernible, and some public liturgy is required to legitimize its incumbent. A "legitimate" leader—one who is officially recognized by the institution—may have an abundance of talents or nearly none. Leadership would presumably be better under a gifted leader, but the less gifted can rely on the authority stemming from "legitimacy" to a degree impossible to the leader of a "community."

In Moses, Israel had a "charismatic" leader. He performed all three functions Israel's community life required: he was ruler, priest, prophet. As the ruler, he mediated the Law of Yahweh to Yahweh's people; as the priest, he represented the people before God and acted as a buffer between Yahweh's holiness and their humanity; as the prophet, he spoke Yahweh's word to specific situations—the golden calf, or Korah's rebellion.

When Israel became sufficiently institutionalized to require a king, the three leadership roles could no longer reside in one person. At first, the king could still function as priest, but ultimately the roles were separated. The king represented Yahweh's rule, and the priests offered the sacrifices to God for the people. Both king and priest had to be legitimized. Saul and David were still cast in the charismatic mold, but after their time it no longer served. The "house of David" became an institution; dynastic descent and the liturgy of anointing were required. Solomon may not have been the most able of David's sons, but he was the one on whom the succession rested—so it was he who was anointed king. The priests also had to be in the proper line of succession, as evidenced in the rivalry between the Aaronic and the Zadokite lines throughout the Old Testament. Priests were anointed, as were the kings, as a public sign of their legitimacy in office.

The liturgies that established these leaders were seen as conferring gifts from God to enable the persons selected to perform their tasks. No office in Israel could be carried out apart from Yahweh, and all required his approval and help. The liturgies became necessary only when public recognition of the leaders had to be proclaimed rather than taken for granted as it had been in a community.

The prophetic role was by definition charismatic. No liturgy can establish a prophet in office. The Spirit alone bestows the charismatic gift—anointing with oil would be superfluous.

As long as the Christian movement was small and the congregations bound together by a sense of familial intimacy—for all were newly "adopted" into the family of God—members were not overly concerned about leadership. Although Paul found it necessary to assert his apostolic authority, he did so on grounds that explicitly repudiated "institutional" authorization. He was a "charismatic" apostle, appointed by Christ himself; he was not a deputy from the Jerusalem congregation. No doubt he had a hand in selecting local leaders in the congregations he established, but he shows no particular interest in the process, either in his own letters or in the Acts accounts of his work. Paul's list of leadership roles in I Cor. 12:28 refers only to functional abilities, all gifts of the Holy Spirit. In no letter does he hint at a specific person or class of persons as the ones who were expected to preside at the community's sacred meal.

By the time the "pastoral epistles" are written, however, leadership roles have become more closely defined. "Elders" and "overseers" are to be respectable, to be chosen with care; "deacons" are to be worthy of their office. The "community" is no longer so easy to discern; rival groups and divisions within the local congregations are asserting claims. The ties that bind Christians together must be noted more clearly—the faith as taught by the apostles must be affirmed, the boundaries of the community more carefully drawn.

When word is heard from Ignatius of Antioch, the institutional pattern of leadership is complete. Ignatius himself may be deserving of the title "saint," but by his own reasoning neither his personal abilities nor even "charismatic" gifts were at issue. What was important was the legitimacy of his office as bishop of Antioch. He was the "head of the family," presiding at the sacred meal because he held the office of bishop.

The documents we possess tell us very little about the other "crisis liturgies" in the early church—marriage, childbirth, and burial. From the glimpses we have, all from post-New Testament times, these liturgies seem to have followed closely the practices of pagan society, with appropriate Christian substitutions for the names of the pagan gods. Essential though they are to any human group, there seems to have been little about them that required a distinctively Christian emphasis.

Hippolytus founded a schismatic church in protest against the moral laxity of Bishop Callixtus. He is remembered further, however, for some important theological writing, which followed very closely the lines of thought developed by Irenaeus. Tradition has it that shortly before his death, he renounced his schismatic bishopric and urged his followers to be reconciled with the newly elected bishop of Rome. Whatever disfavor he may have incurred during his lifetime, his martyrdom in 236 CE earned him a place in the Roman congregation's calendar of saints.

Among his many works is a "Church Order" he entitled *Apostolic Tradition.*[79] With the exception of the *Didache*, it is the oldest of its kind in existence, dating from 215 CE. It is far more complete than the *Didache* in its directions for the liturgical life of a congregation, and, according to the author's foreword as well as the title, is itself based on older traditions. It gives us our clearest picture of life in the church in Rome in the third century and probably as early as the middle of the second.

The *Apostolic Tradition* had an influence over an area much wider than Rome proper. It has been recognized recently as the basis of several eastern Church Orders of a much later date. Up until the beginning of the twentieth century, the document was presumed lost. Modern scholars have found it incorporated into Egyptian and Syrian Church Orders of the fourth century. Since the *Apostolic Tradition* was demonstrated as acceptable to both East and West, we can take it as a sample typical of early church practice.

From the directions for the admission of catechumens (CAT-ah-kew-mens)—people receiving instruction—Christians were not to be outdone by their Jewish counterparts in setting rigorous standards for their converts. Not everyone who sought baptism was allowed even to set foot on the lengthy path of instruction. Unworthy applicants were weeded out in preliminary examinations on the basis of their reasons for seeking baptism. Their occupations were strictly screened; many professions were prohibited. Besides the

---

79. A translation of *The Apostolic Tradition of Hippolytus of Rome* can be found at www .bombaxo.com/hippolytus.html.

obviously immoral occupations, applicants also had to give up any way of life that would bring them into commerce with pagan idolatry or that would entail violence and the taking of life.

If the prospective candidates were deemed suitable, they were admitted to a three-year "catechumenate," a period of intensive study. During this period, the catechumens were examined concerning their daily lives to determine their fitness for baptism—"whether they have lived devoutly during their catechumenate, whether they have respected widows, visited the sick, practiced all the other good works" *(Ap. Trad.* 20).

Only after thorough instruction in these matters were they finally allowed to learn the gospel itself. Once they had been chosen for baptism, the preparation became more intense. Every day they received the laying-on-of-hands to exorcise the demons of paganism. As the day of their baptism drew near, the bishop himself performed exorcisms to determine whether or not they were "pure"—free from demonic possession. Any who were not "pure" were rejected. They had not truly heard the Word with faith, or the demon would not still be there. (The concepts and images used differ from those of modern western civilization, but the exorcisms served the same purposes that psychological tests and therapy do today.)

Baptisms took place on the Lord's day, preferably on Easter. On the Friday and Saturday before the baptism, the candidates were required to fast, and on Saturday evening an all-night vigil was held in whatever building was used for worship. Before the candidates and clergy went to the baptismal site, the bishop said a prayer of thanksgiving over one container of oil, the "oil of thanksgiving," and an exorcism over another, the "oil of exorcism." At "cockcrow"—the early morning watch—on Sunday, presbyters and deacons led the candidates to the water, usually a nearby stream or spring-fed pool. At the baptismal site, the candidate stood facing the west, the symbol of Satan's realm, the land of darkness farthest away from the east where the sun rose, the direction of the eschatological hope. (The "prince of this world" comes from darkness.) After swearing renunciation, "I renounce thee Satan and all thy undertakings and all thy works," the candidate was then anointed with the oil of exorcism.

Now the candidate was ready for the triple profession of faith and the triple immersion. The deacon or deaconess accompanying the candidate asked, "Do you believe in God the Father almighty?" The candidate replied, "I believe." The deacon placed his hand on the candidate's head and immersed the candidate in the water.

After the immersion the deacon asked the second question,

> Do you believe in Christ Jesus, the Son of God, born by the Holy Spirit of the Virgin Mary; who died and was buried and rose again on the third day; who ascended into heaven; who sits at the right hand of the Father; who will come to judge the living and the dead?

A second affirmative reply was followed by a second immersion.

The third profession of faith and third immersion came in response to the question,

Do you believe in the Holy Spirit, in the Holy Church, in the resurrection of the flesh? (*Ap. Trad.* 21)

(The threefold question put to candidates is an example of the "rule of faith." It is also the precursor of a creed called the "Roman Symbol," itself the basis for the one commonly called "the Apostles' Creed.")

Their immersions completed, the presbyter anointed the candidates with the "oil of thanksgiving." They were then clothed and brought inside the building to the bishop, who laid his hands on them and prayed that they might serve God according to his will. He marked their foreheads with the sign of the cross and kissed them, saying "The Lord is with you," and the newly baptized replied, "and with your spirit."

Up until this time the candidates had not been allowed to pray with the congregation. They were dismissed after the scripture readings and sermon at the services of the word. Now they joined in the prayers of the people as the worship of the Lord's day began. The prayers over, they joined also in the kiss of peace. The celebration of the eucharist continued, this time with a cup of milk and honey and a cup of water in addition to the usual cup of wine. The sweetened milk (a baby's "formula") was the food of infants, signifying that the new Christians were but newly born; the cup of water signified an inner "baptism," "so that the inward man [person] who is spiritual may receive the same effect as the body" (*Ap. Trad.* 23). The newly baptized people received the bread, the wine, and the other two cups. The initiation was now completed. (Compare the description of baptism in Justin Martyr's *First Apology*.)

After such arduous preparation—three years of instruction, two days of fasting, and an all-night vigil—the experience was so moving that the candidates really felt they had gone through death and had come into new life. The liturgy accomplished what it set out to do—to fully incorporate new members into the fellowship and with no doubts about what life in the church involved.

The lengthy process of preparation for baptism, from the admission of a catechumen to the final rite itself, contrasts sharply with the brevity of the ordination of a bishop. A new bishop is elected by all the people of the congregation. No mention is made in the *Apostolic Tradition* of any prerequisites, not even that the bishop-elect be from among the presbyters. Presumably, however, anyone chosen to exercise the authority of leadership would be someone who had shown himself capable. But nowhere is it suggested that a bishop, presbyter, or deacon needs training beyond what is required for baptism. Nor is the liturgy of ordination itself nearly as solemn as that of baptism.

A newly elected bishop is presented to the entire congregation on the Lord's day, together with the council of presbyters and neighboring bishops.

The bishops lay their hands on the head of the one to be ordained and pray that God may

> Pour out now the power which has its origin in thee, the sovereign Spirit whom thou hast given to thy beloved Child [Greek *pais*—"child" or "servant"] Jesus Christ and that he has handed on to the apostles who built the church in place of thy sanctuary [the Temple] for the glory and unceasing praise of thy name.
>
> Grant, O Father who readest the heart, that thy servant whom thou has chosen as bishop may feed thy holy flock, may exercise thy sovereign priesthood without reproach serving thee day and night. May he never cease to render thy regard favorable, and offer to thee the gifts of thy holy church. In virtue of the Spirit of the supreme priesthood, may he have the power to forgive sins according to thy commandment.
>
> May he distribute the shares following thine order; may he loose every bond in virtue of the power that thou hast conferred on the apostles; May he be pleasing to thee for gentleness and purity of heart. May he be before thee a sweet savior through thy Child Jesus Christ, our Lord. . . . (*Ap. Trad.* 3)

For all the importance of the bishop's office, the ordination is complete after prayer alone. After the people have acclaimed him with the words "He has become worthy," the newly ordained bishop, with his presbyters attending him, presides at the Eucharist for the first time with his congregation.

Ordinations of presbyters and deacons are similarly brief. The bishop lays his hand on the head of the one to be ordained a priest, while the other presbyters also touch him. The bishop prays that God may give him "the Spirit of grace and counsel, so that he may help the presbyters and govern thy people with a pure heart." The prayer cites the appointment of the seventy elders as precedent for the office (*Ap. Trad.* 8).

The order for ordaining a deacon is oriented more toward the bishop, "For a deacon is not ordained for the presbyterate, but for the service of the bishop, to carry out his orders." The bishop alone lays his hands on the candidate. The prayer says that God has chosen the deacon "for the service of thy church and to bring into the Holy of Holies the offering presented by the high priests that thou has established for the glory of thy name" (*Ap. Trad.* 9). The latter phrase refers to the deacon's function of bringing the offerings of bread and wine *from the congregation* for use in the eucharistic celebration; the "high priests" here means the people.

During this period, Christianity's growth was due primarily to the witness of the laity. Thoroughly trained before they were admitted to baptism, they were in every way as competent as the clergy to carry out their apostolate to the world. The ordained ministers were commissioned to exercise specific tasks within the church, while the laity did all the rest.

The *Didache* had instructed the members of the congregation to pause and pray at three times during the day—mid-morning, noon, and mid-afternoon. The *Apostolic Tradition* makes provision for seven "hours of prayer":

(1) on arising to go to work; (2) at the "third hour" (nine in the morning); (3) at the "sixth hour" (noon); (4) at the "ninth hour" (three in the afternoon); (5) on going to bed; (6) in the middle of the night; (7) at "cockcrow," the earliest sign of dawn. How faithfully this regimen was followed is impossible to say. The clear intent, however, was to remind Christians wherever they were that in their "diaspora" throughout the workaday world, they remain the church. "Church" is not something they *come* to on the Lord 's day; it is they themselves, every minute of the day and night.

In addition to the "hours of prayer," the *Apostolic Tradition* describes two daily congregational meetings. In the mornings, at least occasionally, there was an assembly for "instruction on the Word of God." The service consisted of reading from the scriptures and instructions about them—"The speaker will teach what is useful for all, and you will hear things that you have forgotten, you will draw profit from what the Holy Spirit gives you through the teacher." The people offered prayers and then went to their work (*Ap. Trad.* 35). This was the "service of the word," patterned after the synagogue worship. It corresponds to the description Justin Martyr gave of the "service of the word" preceding the celebration of the eucharist.

In the evening, a "service of light" *(lucernarium)* was held. A deacon brought a lamp, and the bishop gave thanks for the light that Jesus brought to our lives, and for the light that now illuminates the evening darkness. Then, after the evening meal, they recited psalms and probably read from the scriptures.

The eucharist was celebrated every Sunday. As the rolls of martyrs lengthened, it became customary to observe the anniversaries of their deaths; the eucharist was probably celebrated on those days, but on no other weekdays. It was a celebration of the paschal mystery, to be observed on the day of the resurrection.

Congregations were small, and they usually gathered for their Sunday worship in private homes. By the middle of the third century, and possibly earlier, some congregations had purchased buildings specifically for worship, but the practice was not widespread. After all, it was still illegal to be a Christian. The room in which worship was conducted was open, containing a few chairs—reserved for the elderly and infirm—and a chair each for the bishop and his attending presbyters and deacons. A small table, sometimes not brought in until the offering of bread and wine was placed in the center of the room. The clergy dressed in the same manner as the laity. "Vestments" or distinctive clothing for the clergy had not yet evolved.

On Sunday morning, the people gathered in the room and greeted each other, engaging in conversations until the person appointed began to read from the Scriptures. The readings were often lengthy, sometimes an entire Old Testament book and frequently an entire letter from a Christian writer. When the readings were over, the bishop, seated in his chair at the front of the gathering, lectured on the significance of the biblical passages. The people sat on the floor or on one of the few chairs or stools.

When the bishop's sermon was completed, the catechumens and any penitents who were still excommunicated were dismissed. Then prayers were offered. A deacon would lead the prayers by asking the congregation to pray for the various needs and issues in the congregation's life. Such "bidding prayers" as "I bid your prayers for. . . ." gave direction to the congregation while still allowing each person to offer his or her own petitions. At the close of the prayers, the service of the word was over and the people greeted each other with the kiss of peace.

People who had not been able to attend the service of the word during the week came on Sunday for their weekly instruction. The continuing education of the laity was carried out by these frequent gatherings. The Bible and its meaning for Christian life was the constant "curriculum." Prayers were offered—and as always when the church gathered, the people assembled "in the name of the Lord"—but the primary purpose of the gathering was instruction. Worship in its more usual sense was offered at the eucharist and the hours of prayer.

The service of the word completed, the deacons circulated among the people to gather up their offerings of bread and wine. Frequently other foods would be offered as well—olive oil, cheese, and olives. These were symbolic of the "first fruits," the gifts of the earth offered to God in thanksgiving for the abundance of creation; they were also used for the *agape,* a fellowship meal after the eucharist, and for the poor of the congregation.

The deacons brought the table to its place in the center of the room and spread it with a cloth. Enough bread and wine for the eucharist was put on the table and the rest set aside for the poor and for the clergy. The bishop, with the presbyters gathered on either side of him, stood at one side of the table and the congregation gathered around it. All the people joined the bishop in lifting their hands upward in the gesture of prayer as the bishop began the prayer of thanksgiving. (The bishop did not *celebrate* the eucharist— he *presided* as the congregation celebrated.)

When the prayer of thanksgiving ended, the people shouted "Amen"— ratifying what their spokesperson had said. After the bishop and his attending clergy had received the bread and wine, the members of the congregation came forward to receive the sacred meal. Each person would go first to the bishop to receive a piece of the loaf and then to one of the other clergy for a sip from the cup. When all had received, the deacons took some of the bread (and possibly wine) to the homes of any who could not attend the Sunday gathering. In some places, the people took some of the bread home; they were to eat a piece of it each morning before touching any other food, thereby extending the eucharist through the week.

Week Thirty-one, Reading Assignment for Year One

This section on Micah is extracted from John J. Collins's longer text, *Introduction to the Hebrew Bible*, because Micah is not addressed in the *Shorter Introduction to the Hebrew Bible*, our current text for Year One.

Micah[80]

Roughly contemporary with Isaiah was Micah of Moresheth, a small town about twenty-three miles southwest of Jerusalem. According to the superscription of the book, he prophesied in the days of Jotham, Ahaz, and Hezekiah, and his oracles concerned both Samaria and Jerusalem. In contrast to Isaiah, Micah was a rural prophet and not so closely engaged with the Davidic dynasty. As in the case of all the prophetic books, however, we must reckon with a process of edition and supplementation that may have gone on for centuries. A clear example of this is found in Mic 4:10, where Zion is told to writhe like a woman in labor, "for now you shall go forth from the city and camp in the open country; you shall go to Babylon. There you shall be rescued, there the Lord will redeem you from the hands of your enemies." The initial prophecy that the city would be undone, and that its inhabitants would have to camp in the open country, may well have been uttered by Micah. It is quite compatible with the critique of the ruling powers by the rural prophet. The extension of the prophecy to include the Babylonian exile and the subsequent restoration must have been added by a postexilic scribe, who felt impelled to update the oracle in the light of subsequent history.

The actual extent of the supplementation of the oracles of Micah is a matter of controversy. One scholarly tradition, developed in Germany in the late nineteenth century and still widely influential, attributes only material in chapters 1–3 to the eighth-century prophet, and that with minor exceptions, most notably the prophecy of restoration in 2:12–13. These chapters consist primarily of judgment oracles. The more hopeful oracles in chapters 4–5 are usually dated to the early postexilic period. Chapters 6–7 are also regarded as later additions. At least the conclusion in 7:8–20 was added to adapt the collection to liturgical use. This kind of analysis may go too far

---

80. John J. Collins, *Introduction to the Hebrew Bible* (Minneapolis: Augsburg Fortress, 2004), 321–24.

in denying the prophet any hope for the future. At least a few passages in chapters 4–7 are likely to come from the eighth century. In contrast to this approach, some recent commentaries have tried to defend the essential unity of the book (Hillers, Andersen and Freedman). There can be little doubt, however, that the oracles underwent a process of transmission and that the book, like those of the other pre-exilic prophets, was given its present form after the Babylonian exile.

The Social Critique

The opening oracle invokes an old tradition of the theophany of the divine warrior. In Judges 5 the imagery of storm and earthquake were used to express the terror caused by YHWH going to help his people in battle. In Micah they describe the terror of YHWH coming to judge his people. The wrath is directed against both Samaria and Jerusalem. The focus on the capital cities is significant. The offenses are primarily charged to the ruling class. Jerusalem is derisively called a "high place." Micah makes no distinction between the guilt of the two kingdoms. In 1:6 he prophesies that Samaria will be made a heap. In 3:12 he predicts that "Zion shall be plowed as a field; Jerusalem shall become a heap of ruins." The latter prophecy is cited in Jer 26:18, where its nonfulfillment is explained by the fact that Hezekiah repented. Micah says that he will go naked and barefoot as Isaiah did, but where Isaiah symbolized the captivity of Egyptians and Ethiopians, Micah's action is a gesture of mourning for the destruction of Judah. The statement that "it has reached the gate of my people" recalls the invasion of Sennacherib (cf. Isaiah 1), but it more likely refers to the Syro-Ephraimite war, in view of the date ascribed to Micah and his concern for Samaria as well as Jerusalem.

The initial charge against Samaria and Jerusalem is idolatry. Jerusalem is compared to a high place; Samaria is accused of prostitution (cf. Hosea). More typical of Micah, however, is the accusation of injustice. The statement that "they covet fields, and seize them; houses and take them away," refers to the same phenomenon noted in Isa 5:8, which is addressed to those who add house to house and field to field. The punishment will fit the crime. Their own houses and fields will be seized by the invaders. Micah's condemnation of the exploitation of the poor is more biting even than that of Amos. The rich "tear the skin off my people and the flesh off their bones; eat the flesh of my people . . . chop them up like meat in a kettle" (3:2–3). The punishment to come will be a response of YHWH to the cry of the poor. Like Amos, Micah disassociates himself from the professional prophets (nebî'îm, 3:5–12). These people, we are told, give oracles for money (3:11; rulers and priests are similarly venal). They cry "peace" when they have enough to eat, and mislead the people by saying "surely, the Lord is with us" (3:11). If Isaiah saw this Davidic slogan as ambiguous, Micah sees it as a misleading illusion. We have no narrative of the call of Micah as we have of Amos. It seems safe to assume that he did not consider himself to be a nābî'. Like Amos, his preaching encountered opposition and some people tried to suppress it (2:6). It has been noted that the formula "thus says the Lord" occurs only once in chapters 1–3, and that Micah sometimes speaks in his own name (3:1). Nonetheless, he also speaks in the name of the Lord (e.g., 1:6: "I will make Samaria a heap"), and he claims to be filled with power, with the spirit of the Lord, to denounce the sin of Israel (3:8).

The critique of the cult in chapter 6 is also in line with what we have seen in the other eighth-century prophets and is plausibly attributed to Micah. This passage is cast in the form of a rib, or legal disputation, and can be viewed as a covenant lawsuit. God reminds his people Israel that he brought them up from the land of Egypt and redeemed them from slavery. There is a clear implication that Israel should have responded by serving the Lord with justice and has failed to do so, but the offenses and consequent punishment are not spelled out. While the exodus played no part in the preaching of Isaiah of Jerusalem, it figured prominently in the oracles of Amos and Hosea, even though Amos, like Micah, came from the southern kingdom. Micah too addressed Israel as well as Judah. Many scholars assume that the appeal to the exodus here is the work of a Deuteronomistic editor, but this is not necessarily so.

Micah 6:6–8 considers the misguided reasoning of an Israelite, or Judean, worshiper. The assumption is that God will be impressed by the cost of the sacrifice. Even human sacrifice is contemplated. As we have seen in connection with Genesis 22, human sacrifice was practiced in ancient Israel and Judah. King Manasseh of Judah, son of Hezekiah, was said to have made his son "pass through fire," which is to say that he sacrificed him as a burnt offering (2 Kgs 21:6). Human sacrifice, however, is much less likely to have been an option in the postexilic period. Micah's critique of sacrifice is essentially the same as that of the other prophets we have considered. It indicates a misunderstanding of what YHWH wants, which is "to do justice, and to love kindness, and to walk humbly with your God" (6:8). Most of the positive oracles in chapters 4–5 are likely to have been added by postexilic editors, when the time of judgment had passed and the need was for consolation and hope. Micah 4:1–5 repeats an oracle found in Isaiah 2:1–5, with a variation in the concluding verse. The imagery of tôrāh going forth from Jerusalem and the peoples streaming thereto fits better with the aspirations of Second Temple Judaism than with what we know of the eighth century. The oracle probably circulated anonymously. That it is associated with two eighth-century prophets is striking, but probably coincidental. A more difficult case is presented by Micah 5:2–5, which predicts the advent of a ruler from Bethlehem of Judah, the ancestral home of David. Many scholars take this as a postexilic prediction of a restoration of the Davidic line, and the obscure statement in v. 3, "the rest of his kindred shall return," can be read as supporting this interpretation. But the focus on Bethlehem, as opposed to Zion, may be significant. Micah of Moresheth may have felt that the Davidic monarchy could be redeemed if it returned to the humble roots symbolized by the ancestral village. The prediction of a ruler from Bethlehem would then be a rejection of the ruling king and the Jerusalem court, but not of the Davidic line. The oracle would still have been read in a messianic sense in the postexilic period. In the later context Assyria would be understood as the archetypical enemy. The fantasy of a final defeat of invading nations appears frequently in the later prophetic and apocalyptic books (e.g., the prophecy of Gog in Ezekiel 38–39).

Resources for Listening and Spiritual Autobiography

Spiritual Autobiographies: Some Guidelines

A spiritual autobiography is your life story told with the purpose of discerning and proclaiming how your experience has shaped your relationship with God. Each year in the program you are asked to recall your life story. Later, you are given an opportunity to share what you think is appropriate with your seminar group. A different structure is provided for your use for each of the four years of the program. These structured methods allow you to look at the whole sweep of your life. Constructing your autobiography provides a firm foundation for the continuing work of integrating the content of your year's study with the events of your life. Your experience is a primary resource for your theological education; the yearly review of your life story enables you to hear how the timbre and direction of that story has changed in the last twelve months. Your call, discernment, vocation, and ministry are imbedded in your spiritual journey. This process of telling and retelling your story helps those themes come more clearly into your consciousness.

A spiritual autobiography may contain both religious material—significant people or times within the religious community—and everyday material—people and times in your life that have influenced who you are now and how you understand God's presence or absence in your life.

The work you do on your spiritual autobiography is private, "for your eyes only." This allows you to be free, without concern about how others will interpret either the context or expression.

Preparing a spiritual autobiography each year provides a way to deepen your understanding of both the Christian life and ministry. By virtue of your baptism you were called to ministry, guided and pushed by personal gifts, passions, skills, experiences, and interests.

Once you prepare your spiritual autobiography, you need to decide what you want to share with your seminar group. Martin Buber, a twentieth-century philosopher and Jewish theologian, is reputed to have said that he could never hold a significant conversation with another person until he had heard the other's life story. The purpose of sharing autobiographies is to build trust and understanding within the group and to begin to make connections within your own story. We need the experience of hearing other life stories to know that we are not alone in God's world. By sharing appropriate stories of our lives, we form learning communities that can challenge and support us throughout our lives.

Your mentor will relate her or his own story and help the group structure the time for sharing of autobiographies. Most groups give each member **around ten minutes** to tell his or her story, followed by time for the rest of the group to respond. Spiritual autobiographies are the focus of most of the seminar time for the first few meetings of the year. This is a special time for your group. This component of your group's life will carry you to the next phase of your year together. This may be the first time you've told your story in this way. It may seem a bit daunting at first. Remember that you should offer what you feel comfortable sharing in the group. This is not an opportunity for "group therapy" or psychologizing, so the group should not engage in raising questions about motives or probe for information beyond what you share. Feel free to say "no" or to say that you do not wish to explore questions that others may raise out of curiosity or concern.

Sharing your "spiritual autobiography" is a way to say, "Here I am," and to join your EfM group as a full participant. Over the years in EfM you will probably find that your spiritual autobiography changes. You may find yourself free to talk about things that were previously guarded. You also may find that your freedom to "be yourself" will grow as your personal story, the life of the group, and the story of God's people relate to each other.

Holy Listening

VocationCARE is a program in ministry discernment and design, a sister program to EfM in the Programs Center at The School of Theology/ Sewanee. The method incorporates two rounds of storytelling and encourages deep listening. The acronym CARE stands for

- CREATE *space to explore Christian vocation together;*
- ASK *self-awakening questions together;*
- REFLECT *theologically on self and community; and*
- ENACT *the next faithful step.*

VocationCARE Model for Storytelling/Holy Listening

Tips for First Storytelling

EXAMPLE:

Tell a story about why you do what you do, love what you love, care about what you care about.

BE SPECIFIC

Talk about what actually happened. It helps to begin stories with "One time . . . " or "I remember a time when. . . ."

BE DESCRIPTIVE

Use images, feelings, and places to provide texture, color, and thick description to your story. Use the 5Ws: who, what, when, where, and why.

BE SELF-REFLECTIVE

What was the occasion of your discovering that *this* was what you loved, cared about, or loved doing? Was there anyone with whom you shared this discovery? How did it feel to know this about yourself?

Tips for First Hearing of Another's Story

UNDIVIDED ATTENTION

Make eye contact with the storyteller and give him or her your full attention as if there was nothing else more important than listening to his/her story.

HOLY LISTENING

Listen reverently as if you were in the presence of the Holy and witness the truth of this sacred story. Hold the space with your presence and receive the precious gift in this story. Imagine you are listening with God's ears.

JOURNALING

As you journal: What images, key words, or phrases stand out as meaningful to you? Is there a question you might ask your partner that would move the conversation deeper into "the heart of the matter"? What did you enjoy or find yourself wondering about?

Tips for Second Storytelling

EXAMPLE:

Tell a story about a time when you found a note to sing that was unique and God-given, a time when you heard the echo of the Word in your life.

BE SPECIFIC

Talk about what actually happened. It helps to begin stories with "One time . . . " or "I remember a time when. . . ."

BE DESCRIPTIVE

Use words, images, feelings, and places to provide texture and color to your story description. Cover the 5Ws: who, what, when, where, and why.

BE SELF-REFLECTIVE

Where was I? What was I doing? What happened? Was there any risk or challenge in claiming this inner harmony?

Were there any companions in this discovery? Anyone who could share this joy with me?

Tips for Second Hearing of Another's Story

UNDIVIDED ATTENTION

Make eye contact with the storyteller and give him or her your full attention as if there was nothing else more important than listening to his/her story.

HOLY LISTENING

Listen reverently as if you were in the presence of the Holy and witness the truth of this sacred story. Hold the space with your presence and receive the precious gift in this story. Imagine you are listening with God's ears.

JOURNALING

As you journal: What images, key words, or phrases stand out as meaningful to you? Is there a question you might ask your partner that would move the conversation deeper into "the heart of the matter"? What did you enjoy or find yourself wondering about?

Adapted from Fund for Theological Education's *FTE Guide to VocationCARE* © 2012, pp. 18–19. Used with permission.

Resources for Reflecting Theologically

Theological Reflection Models

The theological reflection models used in Volume A are collected here for easy access and reference.

An Individual Theological Reflection Process

IDENTIFY A FOCUS	RESPONSES

Write a brief description of an incident for reflection.

For this reflection, use something related to "work" in a broad sense. Recording the experience aids in making the identification specific and concrete. Use the criteria of "a piece of your life story which challenged your feelings, values, or way of looking at things."	*For instance: Describe one specific incident of parenting, or income-producing work, or hobby. The criterion is that the incident matter to you.*

List the shifts in action in the incident you chose, and choose one shift for the focus.

"Shifts in action" can be physical, emotional, or cognitive movement. Conscious decisions as well as spontaneous responses are listed. Look over your list and choose one. Any of the shifts will serve as a point of departure. Therefore, choose one that holds a certain interest for you.	*Example: A work-incident of creating a garden that was raided by deer might have shifts such as:* • *I walked out to enjoy coffee in my garden.* • *I saw most of the plants eaten down to the ground.* • *I saw deer prints.* • *I sat down and cried.* *One of the shifts in your incident will have the most energy. Choose that one as the focus.*

IDENTIFY A FOCUS	RESPONSES

Recapture the feelings and thoughts at the moment of focus.

List three or four feelings and thoughts you had *at the key moment of shift of focus identified above.* Often, there is the temptation to project feelings and thoughts into past situations. Recall as accurately as possible what you actually experienced at that moment specifically.

Thoughts	Feelings
Oh no!	*Shock*
I'm going to set a trap	*Anger*
All that work gone	*Sorrow*

Recall another time when you had the same combination of feelings and similar thoughts.

Identifying another time when you viewed life in the same way is important. Metaphors are generated best by comparing two or more incidents. When you recall a past experience, new insights often occur. Briefly record the similar incident, including any insights and awareness.

Similar Incident

Create a metaphor.

Think about both experiences. Allow them to become present again. Consider what they were like. How would you describe them using a single metaphor, image, or simile? List all that come to your mind. Then, choose one to explore further.

Ex.: At the moment of seeing the destroyed garden—Possible images/metaphors that capture what it's like in that kind of moment: "I feel like a wrung-out dishcloth"; "I feel like I've been hit in the stomach"; "I feel like a fallen soufflé."

What images/metaphors reflect what life is like when you had the thoughts and feeling you identified?

Write or draw your metaphor.

EXPLORE THE FOCUS	RESPONSES

Explore the "world of the metaphor."

Explore or question the metaphor from one or more perspectives such as:

"What is life like in the metaphor?" (CREATION)

"What temptations to destroy are there in the metaphor world?" (SIN)

"What brings those in that image up short, takes their breath away?" (JUDGEMENT)

"What changes would be called for?" (REPENTANCE)

"What would be an occasion for celebration?" (REDEMPTION)

These are some of the questions that can be used to develop your understanding of the "world of the metaphor." Don't attempt to give a full account of each question. When your energy begins to slow, take this as a sign that enough work may have been done. Sometimes insights will occur while exploring the metaphor. Write those down.

Ex.: In a world of being hit in the stomach—Creation—what the world/life is like: life is dangerous, needs caution, painful

Sin—what tempts those in this world to be destructive: tempted to seek revenge, to harm in return, to give up because of anger or fear

CONNECT TO OTHER SOURCES OF MEANING	RESPONSES

Bring in the Christian Tradition.

Consider the material that you have been studying as it relates to this reflection. Is there anything from the current reading chapter that comes to mind? Review several of the chapters you have read. Write a few sentences commenting on the part of the TRADITION that connects with the selected metaphor/image.

What stories from the Bible or hymns or prayers come to mind with this metaphor? Ex.: Where in the Bible would there be accounts where someone might feel/think "It was like being punched in the stomach"?

List possible stories and select one. Read it carefully.

Compare and contrast the perspectives of the metaphor and of the piece of Christian Tradition.

Write a short paragraph that compares and contrasts the Christian Tradition with the perspective contained in the "world of the metaphor."

How is the scripture story or hymn or prayer similar to and different from the metaphor perspectives?

Connect to Contemporary Culture/Society and Personal Beliefs.

What examples are there in our contemporary CULTURE of life being like the metaphor you chose? How is God present in those times?

Include any statements or judgments that represent presently held positions or beliefs. How would you state the "truth of the matter" as you see it in this reflection (POSITION/BELIEF)? What does "the truth of the matter" contribute to the relationship of meaningful work and worship?

Record your responses.

APPLY	RESPONSES

Identify insights and questions.

Record insights you now have. Do you have any new questions related to the matters that the reflection brought up for you?

Record your responses.

Decide on implications.

In light of your reflection, what might you do? Are you aware of something you want to change, or study more, or pray about, or talk to someone about? You might want to choose a new way to act out your ministry during the next few days.

Record your decisions.

The Wide-Angle Lens Method of Theological Reflection

Why this title? The Wide-Angle Lens Method begins with a variety of perspectives and focuses on a thread/theme/idea/image that connects them. An individual would start by finding the threads or themes present in several personal incidents, a movie that one watched, weekly assigned EfM reading or the like. The key is that use of this method by an individual requires initiation from something that could produce several themes or ideas. In an EfM group, the beginning point can be themes from the spiritual autobiographies, themes from the week's reading, themes from any on-board time of the group, or some other starting point from which a variety of perspectives can be elicited. The key is to list themes and find a thread that runs through several of them.

Identify

FIND A COMMON THEME FROM EXPERIENCE

Begin with your incidents identified in the Respond section of this week's work.

What are the common themes or elements that emerge? Is there a burning question, struggle, or issue? These threads may be expressed as simple statements, as an image, as a metaphor, or as an issue.

Select *one thread* that connects various themes. For instance, a review of several incidents (either ones identified by an individual or those identified in a group) could yield themes of frustration, tiredness, hurry, and feeling overwhelmed. Those themes would have shown up in two or more of the incidents. Asking, "What ties some of those themes together?" yields a thread that may have run through some incidents; perhaps, "Having too much to do results in impatience with others" could be named as a thread that ties two or more incidents.

Explore

REFLECT ON SOME THEOLOGICAL PERSPECTIVES

What kind of an image could paint the picture of the example thread above or of your identified thread based on your incidents?

Draw that image. Examine the image for what's going on in it.

Write about what's going on in that image.

Which theological perspective (Creation, Sin, Judgment, Repentance, or Redemption) does it seem to indicate? What would Repentance look like in that image? Or Redemption?

Connect

This is the point at which one looks at the various sources in life to help find meaning in matters of daily life and ministry. The object is not to find the worst in the sources, but to find connections that teach us something; what gets taught could be either creative or destructive and sometimes it is difficult to distinguish which is which.

CONSIDER THE CONTEMPORARY CULTURE AND SOCIETY

Focus on **one or two** areas of your culture or society so that the reflection will not be too broad. These connections might come from your local community or the larger world: our work environment, our education system, our health care system, our grandmothers, movies, TV, literature, art, songs, artifacts, architecture, government, the press, to name a few. Just pick one area of our contemporary society with which to connect.

What does the world in which you live teach you about dealing with the identified theme? Where do you find evidence of people dealing with tiredness and anger in the world around you?

What have you learned from your culture that helps you or challenges you regarding the theme?

How do the areas of Culture/Society speak to or about this thread? For instance, what does the world of employment teach us about tiredness and anger?

What about our health care system? What about our advertising? Again, just use one aspect of our society.

CONSIDER THE CHRISTIAN TRADITION

1. Identify biblical passages or other elements from Christian Tradition in which this common thread is evoked or brought to mind. Provide time to find and read passages.

2. Select one text that seems to speak most clearly to the thread that was evoked.

3. Examine the passage with these questions:
   a. What do you know about the meaning of the text in its original setting?
   b. How have others interpreted this text?
   c. What does this text mean to you?

COMPARE AND CONTRAST CONTEMPORARY CULTURE AND CHRISTIAN TRADITION

From the perspectives of Culture and Tradition, what kind of a world emerges?

Where do these perspectives join or compete? Where do they clash or contrast?

Use the themes of creation, sin, judgment, repentance, redemption, celebration, the doctrine of God, or grace to shape your reflection. Likely, there is time to use only one or two of these themes during any one reflection unless there is time for more exhaustive exploration. As an example, if the New Testament passage about Jesus cleansing the temple were used for the Christian Tradition and the work environment for the Contemporary Culture connection, how do those two perspectives compare and contrast? What messages do we hear from either or both?

CONNECT TO BELIEFS, POSITIONS, AND AFFIRMATIONS

What do you do with the messages from our Christian Tradition and our Contemporary Culture?

What do you feel about where this reflection has led?

What do you think about it?

Where are you in the reflection?

What positions or affirmations do you hold about this reflection?

Apply

IDENTIFY INSIGHTS AND PERSONAL IMPLICATIONS

What have you learned about coherence of belief and behavior?

What moves or energizes you? What insights come to mind?

What are you personally called to do differently, to affirm, or to change?

What prayer do you want to offer?

DECIDE ON SOCIAL AND CIVIC CONSEQUENCES

What actions will you take to carry out the implications you have discovered?

What will you investigate further in your community in order to make a difference?

Whom can you contact to join you or inform you?

What action might you take?

Dilemma Method for Theological Reflection

Identify

1. DESCRIBE an incident for reflection

An experience in which you felt pulled in at least two directions over something, and for which there are no decisions pending. The incident is over.

Description of the incident
Ex.: I had looked forward to my best friend's wedding for months and had my plane ticket and my new outfit. We had plans to enjoy the sights and catch up and just have fun. And then my mother got sick, but told me I could go ahead with my plans. I felt so torn. There was no one else there for my mother

2. DECIDE AND NAME the turning point in the incident

What's the central moment of the incident? Where is the tension greatest? What was happening? What were you thinking and feeling at that moment?

Record the central moment in a short sentence.

3. STATE the dilemma

Try to state what's at stake or what the central issue is at the moment of greatest tension.

Record the primary pair of tension statements as "I wanted _____ and I wanted _____ ":

To help get to the dilemma, list declarative statements about what you wanted at that moment or what interests were at stake at that moment.

Ex.: I wanted to attend my best friend's wedding and I wanted to stay to take care of my ailing parent.

Select a pair of statements that best represent the central tension.

Record the central issue/what's at stake. Ex.: Personal fun conflicting with caring for another

Identify what's at issue or at stake in that tension.

4. IDENTIFY another time

Clarify the dilemma by recalling another time when you experienced a dilemma.

Record your additional identification by completing the sentence: "It was a time when. . . ."

Explore

5. EXPLORE the dilemma

What is it like to live in that issue/tension? Use Cost/Promise (Risk/Hope) or Perspective Questions of Creation, Sin, Judgment, Repentance, and Redemption.

Record your responses to the questions using either Cost/Promise or Perspectives:

Cost of each choice   *Promise of each choice*

Perspective example:

Judgment—What choices are there?

Repentance—What might require a change of heart?

Connect

6. TRADITION

Identify some stories from scripture or church history that relate to the dilemma. Or perhaps some prayers or hymns come to mind.

Responses:

7. DIALOGUE between tradition and the dilemma—

Compare and contrast what our Christian tradition has to say about that dilemma. What choices would the tradition support? Not support? Why?

Responses:

8. CULTURE and POSITION

Where is that dilemma experienced in our culture? Have there been news stories about it? Have you read a book or seen a movie that dealt with that dilemma? Is there a political dimension to that dilemma?

Responses

What do you believe about that dilemma? How was your belief in conflict in the issue? What do you hope for regarding the dilemma?

Apply

9. INSIGHTS and QUESTIONS

What do you see in a new way now? What have you
learned from facing this dilemma? What questions
do you have about the dilemma in your life?

Responses:

10. IMPLICATIONS

What do you want or need to do about this
dilemma? Are there social implications? Are there
actions you could take? Is there something more
to learn? What support would help? Where will
you find that support?

Responses:

Theological Reflection Beginning with Scripture

This method of theological reflection focuses on a selection from scripture and uses it as the starting point for reflection. The passage may come from the readings for the week, or the group may select a passage that is of special interest.

Identify

SELECT A PIECE OF SCRIPTURE

A person in the group reads the selected passage of scripture.
Be silent for a couple of minutes.

FIRST RESPONSES

What word or phrase stands out for you? Share this in the group.

HEAR THE PASSAGE AGAIN

Another person reads the selected passage again. Perhaps a different translation may be used.
The group is silent for a couple of minutes.

Explore

EXAMINE THE PASSAGE

What do you know about the meaning of the text or its original setting?

What is happening in the text? What is going on?

How have others interpreted this text? What kind of a text is this? (sermon, parable, etc.)

What might it mean today?

EXAMINE THE TRADITION

What is the world like in this passage?

What human predicament in the world is revealed in this passage?

What indicates a change of mind, heart, or behavior?

What gives rise to celebration in this world?

Connect

MAKE CONNECTIONS WITH OUR OWN EXPERIENCE (ACTION)

With whom do you identify in this passage?

Can you recall a time in your life when you experienced an event or situation similar to the one in the passage? What were your thoughts and feelings?

What does that event or situation mean to you in light of this passage?

In what way does the tradition support, inform, and/or challenge your experience?

LOOK AT CULTURE

What does the Contemporary Culture say about the world described in the passage? Pick one aspect of Culture to discuss this connection, such as what books deal with the concerns of the scripture passage; what is happening in the world around us now that relates to the matter described in the scripture passage; what attitudes of our world of work connect to the concern of the scripture passage; how is God at work in our world in ways that relate to the scripture passage's concerns? Other ways that Culture can provide some help in reflection is to think of what movies are dealing with the scriptural issues under discussion; what family or social wisdom speak to the issue?

WHAT IS MY POSITION?

Where do you stand? What do you believe about the matters or issues raised in this reflection? What is your position on this matter?

Apply

IDENTIFY INSIGHTS

What new insights have emerged as a result of this reflection? What can you affirm or state that you have learned?

IMPLICATIONS FOR ACTION

Is there anything you intend to do differently as you live out your ministry?

What help might you need to carry out your intentions?

What are the consequences for others or for the future?
Example:

Moses was keeping the flock of his father-in-law Jethro, the priest of Midian; he led his flock beyond the wilderness, and came to Horeb, the mountain of God. There the angel of the Lord appeared to him in a flame of fire out of a bush; he looked, and the bush was blazing, yet it was not consumed. Then Moses said, "I must turn aside and look at this great sight, and see why the bush is not burned up." When the Lord saw that he had turned aside to see, God called to him out of the bush, "Moses, Moses!" And he said,

"Here I am." Then he said, "Come no closer! Remove the sandals from your feet, for the

> *place on which you are standing is holy ground." He said further, "I am the God of your father, the God of Abraham, the God of Isaac, and the God of Jacob." And Moses hid his face, for he was afraid to look at God. Then the Lord said, "I have observed the misery of my people who are in Egypt; I have heard their cry on account of their taskmasters. Indeed, I know their sufferings, and I have come down to deliver them from the Egyptians, and to bring them up out of that land to a good and broad land, a land flowing with milk and honey, to the country of the Canaanites, the Hittites, the Amorites, the Perizzites, the Hivites, and the Jebusites. The cry of the Israelites has now come to me; I have also seen how the Egyptians oppress them." –Exodus 3:1–9*

A theological reflection starting from scripture begins in the Christian Tradition/Heritage source area.

Identify a focus point in the passage, i.e., where the key energy/heart of the passage seems to be, what the passage seems to be about. Perhaps the group can agree on an image or metaphor that pictures what the passage focus or energy is, such as the burning bush.

Explore the passage by considering what was going on at the time of this event; what commentaries say about this passage; what you have studied; what is described at the point of the burning bush.

> What questions might occur in the face of such an event? What's the world like for Moses at this point (Creation)? What temptations are there for Moses at this moment (Sin)? What's surprising for Moses (Judgment)? What choices does Moses have (Judgment)? What makes things alright for him (Redemption)?

> What questions would you have in such a moment?

Connect to other Sources/Life Areas as responses occur to anyone—not necessary to go in order or as steps. Just let these connections occur in whatever sequence they may come.

> *Personal Experience*—when have you experienced something that you might call "a burning bush moment"?

> *Culture*—what kinds of groups or events might be "burning bush" events in the world around us?

> *Personal Position/Belief*—what do you believe about "burning bush" moments? What do you hope or doubt?

Apply

What new thoughts have occurred to you? What do you want to think about more? How might you engage in your life differently as a result of this conversation?

Theological Reflection Beginning with a Mind Map

This link, http://mindmap.nu/how-to-do-radiant-thinking-based-on-mind-mapping/, provides information on "mind-mapping" or "radiant thinking." You may also want to look at other sources of information on this process.

Identify a focus:

Construct a "mind-map" by making associations with the centering theme. For example, the mind map below starts with the theme "re-formations" placed in the center of paper. As you make associations from your assigned reading over the past few weeks, write those associations around the theme and draw a line between the theme and each association.

Reconstruct   **Confess**

"RE-FORMATIONS"

After making several associations, study the entire map.

• What images or metaphors express the nature of "re-forming?"

• Select one to explore.

Explore the world of the metaphor/image:

Identify a specific point from which to explore the chosen image. For example, if the image is "jumping into an abyss," then be sure to explore the image from a standpoint such as the person jumping into the abyss. Do not shift to other possible standpoints such as observing someone jump into the abyss or leading someone to the edge of an abyss.

Develop two or three questions and explore the image through those perspectives. For example, what questions would explore the destructive dimensions of the image (Sin)? What questions explore the nature of the world of the metaphor-image (Creation)? What questions bring in the Judgment dimensions of the metaphor? Or the Repentance and/or Redemption perspectives?

Connect with other areas of life:

Begin connecting with your life by briefly stating when you experienced the world depicted in the image/metaphor. Remember to work from the standpoint previously identified. For example, when have you metaphorically "jumped off into an abyss"?

Connect with other sources, such as contemporary culture and the Christian tradition. You may find that something from your reading over the past few weeks comes to mind.

Bring in your personal beliefs. What do you believe? What do you hold to be true?

Apply to your life going forward:
Notice how what you learn from the reflection applies to your life. For example, what light does this reflection shed on how you engage opportunities for ministry?

Theological Reflection
Beginning with a Provocative Word

Identify

SELECT THE WORD

Choose a word remarkable for its ability to call up vibrant emotion (scorned, ecstatic, lost, astonished, etc.), and post it on the board for all to reflect on in silence. Then share any revelations on the meaning of the word, anything it denotes or connotes.

Explore

ASK THE QUESTIONS

Next, ask the six "journalist's questions" about the feeling the word conveys:

WHO was involved when you were feeling _____?
   (Action . . . tell the stories from our lives)

WHAT image comes to mind about feeling _____?
   (Image . . . explore the metaphor)

WHERE does this come from and WHERE is it found in society?
   (Source/Culture)

WHEN does this come up in the Bible, lives of saints, hymns, etc.?
   (Tradition . . . explore the world of tradition)

WHY is this manifest in our lives?
   (Position)

HOW might God redeem any negatives in this?
   (Hope in Christ)

Connect

CONSIDER INSIGHTS AND IMPLICATIONS

What have we learned for the next time we feel _____?

Apply

WRITE A COLLECT

Use the outline:

Dear God _____ (naming of God's aspects)
You _____ (connect situation of the image
to that aspect)
We pray that _____ (petition of our hearts)
So that _____ (result we desire)
Amen.

—Method provided by Patricia G. Bleicher, EfM Mentor

Resources for Community Life

The Respectful Communications Guidelines and Mutual Invitation process are from the Kaleidoscope Institute with whom EfM has been in a collaborative relationship since 2011. Learn more about KI at www.kscopeinstitute.org

Respectful Communication Guidelines

R = take RESPONSIBILITY for what you say and feel without blaming others

E = use EMPATHETIC listening

S = be SENSITIVE to differences in communication styles

P = PONDER what you hear and feel before you speak

E = EXAMINE your own assumptions and perceptions

C = keep CONFIDENTIALITY

T = TRUST ambiguity, because we are not here to debate who is right or wrong

(from *The Bush Was Blazing but Not Consumed* by Eric H. F. Law)

I agree to uphold these guidelines for the time we have together.

Signature _____ Date _____